Living Arrows

Living Arrows

(A Story in Two Parts)

Part I: Vignettes

Part II: My Story

HILDAGARDE SPIELBAUER BROOKS

Library of Congress Control Number:		2009911431
ISBN:	Hardcover	978-1-4415-9368-9
	Softcover	978-1-4415-9367-2

This book was printed in the United States of America.

To order additional copies of this book, contact:
Xlibris Corporation
1-888-795-4274
www.Xlibris.com
Orders@Xlibris.com
57800

Contents

To George and Frances

This dedication needs no further words;
it is justly deserved and speaks for itself.

George and Frances

When a man touches the hand of a woman,
they both touch the heart of eternity.

—Kahlil Gibran

And to our beloved children

Todd Steven Brooks (1958-1981)
Baby John Bolsinger (1958-1958)
Baby Mary Spielbauer (1948-1948)

This writer also wishes to dedicate her memories to the young lost lives in our family—our children whom God has taken as his own. It is said that when God chooses to call one of his young children into his home, there is much rejoicing within the portals of his kingdom.

We give our loved ones back to God,
And just as He first gave them to us,
And did not lose them in the giving
So we have not lost them
In returning them to Him . . .
For life is eternal, love is immortal
Death is only a horizon
And a horizon is nothing
But the limit of our earthly sight.

Excerpt: Helen Steiner Rice

Todd Steven Brooks

She was very weak, but her cheeks were flushed
And her eyes were weak. She told them that her
Boy had been with her, that she need not dig him
A grave now; for she had buried him in her heart,
Which is the best place for a Mother to hold her child.

—Hans Christian Anderson

Prologue

You are the bows from which your children
As living arrows are sent forth.

The Archer sees the mark upon the path of the infinite,
And He bends you with His might
That His arrows may go swift and far.

Let your bending in the Archer's hand be for gladness;
For even as He loves the arrow that flies,
So He also loves the bow that is stable.

Excerpt: The Prophet
Kahlil Gibran

My first intent was to write this story for you, my dear brothers and sisters, and for myself. At least that is what I thought. But now, as I progress through its pages, I realize that in actuality, this story is not for you and me, but for our children and our children's children. It is my one small effort to "reach out and touch"—to reach into the future and to touch the minds and the hearts of all the children to come after us—to give these yet unborn descendents a heritage of a once very real and very alive generation.

George and Frances and their large family lived real hopes and dreams, joys and sorrows, laughter and tears, and, yes, successes and failures. It would be a sad thing if we were all to be remembered as just another faded photograph collecting dust in someone's stuffy old attic. Worse yet, to be eternally immortalized with a simple epitaph, engraved upon a weathered slab of cold granite resting in some deserted and desolate cemetery and to be visited (by a duty bound) only on Memorial Day.

We *are* a real people! The nucleus of our family was of course, first and foremost, our own little white-haired mother, Frances, and in respective order, the small river town of Guttenberg and the two-story house where Brother John now resides.

I always think of it (John's house) as "going home" and know that you all do too. It is a quiet house now—if one listens very carefully, one might be fortunate enough to hear the pages of a western paperback being silently turned by our brother, the coffee pot perking on the front burner of the old gas stove; an occasional can of beer popping open, the TV set blaring out its usual sordid six o'clock news of the day, or perhaps a "play-by-play" of some basketball game. But, the walls and the woodwork of that old house are filled with memories of a very large and once very noisy family working, playing, and praying together—kids of all ages running up and down the stairs, opening and closing windows, and banging and slamming screen doors. How many times have we heard our mother say, in reproach, "Don't slam that door!" Usually, too late! However, we were always kept in line, more or less, by the gentle quiet voice of Frances and the kind-hearted, hard-working Father image, George.

Many years have hence come and gone; the children of George and Frances are scattered far and wide. We have traveled many highways—many byways—and yes, even many skyways, since young George Spielbauer drove his rusty old Model T (for that one last time) from the Petsche farm into the town of Guttenberg to our Grandma's house.

In the words of the poet, Gibran, we, the children of George and Frances indeed are the "*Living Arrows.*"

We must fly swift and straight
For was not our bow taut and steady?

No other aim could have been more true
For was not our Archer none other than God, Himself?

This is my story

Part I
Vignettes

Webster's Dictionary defines "Vignettes" as follows:

Vignette, (vin-yet'): A portrait of the head and bust only.

(vin-yet'): A short literary composition.

Dear reader, this section is merely a cast of characters or an introduction to same. The ink drawings that appear on the following pages are a sampling of our sister Kathleen's artistic talents, and as you can readily see, they are copied from our graduation pictures (our mother's most personal and notorious "hall of fame") that still grace the entirety of two walls in Brother John's home. Kathy's sketches serve as the "portrait" vignette and of course, the written synopsis on each brother and sister is but a verbal extension.

Author's note: For those of you who are unfamiliar with the word "playfarmer," which is used at random throughout this manuscript, please understand that it is the English translation of our surname. It is a combination of two German words (spiel, translating to "play" and bauer, translating to "farmer").

Thus, the reference to "playfarmer."

Kathy

We may refill that tiny crib again and still again, and over each new curly head, our fairy castles span. For we have had our ecstasy, we quenched that burning thirst the day we held upon our hearts—"the one God gave us first!"

—Delight Cronin

Kathleen Marie:

June 25, *1925-1994* Aug 24, 1994

As a little girl, I looked up to my oldest sister, Kathy, with much love and admiration. My greatest desire was to one day become as pretty as she, and in later years I was always so thrilled when people would say to me, “Oh, you must be Kathleen.” Most of the time, I would just smile sweetly (as I imagined my sis would do) and pretend that I really was Kathy.

I vividly recall her Graduation Day. I was one of the flower girls and, after the ceremony, the graduating class had been invited to the Nuns’ residence where they were served breakfast by them along with some “parting words of wisdom” (as only good nuns are prone to do). And I am looking around the room, *so* proud because my big sis is by far the prettiest girl (bar none) in the entire class. She has long, black hair, worn in a pageboy style (the fashion of the day); big, brown eyes; the sweetest smile; and is wearing a beautiful white dress that she designed and made all by herself.

After her graduation, Kathy moved to Dubuque, Iowa, where she worked in a box factory. One year for Christmas, she bought me a brand-new turquoise-colored winter coat with matching snow pants and hat (my very own store-bought clothes that were *not* the usual hand-me-downs for the first time in my life!) *Wow*! Did I feel *so* grand!

The best gift, however, was another Christmas—another time. This time, she gave me a little dolly, about six-inches tall, with "real" hair (black curls that I used to brush with a broken toothbrush). I truly loved that dolly. And now, many years later, both big sister, Kathy, and little sister, Hildi, still share a common interest and love for dollies of all ages, shapes, and sizes—just little girls at heart. Kathy had really gone into the doll craze in a big way. She collected them, repaired, and reproduced their bodies, painted china faces, and created authentic costumes to make them perfect in every way.

It is approximately the year 1969 and her two sons, Gene and Lee, pretty much grown, our Kathy convinced that even at age forty-five, one is *not* too old to learn, sheds her old housedress, hangs up her apron, puts aside her pots and pans, mops and brooms, and heads for the Highland Community College. In truth it was not quite that drastic. She had already started her higher education as a part-time student taking classes in Psychology, Sociology, Child Education, etc.—all of which were geared to her job at the Amity Day Care Center in Freeport, Illinois.

This center was for under-privileged children. Her studies and work, however, were brought to an abrupt halt when her husband, Lowell, suffered a severe heart attack in 1972. Kathy gave up her outside interests and devoted all her time to her husband's needs. Shortly, thereafter, she too had a minor heart attack and was forced to slow down even more.

In back tracking once again, I recall that Kathy, as a young girl, had quite a penchant for drawing and sketching, mostly doing portraits if my memory does not fail me. After a short period of recuperation and adjustment to the illnesses that struck her family, our "perennial part-time student" once again returns to her classroom. But, this time her efforts are devoted to something she truly loves and enjoys—her artwork! She had decided that at this late date, she'd be better off at painting (which she loved)—than taking courses (which she hated) in order to earn a degree (which she didn't need).

She has pursued her art career quite diligently in her later years. Her works have appeared in numerous art shows throughout the Midwest and she has been rewarded with much success as an artist.

Not long ago, I was fortunate enough to be able to view Kathy's artwork in person, a painting she'd done for our sister Helen and her husband Don of their farmhouse and surrounding area located just outside of Colesburg, Iowa. I was very impressed with her talents and immediately my devious little mind was hard at work trying to figure out a way that I too could become the proud owner of one of Sister Kathy's canvasses.

Kathy actually did promise to do an oil painting especially for me. It was to be a hilltop view of Guttenberg—a night scene looking down on the little river town with two bright stars in the sky in memory of our baby sister, Mary, and my own dear son, Todd Steven. She had the best of intentions but, alas, Kathy was never meant to see this project to its fruition, for God chose to call her to his heavenly home. We all suffered a tremendous loss when she died of cancer in 1994.

Today, I consider myself extremely fortunate, however, because she did manage to at least complete a charcoal sketch of her intended work. Her artistic talent now graces the front cover jacket and will also appear later in this manuscript. I shall treasure it always—even in its unfinished condition and now say, "Thank you, my dearest sister, for leaving me with yet another cherished memento of yourself!"

Joe

In a rich, happy house a son and heir had just been born and all the family were full of joy! The guardian angel of the house leaned against the head of the bed and spread over it a canopy filled with stars—and each star was a pearl of happiness. "Everything is here," said the guardian angel. "Here—sparkle health, wealth, fortune, and love—*all* that can be wished for.

—Hans Christian Anderson

Joseph Mathias:
1927-

And now to Brother Joe, who has always been the perfect big brother to all of us kids. Now that our father is gone, we must truly dub him the "Patriarch of our Family." There is no doubt in my mind that he is the most honest and *best* man around, a real salt of the earth kind of guy . . .

When I was a very little girl, he used to pay me a penny (a shoe) to polish his shoes when he had a special date. Some big spender, huh? But, not being intelligent enough in those days for arbitration, even in its most archaic form, I was quite content with my miserly pittance and labored diligently at my allotted task. I did think he was just a "tad" too particular, though when he insisted on that "spit polish" shine! Picky! Picky! Dutiful child that I was, I obliged him, nonetheless.

I also have a vague recollection of the large bedroom that Joe shared along with my other older brothers. Model airplanes (dozens of them) all in bright reds, yellows, greens, and blues; big ones and small ones were suspended from the ceiling as if in actual flight. This vivid sight of the handiwork of my brothers impressed me until I was old enough to help with the cleaning and then that tedious job of dusting the fragile wingspans, propellers, fuselage, and other sundry parts became my responsibility—*not* too impressive, then! I was terrified of breaking those delicate parts.

One of my fondest memories is the time I spent a few days of my vacation (I was the young, sophisticated, career girl from Cedar Rapids at that time) on my brother's farm near Volga and eagerly anticipated riding the tractor, pitching hay, milking cows, etc., but as fate would have it, this city slicker wound up spending most of her vacation in bed and at the local doctor's office with severe sore throat and ear infection. The closest I got to being an "old farm hand" was gathering eggs from the hen house. Ahh! But one day I shall return. And that, dear Brother, is a promise! Or, shall I say threat?

Through the years, Joe and Delores have worked very hard (side by side in the fields—theirs is truly a "ma and pa" operation) to develop their farmland. We were all *so* very proud of our big brother when he was honored as "The Outstanding Young Farmer of Clayton County" in the year 1963! Of course this announcement came as no surprise to the rest of the family as we all knew how much Joe loved the farm and how much he and his family deserved this accolade.

The passing years have not been without mishap, however, and some very serious setbacks have occurred. In late October of '76, Brother Joe experienced an almost fatal accident that gave us all a fright. He had fallen eight feet (while in a squatting position from the cab of his combine) and landed on his head, knocking him senseless! On regaining consciousness some time later, he realized a complete paralysis in his body and absolutely no feeling, not even that of pain. At least a mile from the house (and help), alone in the field, and very frightened our brother lay fearing for his life, and he prayed! Somebody up there must like him, for sure,—for a miracle then happened! Approximately some thirty minutes later, sharp pangs surged through his entire body and even though every part of him pained incessantly, he was able to move again.

Sheer guts and determination forced him to make the effort to climb back onto his machine. In low gear—very slowly—and painfully he made, what seemed like an endless trek across the cornfields and the creek to the yard where Delores took over and rushed him to the nearest hospital. He was immediately transferred to the VA Hospital in Iowa City, where an able team of surgeons fused three of his vertebrae together. His was an almost miraculous recovery and even though he still suffers some minor disabilities; Joe sums it up better than anyone with these words, "I thank God every day that I can walk—and work—and enjoy life!" And to that, I say, "Amen! We thank *him*, too!"

Our brother's hard-working years are slowly waning—and today we find Joe and Delores enjoying a semi-retirement of sorts. Oh, they still help out with the seasonal chores but the old family farm has been taken over by their son Lloyd and his wife Becky.

Each winter Joe and Delores ready themselves for a long trip (usually lasting several months) traveling with their pick-up and a 21-ft., 5th wheel travel trailer to New Mexico to enjoy a visit with daughter, Ann and her family. They ultimately end up in a campground somewhere on the banks of the Rio Grande joining a group of their Volga friends and neighbors.

I like to think that as Brother Joe labors diligently in his fields in the picturesque countryside of Northeast Iowa—the Georges', the Josephs', and the Mathias' of yore look down and benevolently bestow their blessing upon this modern-day "tiller of the soil!" Yes, indeed, our "Patriarch of the Play-farmers" has truly lived up to the heritage vested in him by his forefathers!

Rose

Here's to "kind and gentle"
And He will raise you up on eagle's wings,
And bear you on the breath of dawn,
And make you shine like the sun,
And hold you in the palm of His hand!

—Author Unknown

Rosalyn Adele:

March 15, 1928 - Nov 19 2011

Rosalyn was the third child of George and Frances. Not only is she my very special sister, but my very special friend as well. Her gentle manners and quiet nature were always there willing to help anyone, anywhere and anytime! Most of the time, it was me—who needed that help. She was my yesterday's answer to a guidance counselor. I strove to be much like her in those early years and to date, I am still striving.

Rose is six years older than myself and I often wonder just *where* I'd be if she had not been there during those "growing-up times" protecting me, guiding me, and showing me the way. Together, we laughed and together we cried and many were the sisterly secrets we shared.

She moved into her own apartment when I was about twelve years old. This left me devastated. I would sneak off and run to visit her whenever I could get away with it. That first Christmas away from home, she gave me a beautiful red sweater. It turned out to be my very favorite (probably due to the fact that it was the only sweater I owned). I remember having it still in my wardrobe long after I, too, had left home and moved to Cedar Rapids. That sweater (I vividly recall every minute detail of the little Mexican man motif that was embroidered on the left shoulder) stretched right along with my own body. I grew from a skinny, scrawny little kid into a still skinny, still scrawny, and still very much freckle-faced young "lady" of twenty-one. After such a long period of close proximity, my "old favorite" began to show signs of wear and tear, and most reluctantly, I was forced to allow it to find its way to the Rag Bag where it has lain in stately repose for LO, these many years.

I remember Rosy's babies (the three older children) being born almost as well as I remember my own babies. I played "little mother" to Dean, David, and Deb as a babysitter on Saturday nights and visited them often at the farms where Rose and Earl lived. Together, we pulled weeds, picked peas, and strawberries and hoed potatoes in her various gardens. And at the same time, we shared many hopes and dreams, and old memories in those happy, long-ago, carefree hours.

Even though the years have put many miles between us, we still share common interests and not too long ago, my big sister once again "showed me the way"—this time in the art of quilting. Via the US Postal Service and Ma Bell, she led me, step by step and literally, "stitch by stitch" through my first quilt. I couldn't have chosen a more qualified teacher, for Rose, like our oldest sister, Kathy, had also found a way to express her creative talents and has received much local recognition for her quilting efforts.

And again, like Kathy, Rosy devotes much of her time to the growth and development of young children, for she too has a part-time job at a Preschool in Garnavillo. And I'm sure she is exceptionally qualified for her work—for well, I remember how gentle and patient she was with me (as a little child) when she would painstakingly brush and braid my long hair. So gentle, in fact that I refused to allow anyone else to touch it, for Rosy *never* yanked or pulled like the others would do. And, what's more, she would always take the extra time to tie pretty ribbons in my braids.

Ah! Rosy, as you read this, please remember when I take my next Sabbatical (I'll make sure I plan it for the summer months). Then—my sis, you and I have a commitment to keep—together we are going to search for and find the "Big Spring," that Fountain of our lost youth and that's a date! For, you and I, Rose, are not "just" sisters—we are kindred souls!

Note: I am happy to report that my sister, Rose and I did, indeed keep that commitment made so many years ago. Thanks to our brother, Frank (who knew exactly where the Big Spring is located), we were able to physically experience a nostalgic return to what was once a beautiful memory of our childhood. That year was 2003.

Arnie

When through the woods and forest glades I wander
And hear the birds sing sweetly in the trees;
When I look down from lofty mountain's grandeur
And hear the brook and feel the gentle breeze.
Then, sings my soul!"

—Stuart K. Hine

Arnold Albert:

1929-

The passage of time continues on and with it, the patter of little feet continues to rapidly increase. Thus far, these children have established a birth pattern of girl-boy-girl-boy (a pattern that was destined to repeat itself for many years to come). In 1929, the fourth child and second son was born—Arnold Albert!

Tall, dark, and handsome was he. I looked up to him with such pride! (Look up, indeed! We all did—for he was the tallest in the family—at least for the time being). I remember our brother as having that certain "charisma" about him—a special charm that made him the idol of all the dear little old ladies in Guttenberg. "Ma Jaeger" for one (remember her, Arnie?) considered him as one of her own. She never failed to ask about him and would be deeply hurt if Arnie did not rush right over the railroad tracks and across Highway 52 to see her as soon as he blew into town for a home visit. Even our own mother became "putty" in his hands. Arnie never failed to charm her out of homemade cookies or that second piece of cake, and she always gave him the biggest helping of ice cream! When we, the little kids would ask for a cookie, Mom's pat answer would invariably be "No, you'll spoil your supper!" But, enterprising as our little minds were, we soon learned to put Arnie's charm to our own good use and "conned" him into asking for all of us. Of course, we got our cookies, then!

Not only was Arnie dashing and debonair, he also possessed a brilliant mind as well. A veritable "Einstein" right in our own family! He managed to earn enough credits to receive his high school diploma within a scant three years—at least I think he did—but, then again, maybe he just used that good old charisma one more time and charmed the nuns out of that diploma. Seriously, his mental prowess was indeed impressive and even though he didn't have much more than a year of college, he embarked at an early age upon a journey of concentrated self-education, which carried him far down the road of success.

I seem to recall that Arnie as a young lad was already something of a "nature boy." One incident in particular comes to mind—he'd gone mushroom hunting (which as is often the case, did not prove to be lucrative) and instead brought home a bouquet of small white wild flowers (he called them Mayflowers) for our mother. We could all sense that she was deeply touched (no wonder she spoiled him with those cookies!), but she expressed a fear that the delicate blossoms would not last long even in water. "Not to worry" assured our brother, and he promptly proceeded to make a "mess" in the kitchen as he melted paraffin wax over the old wood stove and covered the fragile petals with just a light touch of wax, thus providing a preservative coating that lasted a long time. They were beautiful and our mother was most pleased. I was quite impressed with this gentle and romantic side of my brother that heretofore I had not known existed.

Arnie, I still have the hand-tooled leather purse, which you made for me when I graduated from high school. I used it for years and years and most recently, I resurrected it from cold storage and with just a little saddle soap and "elbow grease," it is every bit as good as it was many years ago. I shall cherish it always—for I can well imagine the sacrifice of your time and talents that went into its making. Once again, I thank you!

Today, Arnie still has a strong interest in the wildlife—he and his wife, Laurie, are avid birdwatchers and share a common interest in outdoor activities, such as canoeing, camping, and "nature walks" in the woods. He has recently combined his talent for woodworking with his love of canoeing and is currently building (to his own design and specifications) his third canoe! Of course, his creative talents are put to the physical test when he and Laurie participate in the local races and by his own admission, he loves to show them (his canoes) off!

Unfortunately, his outdoor activities have been somewhat curtailed these past few months due to ill health. He has recently been hospitalized on several occasions for a heart problem. But now, under the watchful and caring eye of Laurie and subjected to his doctor's strict orders, he has been able to resume some of the more strenuous exercises, such as canoeing (just a little) and walking (a whole lot)!

As a little girl, I always believed there was nothing my talented brother could *not* accomplish as long as he set his mind to it—today, I am more convinced than ever! Hang in there, Arnie! You've just *got* to!

Helen

Somebody said that it couldn't be done, but she with a chuckle
Replied that "maybe" it couldn't, but she would be one,
who wouldn't say so 'til she tried.
So she buckled right in with the trace of a grin on her face.
If she worried, she hid it.
She started to sing as she tackled the thing that couldn't be done—
And she did it!

—Edgar A. Guest

Helen Mae:

1931-

March 29

Nov 27, 2015

In 1931, the third daughter arrived—*Helen*—in all her glory with that bright red hair, which was to be her trademark for the rest of her life! I always was of the opinion that the notorious red hair was the source of our sister's magical power and that of command and control over both man and beast! This power manifested itself in the very early years of her life—one particular episode comes to mind. I was very small and my memory just a little vague and no doubt, greatly exaggerated.

Helen, Frankie, Larry, and myself were squabbling over some minor trivia (a favored pastime that we often indulged in). Grandma Rohner apparently had *all* she was going to take of such nonsense. She "lit" into Helen (probably because she was the oldest). She yanked her by the arm and proceeded to shake the living daylights out of her. I could see old Sport out of the corner of my eye and knew all *hell* was going to break loose in a minute! I tried to warn Grandma, but *too* late. Sport (he wasn't very fond of our Grandma to begin with—nor, she of him) had been dog-napping in his customary spot in front of the cellar door and immediately leaped to our sister's defense. He snarled nastily at Grandma and without further warning, viciously locked his teeth around our grandma's ankle. Helen's self-declared savior held fast and refused to respond to any and all commands to "Let go!" Even our dad's final voice of authority (that which we all feared and highly respected) fell upon the deaf ears of the animal. Old Sport continued to growl ferociously, never lessening the steady grip upon his victim's lower limb. The dear old lady was aghast and visibly shaken with fear! Was this dog mad?

Helen's eyes were fixed in a silent stare—first to Grandma—then to the dog—back to Grandma—again to the dog! After what seemed an interminable length of time, the little girl, obviously in command of this situation and enjoying it immensely decided that Grandma had surely, by now, learned *her* lesson—quietly ordered Sport to "Let her go!" The dog immediately responded and released his hold upon our grandmother, who beat a hasty and silent retreat to the safety of her old rocking chair! Sport walked over to Helen, licked her hand in obedience to his young mistress, and meekly returned to his spot by the cellar door. He promptly resumed his snoring as though the incident had never occurred! Helen eyed the rest of us smugly, as if to say "Let that be a lesson for you all!" Her disdainful look was directed toward our grandmother, as well. And poor old Grandma could only stare at the derelict dog in disbelief, as she gently massaged her bruised and swollen ankle!

School days, how Helen hated them. Many a morning our mother would take a switch to Helen's backside and literally spank her little redhead all the way (3 blocks) to the schoolhouse, where she again struggled to get her inside the large double doors. Once inside, there was no chance for escape on the part of the child, and she would have to cope with the goodly nuns as best she could. Our mother would breathe a sigh of relief but, alas, too soon. For, she'd then spot me happily playing on the big swings at the other end of the playground. Unbeknownst to my mom, I had followed along discreetly at a safe distance, hiding myself behind the trees that lined the streets. But soon, I too, felt the sting of my mother's switch across my bare legs as she headed me in the opposite direction toward home.

As we grew older, it eventually became our lot in life to perform many dreaded (I *hated* housework!) household tasks. Helen was a natural, whereas I was the kitchen klutz! When it came to cooking, her culinary efforts would have put Julia Child to shame! I could not even boil water—and *never* failed to burn the bacon—it took me years to finally realize that one did *not* read "Little Women" and fry bacon simultaneously! At cleaning, Helen was the original "Janitor in a Drum"—industrial strength! I was the type that swept the dirt *under* the rugs! Babysitting created no problem for the little mother—she was always in complete control and had her charges under her thumb. Again, there was Hildi, who usually managed to get herself into more "hot water" than the children she was supposed to be charge of. In the sewing department, Helen, after a few lessons, became an able and dexterous seamstress. My own seams were always crooked—zippers sewed in up-side down, buttons popping off, collars stitched awry—*so* disgusting! Let's face it. I could *never* hold a candle to my sister's capabilities and soon learned to live with my own inadequacies and within her shadow. She was a Betty Crocker—I, an Erma Bombeck!

Frank

It is the generous spirit who when brought upon the plan that
Pleased his boyish thought; whose high endeavors
are an inward light;
That makes the path before him always bright;
Who with a natural instinct to discern
What knowledge can perform—is diligent to learn.
This is the happy warrior; this is he
That every man in arms should wish to be!

—William Wordsworth

Francis George:

1932-

And now, we have Brother Frank—my "cohort in crime" (according to Sister Justiniana, Frank's favorite nun); this opinion being based on the fact that I would never tattle on my brother when he got into trouble at school, which was often! It was Sister Justiniana who would give me notes regarding my brother's delinquency addressed to our mother. Somehow, these telltale notes never reached my mother!

Our Frank alias Frankie alias Francis George alias F.S., the kid alias the Goatman alias Spitzie alias "coach" was dubbed with all of these pseudonyms and many more. Call him what you will! I remember them all—and knew them well!

I guess perhaps my favorite personality was F.S., the *kid*, F.S. was the strong, silent type—he was *tall*, he was *tough*, and he was *terrible*! The six-shooter that he toted had long ago earned him a great deal of respect and much fear from his contemporaries. And like one before him with similar fame, (the Lone Ranger and his well-known silver bullet) our young F.S. left a trail of his ominous presence behind him. His initials, "F.S., the *kid*" were lettered on the covers and pages of his textbooks; imbedded into the peeling paint of his iron bed post; artistically scribed (displaying his own inimitable typestyle) in the beautiful walnut finish of our mother's dining room buffet; roughly scratched into the woodwork of the window sill by his bed; and knifed into any tree trunk or stump that by happenstance appeared on the trail behind him! One always knew he'd just missed contact with the elusive F.S. This notorious trademark was carefully etched into each and every one of his possessions including the handle of the very gun that he wielded with such skill and dexterity!

Of course, that famous weapon was in reality, only a "rubber gun" roughly sawed out of a 1 × 4 with a "pincher" clothespin as its trigger and a ready supply of inner tube bands (with a knot tied in the center forming a figure "8") sufficing as the ammunition. But, not to worry! Even with, or shall I say, "in spite of" his homemade "rod," our hero *never* failed to get his man. For his shot was steady and his aim was true! He was indeed the "fastest gun" in Guttenberg! Known by one and all as one of the good guys!

This macho gun-totin' cowpoke thought it was sissy to play with girls and never would condescend to include me in his adventurous escapades—made me *mad*! But, one day (due to parental coercion on the part of my father), F.S., most reluctantly consented to allow his little sister (boy, was he embarrassed—what would the guys think?) to play with them. Since I was the only female (mind you, ERA would love this tale), I was appointed to act as the "ranch cook." I was thrilled for all of about five minutes. The cowboys (Frank and his buddies) went out to "git the Injuns" and, meanwhile, back at the ranch the elected cook had to, of all things, *Cook*! One had to get up mighty early in the morning to outsmart old F.S.! Now, I would be the last person in the world to call my brother a male chauvinist—but . . . .

"Spitzie! Spitzie! He's our man—if he can't do it—*nobody* can! Rah! Yay! Team!" Somehow after Frank, we were all called "Spitzie," me, Larry, Celie, and John—I'm not sure when and if the nickname ever died out. But that name originated with our big brother and we all made our own feeble attempt to live up to it. That was *not* easy! Frank loved—loves—and lives basketball. He has created his own living legacy in that respect—one needs only to look toward his offspring as positive proof. Of course, he has had the approval, encouragement, and support of his wife, Jackie, through all these years. "Behind every good man, there stands a good woman!" Right, Jackie?

I suppose if I were to compare any one of the nine boys with our father, I would have to say that Frank is most like the young George Spielbauer. He has the same subtle sense of dry humor, that same and by now, famous Spielbauer grin, the same ambling walk, the slow drawling manner of speech, the strong dedication to hard work—I could go on and on listing the "like father-like son" characteristics, but, in short, Frank is truly a chip off the old block!

In the words of my son, Trent, who spent the greater part of one summer with Frank's family: "Frank is really a good guy—he never gets mad and he doesn't talk much, but, when he does, you'd better listen. For an 'old guy,' he can sure play ball, why, he's *almost* as good as Kenny! (Frank's oldest son)."

And in the words of Frank's own son, Mike; "My dad is good—He is the *best*!"

Hildi

Forever earthbound are my feet upon the rocky road ahead,
but high among the clouds my thoughts—and so my heart is
comforted. Too short, indeed, these precious years, to let a dream
die needlessly—beyond tomorrow there awaits a time and place
designed for me. And old hopes rising one by one
are golden wings against the sun.

—Grace E. Easley

Hildagarde Rose: 1934-

The year 1934 was a very good year—for both vintage wine and vintage women! 'Twas the year of my birth. I now turn this vignette over to Brother Jim, who has a much greater talent for expressing himself than "yours truly."

* * *

There were two bedrooms upstairs. The girls' room was the smaller one to the left of the stairway. The door was almost always closed and the keyhole was stuffed with toilet paper to keep the boys from peeking. Would boys peek at their sisters in a good Catholic home? Yes, they would. Not me, of course; it was one of the older boys. Our sister, Helen threatened to "wring his neck" if she ever caught him at it again. It was she who stuffed the paper in the keyhole.

I don't remember much of Kathleen and Rosy's time at home; they married and moved away when I was very small. Soon Helen married her woodsman and then Hildagarde and Cecilia were the only girls left. They were smart and beautiful and I was proud of both of them. Hilda graduated as valedictorian of her high school class in 1952, when I was in fourth grade. She had read the first chapters of Tom Sawyer to me when I was a toddler; so I was early introduced to good literature.

Hilda had wanted to go to college, but with fourteen kids and Dad's job at the Furniture Factory in Dubuque, there was no money for such a thing. In high school, she had worked for the local weekly journal, The Guttenberg Press, folding the newspaper pages, which had been set by a linotype machine, as they rolled off an antiquated printing press. I don't know what her other duties were, but her boss, the editor and owner, must have been impressed with her intelligence for he offered to pay her way through college on a loan, if she so wished. Charles Millham was his name and he strongly encouraged her to further her education at the University of Iowa. He should have known or must have known that our parents would be insulted and never allow her to accept this offer. Also they were very protective and deemed her entirely too young to leave the nest. It was the first big disappointment in Hilda's life.

After high school, Hilda worked for Sammy Meyer, an electrician who kept a store uptown selling TV sets, radios, and kitchen appliances. She kept the books, ran the store when Sam was out and shyly endured the playful flirtatious advances that Sam made toward her—he was known as a "ladies man" and flirted outrageously with all the girls from seven to seventy! It was from this store that she purchased a high-fidelity record player with a bleached mahogany cabinet. She also bought a whole lot of records—mostly 78s. The long-play albums and 45 rpm singles were just starting to come out in those days. You had to have a special spindle for the 45s—they had a big hole in the middle.

Suddenly, the house was full of music—it came from Hilda and Celie's room, where that new phonograph played loudly whenever she was home. Now, at last, we brothers were invited in occasionally where she willingly shared her music with us.

It was a whole new world to us—Louis Armstrong, Woody Herman, Count Basie, Glenn Miller, and Tommy Dorsey. There were new names like Sarah Vaughn and Billy Eckstein, Dave Brubeck, Nat King Cole, Sammy Davis Jr., The Andrews Sisters, Ralph Martieri, and many others. My father didn't appreciate the sounds; he had to rise very early to get to work; so he would holler up the stairs and order us to "turn that damn thing down!" or "off," depending on the hour.

Progressive Jazz was all the rage, then. Hilda subscribed to Downbeat, a musical periodical, which she shared with all of us. I learned about jazz and came to know such names as Charlie Parker, Ornette Coleman, John Coltrane, Thelonius Monk, and Dizzy Gillespie; but those records weren't readily available in the hinterland of northeast Iowa, not in the early fifties. You would have to go all the way to the big city of Dubuque if you wanted such recordings. And you would have to wait a few years, I think.

There was a dancehall in Dubuque called the Melody Mill, and Louis Armstrong played there on St. Patrick's Day in the winter of 1953. Hilda got a ticket somehow and arranged to go there with some of her friends, including our cousin, Gary Hanson. "So, you're going to see the 'Big Satchmo'?" asked Uncle Hanson, amused at her enthusiasm.

"Oh, yes," said Hilda, starry-eyed. "I wouldn't miss him for the world." "He can sure play that horn," Uncle Hanson admitted grudgingly, "but he can't sing a note. He ought to just shut up and let his trumpet sing for him." "Ah, but I like the way he sings," insisted Hilda. "His voice may not be pretty, but it is different and he is a wonderful entertainer!"

Afterward she showed me her trophy of this occasion—the great musician's autograph! She told me how she had been able to speak with Louie, himself, backstage after his performance. He told his young fans how he practiced every day, even when he wasn't on tour—so much that his lips were sore and cracked and he had to use special salves of his own mixture, in order to ease the pain enough to play at all.

Louis Armstrong went on to some bigger city and my sister now listened to other musicians and newer recordings by Stan Kenton, Duke Ellington—artists like Shelley Mann, Gerry Mulligan, and others. Dave Brubeck cut an album called *Jazz Goes to College*. Hilda never got there (college) until she moved to Cedar Rapids and enrolled in night-school at Coe College. But I'm getting ahead of my story.

When she was still at home, her girlfriends would often come by to listen to records. I was allowed to join the group. She liked to show me off because I was intelligent and articulate for a fifth-grader and her friends, Alice Tujetsch and Augusta Handke, thought I was cute "for a little boy." I would sit on the floor listening to the "hot, hair-tossing music" as Alice so dramatically described it—and try to "sneak a peek" at the buxom Augusta (she was one good-looking chick), while Sammy Davis sang

> The red grapes shine like rubies on the vine
> but the fruit has the taste of bitter wine . . .

After a few years, Hildagarde got tired of doing Sam's bookwork and was bored with the "sameness" of the small town lifestyle. She eventually moved to Cedar Rapids with Alice where she found a better job. I hated to see her go—for she took all her wonderful music with her. Augusta broke my heart when she married an "older man" and Hilda soon fell in love with an insurance man from Marshalltown, who was into modern jazz, naturally. In the meantime, I was going through a lot of changes, growing up slowly, and sometimes painfully. But I never forgot that course in Music Appreciation that I learned from my sister and her extensive record collection so many years ago.

"When the music is gone," said Eric Dolphy, "it is in the air; and you can never capture it again." Maybe so, but those vinyl discs sure came close to reproducing it for us, even if they do get scratched and worn out too soon. As somebody else once wrote, "The song is ended, but the melody lingers on . . ."

Thank you, Hilda!

Larry

There is a destiny that makes us brothers—
none goes his way alone.
All that we send into the lives of others,
comes back into our own!

—Author Unknown

Lawrence Robert:

1936-
Dec 18, 2015

Once again, you guessed it—the birth of a baby, and, true to form, another bouncing, baby boy! Larry was the second redheaded child born into the family. I believe the red hair (our mom and dad both had black hair) was finally traced to our Grandmother Juliana Johll Rohner, but when we knew our Grandma, she was already an old lady and her hair was white as snow!

Our little brother soon developed a profusion of freckles—all of us were freckled to some degree or another, but none so well endowed with "angel kisses" as little Larry. He too possessed that famous grin, which by now seemed to be a prerequisite for being born into this prestigious family of "play-farmers!"

Naturally, being only two years younger than myself, Larry played a starring role in most of my early recollections. In delving into the deep dark recesses of my child's mind, I recall the morning Larry and I decided to play "house." Actually, I decided, Larry simply responded with a somewhat intellectual "goo-goo-ga-ga," which I promptly interpreted as acquiescence to my plans. Playing house was innocent enough, of course, but we chose Celie's crib to be our happy home! She was *so* tiny, I can still remember Mama saying, "Now, you kids, be careful of the soft spot," whenever anyone would get near the baby. Celie naturally was "the baby," Larry "the papa," and me "the mama."

It all started you see, because I had received a new little broom from Santa Claus and needed to create the perfect setting for our game of "pretend."

I scooted and shoved Larry up and over the side of the crib and climbed in after him. He was almost two years old and I about three and a half; together we pushed and pulled the baby down to one end of the mattress and turned her sideways at the foot of the bed. We partitioned off (using wadded up baby blankies) a bedroom for our "baby" (she slept blissfully through it all), a living room for "papa Larry" (where he sat and sucked his thumb.) Well, what *else* do you expect a two-year-old papa to do? We also made a kitchen where "mama Hildi" became so engrossed in sweeping the dirty floor, she didn't even notice the *real* mama Frances appearing on the scene! Poor Larry was rudely snatched from his living room and I was literally thrown out of my own kitchen! What a way to treat the "lady of the house!" We were both spanked soundly and sent back to bed!

Seems as though you and I were the recipients of many a spanking in those days, Larry. Most of the time the spankings were justified, as was the case when Dad caught us on the railroad tracks. We could hear the train whistle warning us of its arrival, but couldn't see it, so we thought we had plenty of time. But that old train came zooming "round the bend" at a break-neck speed and by that time, Dad had spotted us on the tracks and well, you *know* the rest! Then there was the time we both got it so bad—and to this day, I swear, by all that is *holy*, we did *not* deserve it! Someone, (I always suspected Albert Jaeger, the ice-man) told Dad that he'd seen you and me playing on the frozen Mississippi River down by the ice house. It was early spring and the river had begun to thaw a little. The part that we were allegedly on broke away and started to float out. We jumped (according to the "report") to a more solid section of ice and worked our way back to shore. However, the more vehemently we denied this accusation, the harder Dad spanked! Now, I could understand his not believing you—'cause you fibbed a lot, but, I *never* lied.

And the games you used to play! Poor Mrs. Ben Voss (we called her "old Mama Fuss") was at her wit's end with those awful Spielbauer boys living right across the alley. Now Larry, you knew darned good and well, that little apple tree was her pride and joy! Especially when it reached the maturity to bear fruit. Its very first harvest was just one perfectly formed apple that hung by a most delicate stem in the very center of the tree. "Mama Fuss" checked on its development each and every day. Alas, one morning, she observed that someone had (oh, so very carefully) taken a large bite out of the apple and amazingly enough, the apple was still precariously hanging from its branch! One could still see the culprit's teeth marks. Who could be so dastard as to commit such a terrible act? We all knew it had to be someone with a great deal of dexterity and finesse to be able to manage that "not-too-easy," albeit evil task! Not one person came forward and confessed. But, *you*, Larry, you always got that Cheshire-cat grin on your face every time the apple incident was mentioned, even in later years. I don't mean to point any fingers, but I have always had my suspicions!

Note: June, 2004 (John confesses)

I am so chagrinned! And, Larry, I truly owe you my deepest apologies! Our Brother John finally confessed to Rose and myself after all these years. Neither of us could believe that he was the guilty party. Worse yet, it was a one-man crime!

It seems as though our little brother created a makeshift scaffolding out of some nearby stacked firewood directly beneath the apple tree. He made it high enough so his mouth was in direct contact with the hanging fruit. He placed one arm around the nearest branch for balance and holding the apple in his other hand, carefully bit into it without breaking the stem! Larry, you are hereby exonerated of all guilt!

Celie

To perfection—and to beauty—and to soul.
Long were you a dream
In your mother's sleep;
And then she woke
To give you birth.

—Kahlil Gibran

Cecilia Margaret:

1937-

A Bopsy is born! "What is a Bopsy," you ask? We'd probably have to ask Uncle Hanson, since he was the one who gave Celie the nickname; my guess would be someone *very* special, someone *so* sweet, precious, loving, and loved! She is the apple of her mama's eye and her papa's pride and joy!

She is everyone's sweetheart. A "Bopsy" is most decidedly the baby sister—and the one daughter most like our own mother. I do believe that each of us girls was fortunate enough to carry on just one small trait of our mother's marvelous personage; however, our Celie has inherited them all! Thusly, she is a composite of all her older sisters. She is . . . .

Kathy's . . . sweet and pretty
Rosy's . . . kind and gentle
Helen's . . . strength and fire
Hildi's . . . I really don't know what—perhaps my tears and sensitivity.

However, and on this, we all agree; she is the pick of the litter! If our brother Frank is a "chip off the old block," then young Celie is indeed our mother's child—our own "little Francie."

No question about it, Cele was always our father's favorite—she never, *ever* received a spanking, not once in her entire lifetime. I remember the rest of us getting the old switcheroo from time to time and being in the doghouse on more than one occasion, but *never* the Bopsy! Truth is, she never needed to be reprimanded—she was just naturally good! And even though the rest of us fought amongst ourselves in good friendly sibling rivalry, none of us ever had recourse to be at odds with Celie—we just loved her too much! Baby sisters indeed are "special!"

Celie and I were very close and grew up together, pretty much on the same wavelength. Remember those apartment days in Cedar Rapids, Celie? Just two little "green as grass" small town girls venturing forth, hand in hand, into the cold cruel social world of the big city. Unprepared for what lay ahead, one blindly leading the other. We stumbled and we fumbled—you bet we did, on more than one occasion! But, we managed to get through it all OK—didn't we, Sis? We always resented the strict manner in which our parents brought us up during those formative high school years, but as time passed on and we both got a few more "smarts," we appreciated that earlier curtailment. At least, that is what I tell my own kids today—and I'll bet that you do too, don't you, Celie?

I was always so proud of my little sis and loved to "show her off" to all my friends. All the guys in C.R. wanted me to fix them up with Cele on blind dates, but I refused to do so. First of all, they were nowhere near good enough for her (at least in my estimation) and second, she was already loyal to Vern. My proudest moment was the time her coworkers from Quaker Oats selected our sister to represent their company in a city-wide beauty contest "Industrial Queen of Cedar Rapids." In 1957 or '58, I think. This was quite an honor and Celie really should have worn that crown. She was, by far the prettiest and best all-round candidate, but unfortunately, she lost by only a small margin to a girl who worked in my own office at Cryovac. But, in my book, Cele was always the winner!

We shared a lot together, my sis and I, in those single apartment days. The same friends, same clothes (we both were identical in size then—and I think, still are), the same experiences, laughter, tears, and good times. Remember when I conned you into taking a Beginning Calculus course (night school) at Coe College (approximate time again '57 or '58). You were not much interested in advanced math and, I must confess, neither was I, but I had this mad crush on the professor who looked somewhat like Burt Lancaster and who at the time was my favorite "tough guy." But after a few weeks, and much grumbling on your part, I must have become bored with either the professor or the course, or both and we dropped out—much to your relief!

Somewhere along the way, during those C.R. days, our big sister/little sister roles got reversed. Even though she was the younger one, Celie always had her head on straighter than I did, and more often than not, she played the role of mentor to her older sister who was most often in need of advice. Someday soon, my *big*-little sister, the two of us must get together and reminisce about those good old days. Confession Time—I have an ulterior motive and a method to my madness, I just feel the need for some sisterly advice—one more time!

John

The strong men keep coming on
They go down shot, hanged, sick, broken.
They live on fighting, singing, lucky as plungers
The strong mothers pulling them on.
The strong mothers pulling them from a dark sea,
A great prairie, a long mountain.
Call hallelujah! Call amen! Call deep thanks
The strong men keep coming on.

—Carl Sandburg

Loras John: 1940

As we move on down these ever-lengthening stairs, we once again follow suit in the girl-boy procession of new babies. Our little brother, Loras John, has arrived. Johnnie holds the unique distinction of being the first, of only two babies, born in a hospital. While our mother was out of town—all the way to Iowa City—for this occurrence, we were watched over by a certain Mrs. Helen Krogman (a cousin of Mom's, I think. And that is another story, all by itself!) We shall return to Mrs. Krogman later in this book.

From day one, we (the children) dropped the Loras from our baby brother's Christian name and henceforth, he has been affectionately known as Johnnie. Indeed, he is our own "dear John" and undoubtedly the favored one of all of us.

Dear John, I have always thought of you as the mainstream of our family; constant as the old Mississippi; never changing course; sometimes meandering lazily, but more often flowing steadily and silently to the sea. The rest of us have each traveled our separate pathways, for we, in essence, are no more than tributaries of sorts, wending our way in whatever direction destiny has chosen to lead us.

Yet, we all bask in the comfort and knowledge, John, that you are there, as you always have been since our father passed away; our mother's right hand and her one reliable source of strength and stability! And you are an important part of "going home" to each and every one of us, John. We are all indebted to you for maintaining a very precious part of our childhood (the house that most of us) grew up in. Granted, it may not be much by today's housing standards, and those smooth talking glib-tongued Real Estate agents might not exactly sing "*Glory to its Name.*" But, that old house, dear Brother, has a heap of memories and as the old songwriter says, it has known some "*sad times*"—some "*good and bad times*!" Her memories are worth more than money could ever buy! Going home means more to us than you shall ever know. Dear John, thank you for being there and keeping us together.

And, who among us can go home and not help him or herself to John's lavish lending library of paperbacks? Yes, indeed, the old "dormer" bedroom that once was over-run by a passel of rough-neck, rowdy, pillow-fighting brothers has dramatically been transformed into a subdued and quiet study. Shelves and shelves of John's paperbacks now line the walls and overflow into whatever available floor space that remains.

Each trip home finds me closeted within the confines of this room, delving through volumes of delicious literature and I usually end up taking at least a six-month supply of reading material with me when I leave. And I am not alone—brothers, sisters, in-laws, nieces, nephews—all of us have been, at some time or another, the recipients of Brother John's gracious generosity. The only "law of his library" is unwritten and that is simply to return any and all books "on loan" only to make them available to some other avid reader.

Johnnie, being the oldest of my entourage of baby brothers, is extra special to me because I remember him best as my little assistant in keeping the others in line. It is at this point, in time, that I began to think of my five little brothers (as one) collectively rather than on an individual basis. From the time I was about twelve years old, I had them "in tow" at all times. Just like Mary and her little lamb, "my" boys were sure to follow! Oftentimes, I felt just like Mother Duck as these "five" strung out behind me in single file!

I was much like a combination big sister/teacher—surrogate Mom and built-in babysitter in those days. However, I could always rely on little John (he was very studious and serious and displayed a strong sense of responsibility even then) for his help. He was very capable of taking charge of the in-between ages (this would have been Tom and Jim) and I, of course, would handle the baby, David, and without fail, always have a firm grip on Danny, who was the mischievous one! I could *never* trust "that one" out of my sight—but that, folks, too is another story!

And now, on to Danny!

Danny

A boy is truth with dirt on its face; beauty with a cut on its finger, Wisdom with bubble gum in its hair and the hope of the future with a frog in its pocket. Nobody else is so early to rise or so late to supper. A boy is a magical creature—you can lock him out of your workshop; but you can't lock him out of your heart!

—Author Unknown

Daniel Lee:

1941-

You may find it hard to believe that I ever run out of words—but on rare occasions, it does happen. And, frankly, right now, I just don't know how to express myself—except, "Dammit, Danny! You were *supposed to be a girl*!"

And your name was supposed to be "Danielle Leigh"—*not* Daniel Lee! You broke our pattern—you ruined our image. They (Dad and the older kids) told me you were a little boy and I would not believe them. At least, *not* until Mom brought you home from the hospital in Iowa City and I watched her change your diapers for the very first time and—*whoa*! I was faced with the bare facts—with stark naked reality! Then, and mind you only then, did I cease to call you Danielle Leigh and most reluctantly accepted you as her male counterpart, Danny Lee.

You were born with the very devil in your eyes and the very devil in your grin—you were just full of it, such a tease, but I must admit, at the same time you were an adorable toddler! I could never really stay upset with you. I remember well the "terrible twos" you went through, and what the family went through; I didn't think any of us would survive—it seems as though you did not grow out of that stage for at least 10-15 years! Even though you infuriated me, my heart would ultimately go out to you whenever you were punished (which you so often and so richly deserved). When you did get a spanking, you would always crawl under Mom and Dad's big bed (like a little puppy crawling off to lick his wounds). I couldn't stand to see your tears, so I too would crawl under the bed to comfort and console you!

Oh my god! I almost forgot! Our house (the one in the alley) had just two large bedrooms upstairs. The boys had the biggest one and it was furnished just like a dorm with double beds lined up all along one wall. The girls' room only had two double beds—Helen and Celie shared one and Rosy and I, the other—which actually was nothing more than a wide cot. Well, after Rosy left home, I had the *whole* bed to myself! But, alas such luxury could only be short-lived. The boys' room was already full to overflowing with brothers, so wouldn't you know it? I was forced to share my bed with my little brother! (Dammit, Danny, one more time! You were *supposed to be a girl!*) And, of course, you just had go to school and tell everyone that you slept with me and I was *so* embarrassed! I shall *never* forgive you!

"Blessed are the poor! For the Kingdom shall be theirs!" Danny, you are truly blessed, thrice blessed, as a matter of fact. I was to take all five of my little brothers to church after school to have their throats blest. On February 3, the Catholic Liturgy pays homage to a goodly and kind man by the name of St. Blasé, who as legend or perhaps the bible has it, became canonized into sainthood because he blessed the throat of a young lad (who had swallowed a fish bone). Thus, he saved the boy's life.

So here we are—en route to the church to partake of this holy ritual. Now, I was well aware of the fact that I would be unable to monitor all five little brothers and still keep an admonishing eye transfixed on Danny's person at the same time. The only recourse I had was to make several trips to the altar, leaving Johnnie (good old dependable John) in charge of the little ones who remained in the pew. Naturally Danny, unable to be trusted outside of my visual scope, was forced to make each trip to the altar with me and thus received the Blessing of the good St. Blasé on each occasion! Danny, you are indeed, the *most blessed* person I know!

Seriously, Dan, you were not nearly as "terrible" as I have jokingly sketched you. Even as a little boy, I could sense a kindness and sensitivity developing within you. You had a certain protective love and caring directed toward your younger brothers. And I now take the liberty of quoting your own little brother Jim, who says it all so much better than I.

Dan was the brother closest to me in age. He was my shield and protector in a lot of nasty situations; especially around the school. He bore the brunt of the cruel social war that children play when they don't know any better. He was a good athlete, tall and big of frame, but somehow more vulnerable than me. He cared about the ostracism and pecking-order games of the social world. He learned to run faster, fight harder and talk louder than his schoolmates. He saved me from drowning once, but could never stand my incessant philosophizing.

Jimmy

They said he had the pip—and must have pepper and butter. But, he got kisses, and he was a poet; and was buffeted and kissed alternately, all his life. His thoughts took wings and flew up and away, like singing butterflies—the emblem of immortality!

—Hans Christian Anderson

James Leonard:
1942-

The year is 1942—and, would you believe another man-child again graces us with his presence? What is it with this male population explosion? I knew my mother always said she preferred raising sons to daughters, but this is getting to be a bit of a bore.

Brother Jim was an angelic cherub as a baby—and my own personal "little luv." I shall never forget his endearing smile and those soulful eyes. Even before he could talk baby talk, those limpid pools of wisdom spoke volumes of words and asked a multitude of questions that *not* one person in the world was able to answer. He already was a little scholar from the moment of his birth and continuously quested after knowledge and forever sought the reason "why"!

Once he even asked me "why" Jesus on the Cross wore diapers instead of regular clothing. I had been reading Bible stories to him and he'd become entranced with a Holy picture of the Crucifixion. Well, I gave it my best shot—but the more I tried to explain, the more inquisitive he became, and I soon found myself bombarded by an onslaught of rhetorical questions that reached far beyond my intellectual capacity. Finally, in a moment of defeated desperation, I told him the clothing in question was not a diaper, but was referred to as "swaddling clothes," and (I continued to explain) the Virgin Mary wrapped Baby Jesus in them before she laid him in the manger, etc.

Well, this very young, astute student of philosophy gave me a somewhat sardonic look that smirked of superior intelligence. The originator, or perhaps a better choice of words, prevaricator of "The Tale of the Holy Attire" (namely me) could only hang her head in abject, not to mention, remorseful shame! Alas, this was *not* the only (albeit the first) time that I was to be "bested" by the mastermind of my little brother.

Jim as a little child existed in an imaginary world created by his own ingenious mind. I loved to tell my five little brothers bedtime stories; but it wasn't long before Jimmy took over. He started out first by adding just a little at a time, but soon became so adept at the art of storytelling that I often found myself listening with rapt attention to his own embellished versions.

Jim, (like many toddlers) had his favorite baby quilt that soon took on the typical, tattered, threadbare, raggedy appearance of most cherished "blankies." To our little brother, this bedraggled piece of nostalgia became a "Magic Carpet" that carried him to far-off exotic lands each and every night as he closed his eyes in slumber, and gave way to his vivid imagination. It became his own dream machine and he would willingly relate these visions of grandeur to me in glowing detail the next morning as he sat in his high chair and consumed bowls of milk and bread and sugar, his favorite repast.

As I recall, he had a little difficulty differentiating between fact and fiction; thusly, much of his childhood was lived in a fictional state of mind. He'd heard the old story (from our mother) of how Dad, as a young boy, lived in a log house in Buenie. And from that one single truth, he created a make-believe story of our mother, our father, and good old Honest Abe growing up together and living happily ever after in what else? Log cabins, of course! And, of course, they *never* told a lie!

I don't think our mother appreciated being portrayed as "aged" as the good Mr. Lincoln, however, especially when Jim went to school and told the nuns that his mother was a personal friend of Abraham's and knew him well from the "olden days"!

Helen reminds me of the time when Jim and his friend, Chuckie Zapf, were playing "cops and robbers." Jim kept shooting Chuckie with, what else, a rubber gun! And, much like his big brother, F.S., the *kid*, Jim's shot too was steady and his aim was true; but Chuckie would not cooperate and refused to "fall down and die" like bad robbers were supposed to do. This total disregard for the rules of the game on Chuckie's part sent our little brother running into the house in a tearful rage!

My mind conjures up yet, another image of young Jim. Yes, I recall with great fondness the cherubic little altar boy clad in his black cassock and white lace-trimmed surplice, hands devoutly folded and eyes reverently downcast—one could just envision a halo of holiness hovering above his head. Even then, our brother Jim had a dream—never lose sight of that dream, Jim, you are gaining on it more rapidly than you know. And one day, brothers and sisters, hear me—and hear me well—we will all be able to say "I knew him—when!"

Tommy

Blessings on thee, little man
Barefoot boy with cheek of tan!
With thy turned-up pantaloons,
And thy merry whistled tunes;
With thy red lip, redder still;
Kissed by strawberries on the hill.
Ah! That thou couldst know thy joy,
Ere it passes, barefoot boy!

—John Greenleaf Whittier

Thomas Michael:

1944-

And a little man indeed was our Tommy. My memory recalls that he was the biggest baby our mother gave birth to, weighing in at approximately 12 lbs., and ultimately one day, to become the tallest of her nine sons. He was a very handsome lad, quiet, and reserved—a serious student—and always a perfect gentleman. Tommy, in my estimation is much like our brother, Arnie. Not just the "tall, dark, and handsome" part, but the intellectual side of our older brother as well. Both of them possess a keen analytical mind and have an exceptional superior ability in the solving of mathematical problems.

I was almost into my teens when Tommy and little David (born two years later) were toddlers and they soon became like my own babes. I sang lullabies and rocked them to sleep on a regular basis. They were beautiful little boys and I loved them dearly, lavishly spending my hard-earned babysitting money on store-bought presents for them.

Kuempel and Lakes's Hardware store was, at that time, Guttenberg's only answer to a Toy Store, especially during the holiday season. I frequented it often. How excited I was, when I had finally saved enough money to purchase cowboy hats and a set of guns and holsters for each of these two youngest brothers—just in time for Christmas!

Actually, I loved to buy things for all five of my little brothers. I felt they deserved to have the playthings that most other children took for granted, but were very hard to come by in our large family. When I began to earn a weekly paycheck on my own, I was able to present them with much nicer gifts—like that electric train set. Even our father got down on the floor to play with the boys then and had actually assisted them in permanently mounting the oval track to a large piece of plywood for easier set-up. But, the best present of all was the bright shiny, red and white 2-wheeled bicycle, which of course had to be shared by all five little boys.

Mom had tried to talk me out of it—saying, "It's *not* a good idea. They'll just be fighting over it most of the time." But, such was not the case. For these little boys, like their older siblings, had learned at a very early age how to share and willingly took turns throughout their entire childhood riding that bike. Ah! But one special day, my little brothers decided that "turnabouts is fair play" and much to my surprise, they emptied out their "money jars," pooled their resources, and proudly presented their big sister with an awesome twenty-first birthday gift! I was deeply touched!

The following story has been told to me by Juanita Kann. She along with her husband, Carl, owned an exclusive gift shop known as Kann's Imports. Please bear in mind that this store did not exactly cater to such rough-neck, barefoot, rowdy little boys, as my brothers; but like it or not, they made their grand entrance into Mrs. Kann's shop, proudly carrying a canning jar filled with loose change that was the accumulation of all their worldly wealth.

As Rich As Rockefeller

(as told by Juanita Kann)

It was the start of Labor Day weekend, late Friday afternoon. Carl and I were sitting on the bench out in front enjoying the balmy afternoon. The traffic had become more congested in the past hour, with the usual tourists and island dwellers towing boats and campers already descending upon the town. I had just mentioned to Carl that it was almost time for me to lock up for the day, when around the corner, here they came—those little Spielbauer boys, all talking at once!

"Are you still open? We want to buy a birthday present for our sister," said one. "Yeah, and we need it for tonight, 'cause she's coming home for the weekend. She likes earrings," said another. "She is really picky, though," piped the third. "And, she doesn't like "fake stuff," another voice spoke.

Then, Johnny (the one holding the money) motioned to one of the older boys and said, "Remember what Mom told you. You and Dave are supposed to stay out here and visit with Mr. Kann." He now looked in my direction and continued, "It's just 'cause Mom is worried that he," pointing to the smallest child, "might accidentally break something really expensive."

"Your Mother is a very wise woman," Carl quickly spoke up, and then patted the seat beside him, motioning for the boys to come and sit with him. "We'll just stay out here and chew the fat."

"Yeah, come on Dave. They don't need us to pick out some 'dumb old doodads,'" Danny offered. "That 'girl stuff' makes me nervous. I never did like shoppin' anyway."

The other three boys followed after me in single file as I entered the shop. First, there was John (the money man), who promptly and carefully emptied the coin jar onto my shining glass display case and proceeded to sort the money into one dollar stacks.

Next came Jim (who was most concerned in buying something that was *not* "fake stuff") and young Tom, who up to now had been the most quiet one in the bunch. Jim had, after much deliberation, decided on a pair of copper earrings.

Of course, I had to reassure him that they definitely were "real copper," but John (still counting the money) was worried. "Now, just hold your horses, here. We might not have enough money."

Those two boys continued to banter back and forth as they counted out their coins. I was hoping this wouldn't develop into a heavy argument, when suddenly young Tom steps up to the counter between them. Then, to my amazement, this little barefoot, T-shirted, dungaree-clad child flamboyantly threw his arms into mid-air and dramatically spoke as though he were a direct descendent of J. D. Rockefeller, himself! "Money is *no* object, here! I say we buy 'em!"

* * *

As it turned out, the boys were just eleven cents shy of the amount needed to purchase my twenty-first birthday present; but Mrs. Kann graciously gave them a "spur of the moment" sale price and even wrapped the package for free. Needless to say, I still have those "real copper" earrings and yes, dear brothers, I still wear them.

Well, that good-looking "big spender" of my youthful memory has now grown into a handsome young man. However, Tommy shall always remain in my heart as that little barefoot boy with "cheek of tan," who stood straight and tall with his big, brown eyes that even way back then, hinted of his manly strength of character and shyly spoke for him, "Look out world—here, I come!"

David

I am the child
All the world awaits for my coming,
All the earth watches with interest to see what I shall become.
Civilization hangs in the balance
For what I am, the world of tomorrow will be.

—M. G. Cole

David Edward:

1946-

"The child" was none other than little Dave. Perhaps, not all the world or all of the earth awaited his coming with interest; but let me assure you, at least eight older brothers and five devoted, not to mention, doting big sisters eagerly anticipated the birth of this child with (you got it) bated breath.

For he was the "last of our clan" and one more time (the third) red-haired offspring born into this family. He too was a picture of angelic innocence with large searching eyes and an uncontrollable mass of soft, curly ringlets that formed a living halo around his face. At first, these ringlets were a golden blonde, but in a short time, they deepened into a beautiful auburn shade and of course those inevitable freckles soon appeared.

I do not recall which one of my brothers initiated the tree house projects, but I remember well how Davey, as a little toddler, became greatly fascinated with climbing. Unfortunately, he also suffered from an inborn fear of heights. Actually, there were two tree houses: the first was nothing more than a platform floor wedged amongst and in betwixt the high central branches of the tree and nailed to the branches themselves. This first attempt at construction left much to be desired as it could only "house" one person at a time and was not very sturdy. However, my creative brothers managed to erect a second and more permanent dwelling, supported by four posts cemented into the ground. Now, they were able to add four walls, a roof and even a front door. A makeshift ladder led straight up to the elegant portico.

I think it was Jimmy who came up with the name "Castaway Castle" and he actually painted the name above the entrance. The boys also made a sign that read "*no girls allowed*" and secured it to the front door. This house rule was, of course, highly respected and obeyed by our entire family.

Davey loved to scamper up the rungs of the ladder like a frisky squirrel. But, once he reached the doorway and looked back down, he would without fail begin to panic, whimpering and whining, while frantically clinging to the top rung until an older sibling came to his rescue. On one such occasion, I was in the backyard hanging up laundry and he started yelling at me to come get him.

Now, I must confess, I couldn't help but tease him just a little so I responded by saying, "But, Davey, remember I am a girl—and girls are not allowed to climb up into the tree house. I can't save you."

After a short time, his brothers got fed up with his incessant crying and gave me the OK to rescue the toddler, who clung to me in panic as I carefully guided him to the ground. This actually allowed me to obtain a sneak peek into the interior and that, dear reader, is as close as any female ever came to entering "Castaway Castle."

David pulled this same old trick so many times that the other boys got sick and tired of his game. He'd been up on the highest step hanging on to the floor and door of the house, bawling so loudly that it alerted his little dog, Jinxie, who immediately began running in circles around the base of the tree house and barking loudly. Still, there was no help from his older brothers. Finally, David in desperation slowly and gingerly began to back down the rungs of the ladder still crying and shouting to the dog, "I will save you, Jinxie! I will save you!" Thus, it was that our little brother lost his phobia for heights and soon became very adept at scaling the rungs of that ladder in both "up and down" directions!

The little boys are all grown up now, and that old tree house is long gone. I vaguely remember someone telling me many years later a young father by the name of Marty Hefel sawed the tree house down and hauled it off to his backyard where he was able to reconstruct it for his own little boys. I'm sure they enjoyed it as much as my brothers did.

But, I shall always have that mental picture of a small boy dressed in blue denim dungarees and a home-made flannel shirt (lovingly stitched by Mama Frances), sitting on the outside cellar door with his arms protectively wrapped around a small black and white puppy whose name was Jinx. It was a toss-up as to "who loved whom" the most, for the two of them were inseparable. That dog was always at the heels of our little brother, nipping playfully at his pant leg, demanding the constant attention that he knew was his, but for the asking!

Baby Mary

Mother—the bells of Paradise are ringing, said the child.
"Mother, the sun is shining!"
And an overpowering light streamed forth upon her, and LO!
The child was lifted up!
All was cold around the mother;
She lifted her head and found herself lying in the churchyard . . .
Among the flowers of her child's grave.

—Hans Christian Anderson

Baby Mary:
1948-1948

August 17, 1948, dawned bright and beautiful. It was a perfect summer's morn—the sky was a clear and shining blue—the air was fresh and clean. Mother Nature had taken great pains to attire herself in her most lavish of gowns for today was truly a special day.

The sights and sounds of the little river town came through loud and clear. Dogs were barking—children laughing at their play—somewhere a train was whistling and somewhere a car was honking. White, bright clean laundry whipped freely in the wind as it hung from backyard clotheslines. In the distance, a river barge emitted several long loud blasts in greeting to the lockmaster in control of Lock and Dam # 10. The bright and happy faces of summer's blossoms bobbed a friendly "good morning" to any passerby who cared enough to glance their way. Butterflies flitted from flower to flower—birds were singing—and *so* was my heart!

For this new day that had so beautifully dawned only a few hours earlier was fast developing into a "new baby day" within the Spielbauer household. Soon it would be time to summon Mrs. Ferris. This very dear and ever sweet lady had helped our mother through many a "birthing" time in the foregoing years and was, more or less, our mother's own personal midwife. My pre-arranged responsibility was to gather all my little brothers and Celie. We were to go to Mrs. Jaeger's house and remain there until someone called us home. Yes, my heart was singing—for, ever since Mom had told me of the new arrival, I'd been praying for a baby sister! And today, I was going to get her! I just knew it!

I stayed close to Mrs. Jaeger's phone all afternoon, waiting impatiently. Gosh, it sure takes a long time to have a baby, I reflected. Finally, word from home! Celie and I quickly collected all the little brothers and herded them across Highway 52 and the railroad tracks. Just as we turned into the alley where we lived, we met Doug Gueder riding his bike. "Hey," he called, "Did they bury your new baby in a "regular coffin" or just an old cardboard box?"

My heart stopped beating! I looked at Celie—she, at me! We grabbed each other's hand and made a mad dash for home. We didn't even bother to answer Doug, nor did we stop to worry about the little boys; we were close enough to home by now, they could fend for themselves. We reached the front steps and stopped instantly. We listened intently. There was no sound to be heard. Silence reigned.

No longer the sound of dogs barking or children laughing—no more street sounds—or nature noises. Not even the sound we longed to hear—that of a new baby crying! Fear gripped our hearts, for only the sound of sadness and that awful stillness remained to greet us. Death, indeed, is a sneaking thief—even in broad daylight!

We crept quietly into the house. We didn't even let the door slam. Our father was slumped in a kitchen chair at the table, his head bowed in anguish. I asked, "Daddy, the baby, is it true?" He said nothing—only nodded his head. Celie and I slipped into the bedroom. Mrs. Ferris wouldn't look at us either, just kept fussing with Mom's blankets and smoothing the pillow under her dark hair. Our Mom looked so sad and white. So frail and tired. Her eyes were moist with unshed tears. Yet, she answered the question we were unable to ask of her.

"It was a baby girl. And, she looked a lot like you, Hilda, lots of dark hair." I sobbed, dashed out of the room, and up the stairs, threw myself on the bed and cried and cried! It was all my fault, you see. I'd prayed *too* hard for a baby sister. I should have just prayed that the baby be healthy and strong. Our new baby sister had been too tiny and delicate to survive the ordeal of her birth. I was truly heartbroken! "Oh, Mama, can you ever forgive me?"

Mom said it was not my fault—that, she too had prayed for a girl child. She thought it would be nice to have a little girl once again after five boys in a row. I was not to be consoled, however, and I would always feel my guilt!

Our little baby had already been baptized "Mary" and was buried that same afternoon—yes, in a "regular coffin" at the foot of Grandma Rohner's grave. We were not allowed to see her, which saddened me, even more so; but we all know that our Baby Mary has gone to "where the angels sing" and there she remains—the brightest and shiniest star in the heavens that hover over the little town of Guttenberg! And to this very day, when I am so deeply down and desolate, I look toward those heavens and search for our own shining star—our beloved Mary—and . . .

"Not until each loom is silent
And the shuttles cease to fly
Will God unroll the pattern
And explain the reason why.

The dark threads are as needful
In the Weaver's skillful hand,
As the threads of gold and silver
For the pattern which he planned!"

Author Unknown

Part II
My Story

Now, that you have met the family of George and Frances let us move on to the story proper; a story based on the growing up years of the children; a period of time that spans approximately fifty years.

Chapter I

Buenie

The dark-haired young farmer leaned his long and lanky frame against the doorway of the small clapboard house and with his right hand raised to shield the glaring late day sun, allowed his eyes to traverse the landscape before him, as it ascended upward into hilly terrain and then suddenly, without warning, dipped downward, creating low valleys. Huge boulders surrounded by small clumps of wild flowers dot what little grassland that exists.

He gazed at the panoramic view of the "Buenie" countryside. Geographically, the town of North Buena Vista was much too small to appear on the Iowa map; nonetheless, it was very well known due to its magnificent scenery. Someone had said that its literal translation means "good view" and, indeed it was all of that; however, "Buenie" was the local term of endearment for this friendly community. Everyone around here was related either by blood or marriage. George's own Ma lived just down the road a mile or so in the actual town itself.

This was a typical river town, located on the banks of The Mighty Mississippi, consisting of dirt roads, frame houses, and a Catholic Church, known as The Immaculate Conception, that in ensuing years would become famous or, perhaps a better choice of wording, infamous; thanks to its permissive gambling (*bingo*)!

And heaven forbid—the consumption of an alcoholic beverage (*beer*) on holy ground! This notoriety could only be blamed on the presence of the "beer tent" that was set up on the church property during its Annual Labor Day Picnic as a fundraiser for the parish. As I recollect, it did, indeed raise a lot of money!

The young man smiled to himself as he allowed his thoughts to wander once again to The Catholic Church and that one time when he had confessed his weekly sins to the good priest, Father Schmidt, the day after a severe snow storm had hit the area. He had fully expected the usual penance of six Our Fathers and six Hail Marys that Father consistently gave to his parishioners when they violated the Ten Commandments. And he was taken amiss when the priest said, "And now, for your penance, I want you to go down to the basement and fetch the snow shovel from behind the furnace. Go out and clean all the snow and ice off the sidewalks in front of the church. Be sure to chip the ice off the front steps too. That old Mrs. Engling has trouble getting round and she is always the first one in church on Sunday morning. We sure don't want her falling down on Church property!" It would have been much easier to pray the usual Our Fathers and Hail Marys, George reflected, to himself.

But, let us return to Buenie. Across the street from the church was a large one-room building that served as a General Store, the Post Office, and the local tavern (all rolled into one). On occasion, it even served as a dance hall on Saturday nights. There was always "cream sody" available for the women and children; but most of the men preferred to indulge in "tap" or home-brewed beer.

George's cousin Fritz Brimeyer (and his, wife, Hilda) owned the farmland next to his own. He and Fritz were good buddies when they were younger, just "this side of bein' on the wild side." They nearly drove their mothers to insanity! But enough of this reminiscing, it is time he looked to the future. He had to make this farming thing work! It was one hell of a tough, hard life, scratching a living out of this land; this rocky soil was enough to break a man's back—and, a man's spirit, as well! George sighed deeply as he headed out to the shed to find a pitchfork and bushel basket. He promised to dig up some new potatoes for Frances.

It was the fall of '27 and young George Spielbauer was worried about the long cold winter that was inevitably creeping up on them. He gathered his tools and headed toward the garden patch that darn near drove him crazy with those "damnable" weeds. Little did he know that for the rest of his life he would forever wage his personal vendetta in a private warfare against those "damnable" weeds!

The pretty little toddler (two-year-old Kathleen) kept up a steady stream of baby prattle as she gaily skipped and hopped her way along the path beside him. Her short, chubby baby legs were forced to work three to four times as rapidly as George's in order to keep pace with his giant strides. Together, he and the child labored over the small hills of dried up leaves and stalks, or rather, he labored—the child played. Each mound of dirt he uplifted brought forth an abundant count of new potatoes and little Kathy delighted in picking them up and placing them into the basket as they worked their way down one row and back up another. His shoulder pained him as he leaned on his fork and looked backward at the many potatoes his little one had overlooked.

It was only a game to her as she pretended that one potato was "too big" and "too heavy" for her to carry. "Papa, you gots to help me," she scolded. George hurried her along and together they finished the evening task. He quickly pulled a few carrots and onions and one large cabbage head for tomorrow's meal, so Frances wouldn't have to make a trip to the garden patch the next day.

Ah! Frances! And his thoughts turned to his slender young wife—slender everywhere except for her abdomen, slightly protruding now with just the smallest hint of a new life once again beginning to develop within her. It was much too soon after the last birth, which had almost been a disaster for them all. George's thoughts began to regress once again—this time, to last winter when little Joey was born.

They had been living in Dubuque and he was employed at the Farley Lumber Company. Frances had been having a rough time with her pregnancy all through the Christmas holidays and never really snapped out of it. Kathy began sneezing and sniffling, which, at first, they thought was just another winter cold coming on, but the symptoms had persisted and developed into a raging fever and hacking cough. Even as Frances was delivered of a beautiful, black-haired baby son, their tiny daughter lay sick and frail in her white, iron baby crib. In spite of the worry over his family's health, George was elated with his first man-child and immediately named him Joseph (after his own father) and Mathias (after his grandfather), thus carrying on a tradition that was typical of the old German families. (And, incidentally, Mathias was also the name of baby Joseph's maternal grandfather as well, so it carried a double impact!

Frances lay back in the big bed exhausted after her difficult labor, but smiled happily when Edwina (George's older sister had come over for a few days to help out) placed the newly born babe in his mother's arms and soon both Francie and the infant were sleeping peacefully. George sat next to the bed and watched over them. He was overcome with emotion and could no longer contain his pride! He rushed out into the brisk winter sunlight to tell his coworkers at the lumber company about the birth of his son! What joy!

But alas, a few hours later, his elation gave way to a new emotion—*fear*! The tiny baby was showing signs of very labored breathing. Frances was the first to detect it—almost with a sixth sense, she knew the infant was seriously ill. Edwina and George rested very little as they cared for the sick family through the long dark hours of night. By morning, they knew the baby was in grave danger and again the doctor was sent for. He took George aside and informed him of the dreadful disease—Whooping Cough!

The little girl, the doctor said, would be able to fight it with her own natural immunity and medication; but the baby did not have that built-in strength as yet, and the next few days were going to be critical for their little one. The young parents were frightened! The priest was called in and the Sacrament of Baptism (with Aunt Edwina and Uncle Albert Rohner as sponsors) was administered over little Joseph Mathias, now fighting for his very breath! "Oh, dear God! Please don't take our son!" They prayed—harder than either of them had ever prayed in their entire lives.

"Hear, Oh Lord! And answer me!"

Ah, indeed, God had heard the prayers and had answered them! Within a few weeks, the young family was well on its way to recovery. Kathy was the first to bounce back and just as soon as Frances had gained enough strength to better nurse the sickly babe, it wasn't long before that little guy became "fat and sassy" to the delight and relief of the young parents.

When Joey was one month and one day old, the long awaited move to the country (Buenie) finally came about. The first few months, Frances and the babies traveled to Guttenberg to live with her mother while George stayed by himself at the farm. This gave him the opportunity to make some necessary improvements on the house and barns and prepare for the spring planting, which would take place in another month.

The time passed quickly and soon the young family felt right at home in their new surroundings. George's youngest sister, Tootsie, moved in with them and helped Frances with the children and household chores. She was a great help and the two of them worked well together. They had the cellar shelves filled with jars of canned tomatoes, green beans, corn, peaches, apples, jams, and jellies—a more than ample supply of food that hopefully would serve them well in the long winter months ahead.

The evening sunset was slowly descending behind the highest hill and the cool air was refreshing to George. He would have liked to linger in the garden, but his tiny barefoot daughter shivered in the cool air. He quickly scooped her up and plopped her on top of the potatoes in the basket, which sent her into a giggling frenzy and he carried produce, babe, and all to the house and to Frances. His wife with her ready smile was waiting on the stoop with a basin of warm sudsy water and a flannel nightgown to ready little Kathy for her early bedtime. The baby, smelling of soap and clean pajamas, gleefully clapped his hands at the sight of his sister and as George eased his tired body onto the porch steps, his young son crawled into his arms and contentedly relaxed in the comfort of his father's strength.

The happy family sat in silence for a short time enjoying the quiet beauty of the evening—soon Frances rose up, pitched the basin of water to the earth. She took the baby from her husband's arms and asked, "Would you bring that heavy basket of potatoes up on the porch for me? It's time I put these little ones to bed." She balanced Joey on her hip, took Kathy by the hand, and headed into the house. George observed this tender scene in silence and as his gentle wife carried the actual physical weight of his little ones, his immense responsibilities, he, himself felt a much heavier weight—the weight of the world coming down upon his shoulders. He glanced backward toward the direction where the setting sun had now totally disappeared—another long, hard day had come to its close.

* * *

December 24, 1928. It was a clear, bright, brisk afternoon and the brilliant sun made the snow covered ground glisten as if covered with a fresh coat of shiny pearly white polish. George breathed heavily as he loaded the big Christmas tree onto the back end of his sleigh and inwardly congratulated himself on his "find." He rejected at least a dozen trees of various sizes and shapes prior to finding this perfectly formed specimen over six-feet tall—of course, it was *real* cedar! Its aroma would permeate the entire house! He giddy-yapped to the horses and the steel runners of the sleigh crunched swiftly along the hard sleek snowy crust as he headed homeward.

The children would be taking their afternoon naps, so he'd be able to bring the tree right up to the house and if he hurried, he might have time to build the stand before they woke up. Then he could hide it on the side porch and later tonight with help from Frances, drag it into the living room. George reined in his horses as close to the shed as possible before he loosened their harness. He hurriedly brought them into the warm barn and gave them oats and water. Old Birdie had to be led by the bridle about her neck as she could no longer see due to the cataracts that had grown over her eyeballs. She was a good horse though in spite of her handicap. And, as long as her helpmate was able to take the lead, she was very capable of pulling her own weight.

George struggled with the large tree and managed to half-drag and half-slide it up to the house. He retraced his steps back to the sleigh and with a sly grin, reached down under the front seat and retrieved a big jug of wine. He had stopped by his cousin's farm earlier that afternoon and picked up a gallon of the homemade grape wine that he and Fritz had made last fall. They always managed to save some for the Holiday Season. He looked forward to tonight and perhaps even Frances could be persuaded to join him in a glass, while they decorated the tree, just to celebrate the season.

The kitchen was warm as toast—and his chilled body quickly absorbed the heat as he stood with his back up against the cook stove. Frances had been baking his favorite "filled cookies," which were her Christmas specialty. She'd cut small circles of sugar cookie dough and then dropped a tablespoon of cooked filling with nuts, dates, raisins, brown sugar, and delicious smelling spices in the very center of one circle. She would then top it with another circle, pinching the edges all the way around to seal in that wonderful filling while the cookies baked to a golden brown. The cookies resembled miniature pies and tasted even better! Yum-m-m! George sneaked his handout and quickly grabbed one and had it almost entirely wolfed down before Francie caught him with an admonishing eye.

"You're the biggest kid I got," she teased him. "It's just that I can't resist your good cooking," he responded. "I'm going back out to the shed, as soon as I get warmed up and build a stand for the tree. It's a beauty! At least six-feet tall and the cedar that you like so well." George knew she was pleased.

"I hope we have enough ornaments and lights for such a big tree," she spoke. "Maybe I can make some popcorn chains and cranberry ropes to fill in," she offered. Ah, they were both beginning to feel the Christmas Spirit! George grinned as he pulled his work-worn gloves back over his fingers and buttoned his black and red plaid barn coat as he headed once again into the cold temperatures.

He awoke early the next morning, but took advantage of the warm cozy quilts for just a few minutes longer as he lingered in the semi-darkness, procrastinating against getting out of bed to stoke the dying fire. He'd been up two to three times during the night to throw more logs on, one at a time—just enough to keep the fire from dying completely out and just enough to keep the bitter cold from creeping into the drafty house. But soon, the children would be stirring and oh, my goodness! George quickly jumped out of bed for he just realized that today was Christmas Day! And there would be no containing the little ones in their beds (even if the house was cold) on this Day of days!

George could see his breath cloud over as he quickly pulled on his clothes. He hurried into the kitchen and soon had the wood stove blazing away. He put the pot of coffee on to perk and told his wife to stay in bed until the house warmed up a bit. He then carried an armful of bigger logs into the living room and added as much as he could into the round, potbellied stove. It would soon become red-hot around the middle, and, in no time at all, the small house would be warm as toast!

And, it did not take very long before the coffeepot was giving off its tantalizing aroma of freshly brewed coffee. George poured himself a cup and just as he was savoring his first hot sip—his early morning sustenance—he remembered communion! Darn! Too late, now! He wouldn't be able to receive the sacrament on Christmas Day! Frances was not going to like that! Oh well, since the damage was already done, he might as well sit back and enjoy it. He poured some of the steaming liquid into a saucer, where it cooled much faster and very carefully sipped it out of the shallow dish.

Frances came into the kitchen with their youngest child, Rosy, who at the sight of her daddy, reached out to him with open arms in anticipation of being coddled and cuddled. George called her his "dimpled darling" and held the little one on his lap while his wife proceeded to prepare an oatmeal breakfast for the children. She eyed his coffee cup suspiciously and queried. "No communion this morning, George"?

He grinned sheepishly at her, "I forgot! I thought I'd surprise you with the coffee already done by the time you got up, and then, just as I took my first sip, I remembered. I just wasn't thinking. Do you want some?"

His wife declined, but George did notice that she was smiling—so obviously, she wasn't too upset with him. Certainly not on Christmas Day! The conversation ceased when both parents heard the excited voices coming from the bedroom. George hurried into the living room and plugged in the tree lights, just in the nick of time, for here they came, running in their bare feet into the living room, "oohing and aahing" and squealing with delight at the sight of the beautiful tree! Its bright shining baubles and brilliant bits of light twinkled like stardust in the dim, early dawn!

Way up high on the tree, they spotted their favorite ornament—a tiny horn made of delicately blown glass, which really "tooted." It was traditional for each child to take a turn at "blowing the horn!" After which, they watched in awe as Papa would very carefully hang the fragile ornament back on the tree, tucking it safely into a high branch where all could see, but none could touch!

And then, it was time for the presents! Kathy's joy knew no bounds when she discovered her "most beautifullest" baby dolly dressed in an exquisite gown and bonnet of yellow taffeta with matching panties and slip, all trimmed in real lace! Little Joe immediately laid claim to the tiny replicas of farm machinery that he found under the tree. Of course, they were meant for him; girls did not "play farmer." (Even if their surname was Spielbauer!) Dimpled baby Rose, too joined in the gaiety when Frances placed a soft rag dolly into her eager waiting arms. She hugged it to her bosom and laughed delightedly.

George glanced at the clock—nearly 7:00 a.m. and even though the world wide over was celebrating the birthday of the

Savior, duty called to our young "playfarmer." He bundled up against the chilly morning and went off to the barn to milk the cows and perform his other chores. Usually, Frances helped with the milking, but he decided he would do it alone today. She had a lot to do in the house before they went to church. And, besides, when Frances helped, they would bundle Joe into his warmest snowsuit and take him along, leaving Kathy to watch over the baby for a little while. They put the baby into the large wicker buggy and little Kathy would sing to her and gently bounce her up and down until she fell asleep. But, that was not going to happen today—Papa had to do it all by himself.

Mama left the little ones playing with their new toys and returned to the kitchen where she finished preparing the first meal of the day for her children. She didn't call them to breakfast until she had the steaming hot cereal portioned into the bowls, covered with rich cream and sugar, and a tiny plate of fresh orange sections (another Christmas tradition) by their places at the table. Each child was allowed to choose a favorite frosted cutout cookie from the large platter in the middle of the table. Kathy immediately selected the Christmas Star with pink frosting and silvery sprinkles of sugar on it. Joe (our little lad of husbandry) naturally chose the decorated reindeer that was iced with fudge frosting—his "best" kind. Baby Rose, sitting in her high chair(patiently waiting to be fed), was still too small to make a decision, so Kathy and Joe picked out the angel for her. "Cause," Kathy said, "She is our own real angel!" But only after they had completely scooped up every spoonful of oatmeal were they allowed to savor their Christmas delicacy, which to these little ones, magically became a "manna" from heaven!

As soon as she was through with breakfast, Kathy begged her mama to let her get dressed for church. The little prima donna couldn't wait to try on the pretty red dress she'd received for Christmas. Frances had managed to find the time out of her busy schedule to sew new dresses for both girls and a warm flannel shirt for Joe.

Kathy struggled out of her nightgown and into the pretty dress. It had a white lace ruffle around the collar and she loved it! She couldn't reach the buttons in back, nor could she tie the belt into a big bow behind her, but she'd get Mama to help. She went ahead and pulled on the long cotton stockings (how she wished they could be white instead of that "yucky" tan color). She hated them! She had to keep them from falling down by wearing a circlet of elastic (Mama called them garters) around the tops of her legs. The child sighed in disgust—well, at least, she wasn't alone. Everybody, even big ladies like Aunt Tootsie had to wear the long stockings in the wintertime just to keep warm! And, besides, she had heard Papa say they would be taking the sleigh into town. It was such fun to ride behind the team of horses as they trotted lightly over the snow. But, it was a *really* cold ride. They'd all have to bundle up in their warmest clothing and even then, Mama would tuck that big quilt around them all. It was a heavy patchwork quilt that she'd made out of old coats all pieced together. Wherever the squares met into a corner, she had tied through all layers with bright red yarn. It was very colorful and very warm!

"Hurry. Kathy," called Mama from the kitchen. "I need you to watch over Rosy while I help Joe get dressed." Kathy quickly pulled her shoes on, but she too would have to ask Mama for help in tying those troublesome shoestrings, for she had not yet mastered the art of making a bow. She could hear Joey still playing in the living room and ran back in there first, just to take one more look at the pretty Christmas tree. She hoped she would be able to remember every tiny detail of its shimmering beauty. Because one day when she was bigger and able to draw much better she was going to become a famous artist and then, she would paint this gorgeous tree, just as fine as she remembered it—and, then, it would last forever and ever!

She bounced through the doorway—but hark! Suddenly, her happy little world had turned all topsy-turvy! Her usual cheerful nature gave way to livid rage! She pitched a fit! She screamed! "Mama, come quick! Joey's breaking my dolly!"

"Joey, you mean old brother, you stop that! She is *my* baby!" Her little brother had stripped her beautiful dolly "bare naked" and had carelessly strewed the beautiful clothing all over the floor. How could he be *so* cruel? He had tied an old piece of dirty rope around the dolly's neck and was now engaged in pulling the doll on her bare tummy across the floor pretending that it was a dog!

"Here, Pickles! Here, boy!" He shouted with glee as he ran round and round in a circular direction, pulling the doll behind him. "Come on, Pickles! Good dog!" Kathy was heartbroken and rushed to save her baby! Frances, on hearing this commotion, quickly hurried into the room. She could barely suppress her laughter, as she surveyed this comic tragedy before her. However, she did realize just how traumatic this was to her oldest daughter and admonished Joe even though the little boy was unable to see that he'd done something so terrible as to warrant such wrath from Kathy.

Kathy was soon consoled, however, as Mama helped to redress the dolly. To further placate her, she even allowed the child to "borrow" one of Rosy's baby blankets (a square of yellow flannel that matched the doll's yellow dress and bonnet). Mama carefully showed the little mother how to wrap her baby, bringing up three corners of the blanket over the top of the baby and lastly folding the remaining corner over the face of the baby to protect her from the cold wind. Kathy was happy once again, and by the time Frances had finished tying her dress and shoelaces, she was even willing to forgive her little brother;

but, only after he had made a solemn promise, "I'll never do it again, Kathy! I'm sorry!"

Her husband had already brought the team of horses and sleigh from the shed. Just as he entered the back door in a flurry of wind, Frances urged him to, "Hurry up, George, we don't want to be late for Mass on Christmas Day!"

The long, cold, isolated days of winter grew into weeks and the weeks into months. Time moved slowly on. Indoors, Frances hustled and bustled about answering to the needs of her growing family. She cooked, cleaned, sewed, mended, did the laundry, and the baking—and always managed to keep a cheerful smile on her face and a happy song in her heart, even though she was once again plagued with the morning sickness that left her weak and worn-out for a goodly portion of the day. Her one consolation was that, at least this new baby would present himself in good weather, early September, and she would not have to contend with another one of those winter births this time around.

The frigid weather did not permit the family to get out much during this interim; however, Sundays usually meant a trip into town to attend church and afterward a visit that oftentimes ended up as Sunday dinner with Grandma Spielbauer. The children called her their "black grandma" due to the fact that Mary Spielbauer's hair had remained a shiny jet-black in its color in spite of her aging years. In contrast, their other Grandma was known as "white grandma" as her hair had by now turned white as snow!

In the meantime, George kept busy with the daily demands of the farm animals and the ever-necessary maintenance to house and outbuildings. Many hours were spent on the farm machinery and equipment that seemed to be in a constant need of repair. At least once or twice a week, George would go off alone into the woods in search of small game to replenish the meat supply of his young family. His only companion on these sojourns was his faithful dog, Sport. His brother-in-law, Frank Rohner had given the dog to him. George grinned to himself as he remembered how Kathy from the start had always called the dog her "orange dog." George had to readily agree that the dog's coloring was a bit unusual, but thought to himself that "yellow" might be a more appropriate description.

Sport had already earned the reputation of being a "good hunting dog" and George highly valued the animal because of his retriever capabilities. The man and his dog had established of sort of quiet camaraderie as the two silently stalked their quarry. They both held a mutual respect for each other as well as for the land and what it provided. They were hunters in the truest sense of the word, taking only what was needed, and no more. George had come from a long line of hunting men before him and to him it was a game of necessity and not of "sport" (no pun intended—in all due respect to our canine friend).

Bye, baby bunting
Daddy's gone a-hunting
To fetch a little rabbit skin
To wrap the baby bunting in!

The little children would gaily sing this ditty whenever they saw their papa put on his huge tan hunting jacket that possessed many pockets stitched into it—little ones where the bullets snugly fit and larger ones that held the rabbits and squirrels that he would bring home for supper.

One particularly warm sunny day in early spring, George and his dog took off over the hills in search of a couple of rabbits. They headed south in the direction of Benda's Bottom where the spring fed into a little stream teeming with fish aplenty. The Bottom was a favorite family picnic area and had hosted many a friendly neighborhood fish fry in the warmer months.

Sport was enjoying the freedom of the outdoors and bounded from boulder to boulder—from tree trunk to brush! He sniffed strange smells, darted off after shy rabbits, and chased chattering chipmunks. Sometimes, his master would have to call him back and sometimes he would have to urge him onward. The dog was a natural aggressor and obviously was becoming very disgusted when George repeatedly allowed his prey to get away.

But, today the man had another purpose in his stride. He was sure he knew just where a lush growth of watercress grew wild around the base of the rocks right where the spring tumbled into the smooth flowing stream at the foot of a small hill. He had brought along a paper bag in hopes that it would be ready to pick. He was certain it would be, because the weather conditions had been just right the past week. Sure enough, there it was! He had to break through a thin sheet of ice in order to harvest the tiny leaves and selected just enough of this crisp, cool green for Frances to make her special "wilted salad" for supper. It was a gourmet addition to any meal and along with the rabbits he would bag on the way home, the family would indeed have a feast tonight.

Now, he stopped to look around at the beauty of this land. It never ceased to amaze him. The rolling hills, the fresh, spring green just breaking through the dead brush of winter—and what is this? Some dainty, pale purplish flowers—so tiny and fragile, barely peeking through the ground on the shady side of a huge pile of rocks! He thought of Frances, who always loved the first signs of spring and picked a huge bouquet for his wife; mixing the shades of blooms—some so pale in color as to be almost white and others a deep, velvety, passionate purple. He pulled out his red bandana, dampened it in the spring waters and carefully wrapped the flower stems in the moist material and placed it on top of the watercress in his bag. The man and his dog retraced their steps toward the farmyard and on the way, much to Sport's satisfaction, George's prowess as a hunter was once again reaffirmed in the eyes of the dog.

They were soon back in the warm kitchen and Frances' blue eyes twinkled with delight as she found a cut glass vase to put the flowers in. They were, to her, the very first harbinger of spring and a fresh new promise of warmer weather and bright golden days of summer ahead of them. Her greatest pleasure, however, was the fact that George had been considerate enough to think of her. George was pleased that he "pleased" her. Kathy too, showed her delight and begged her papa to "always bring flowers home to Mama" each and every time he went a-hunting!

Yes, the lavender and purple blossoms of the wild violets had kept their promise as predicted. Spring did arrive on the gentle sloping hills and in the low valleys of the Beunie countryside. The sun shone bright and warm and the patches of snow diminished into nothingness leaving in their wake small clumps of greenery pushing through the dark brown crust of the earth. The birds, hesitantly, at first began to trill the songs of spring and as the days gradually lengthened, small woodland creatures became more courageous and ventured outside their winter havens. The sounds of spring grew steadily stronger.

The children's cheeks became red and rosy as they too spent more and more time outdoors. Frances, with the arrival of warm weather and the sight of the healthy glow on the faces of the little ones, had by now given up administering the daily dosage of (yuck!) castor oil; that liquid pariah that was supposedly the cure-all and prevent-all of most childhood diseases and more than likely the precursor of our modern day vitamins. She, of course, would be forced to resort to cajoling, pleading, and outright trickery in order to get this bitter vetch into the mouths of the children. One of her ploys was to first give them the medicine in a doll-sized teacup and then quickly "chase" the dosage with a shot of apple juice, which was meant to remove all traces of the horrid aftertaste. However, this added attraction never quite succeeded in its mission. Yuck! Another one of her methods was the "spoonful of sugar" or honey, if you prefer, which, as everyone knows (and I now quote that remarkable authority on this subject, Ms. Mary Poppins), "makes the medicine go down, in a most delightful way!"

Well, Baby Rosy soon developed a real fetish for this nature's own sweetener and it was not at all uncommon to find the little girl sitting cross-legged inside the bottom half of the kitchen cabinets, attempting to satisfy her insatiable appetite for the sweet, amber syrup-like liquid. She would painstakingly remove all the pots and pans, then crawl inside the cupboard, pull the door almost shut, and conceal her little person there, along with the jar of honey clutched within her sticky little hand. There, she'd sit, scooping out honey to her heart's content.

Those hazy, lazy days of summer found the children barefoot, freckle-faced, and golden-tan, out of doors for most of these waking hours. Summer days were both happy days and busy ones for both young and old alike. Neighbors in the surrounding community helped each other at times of threshing, harvesting, and butchering. They'd combine their physical strength, believing in that old adage, that "many hands do light work make" and progress from farm to farm assisting each of the landowners in turn. As the men labored in the fields, their womenfolk prepared mountains of home cooked foods and baked goods to appease the hungry appetites.

The children richly enjoyed the companionship of friends and cousins "by the dozens" during these occasions and convened often at the base of the big shade tree where they spent many happy hours of "play and pretend." Papa had made a swing that hung from one of the lower branches and, if you let yourself go high enough, it would take you flying out over the creek that bordered on the backyard and the thrill of it would nearly take your breath away!

Sometimes, Aunt Martha and Uncle Pete (Duehr), along with their children would come out to visit on Sundays after church. Kathy and Joe watched in awe and fright when their bigger and more daring cousins, Billie and Rita, would swing out so far that they'd go sailing clear across the creek. They'd jump from the swing and land on two feet on the soft grass on the other side. It looked very dangerous and Kathy and Joe were *not* about to try that feat—not for all the coaxing in the world. At least, *not yet*!

It must have been about this time in young Joe's life that, the mean old rooster reared his ugly head. Kathy did not mind him so much. She actually laughed when the old bird pecked at her feet and bare legs, egging him on poking back at him with a long stick. But, little Joe *hated* that old bird! With a passion! The rooster was undaunted, however, and determined to harass the boy. Every time he spotted Joe in the backyard, the old bird would come a-running and a-squawking, and a-scolding and a-pecking at the little boy! Poor Joe! He'd take off on a run for the safety of the house, but was never quite fast enough. The mean old rooster chased him right into the house (before he could get the door shut) and all the way to the back bedroom where he'd hide under the bed thinking he would be safe. But the bird continued his attack and Joe was forced to beat him off with arms and legs and feet and whatever extra strength his little body could muster up!

Finally, one day Papa decided, much to the satisfaction of little Joe, that this rooster was meant for other things. Yes, indeed, it was with much relief, not to mention, relish that, on the following Saturday night, young Joe sat down to his place at the supper table and delighted in savoring and sipping the steaming hot bowl of "Banty rooster soup" his mother served to her family. "This is the *best* supper I have ever had," he grinned happily at his mother.

September was fast approaching and Frances looked forward to the arrival of her new baby. "Nothing could possibly go wrong this time," she mused. No snowstorm—no frigid blowing winds—no winter illnesses. But, George was taking *no* chances. His mind backtracked to little Rosy's birth in March of '28. The weather was very cold, and there had been more than the usual amount of snow piled along the roadsides and filling up the ditches.

The doctor who delivered her (Dr. Schroeder by name) had to drive from Holy Cross, a little town along the highway leading to Dubuque. Since Buenie was unable to boast of its own doctor, the rural community had to seek medical service elsewhere. As soon as he had pronounced both Mama and baby doing fine, our good doctor gathered up his small black "doctor bag" and informed Frances that his next stop was down the lane to check on Hilda Brimeyer and her new son of less than a week. The Brimeyer family too had been keeping up with the young Spielbauers and growing by leaps and bounds. This latest addition to their family was Nicholas L. who beat our sister into this world by a mere four days.

Back to the present, as these September days grew closer to the delivery date, George took the older children to Guttenberg where they stayed with their "white grandma" and Frances would be staying in Dubuque with his sister, Edwina. The doctor lived only two blocks away and could be there in a matter of minutes. Frances was reluctant to do this, but George was adamant!

She had been at her sister-in-law's just a few days, and in the middle of the night on September 11, she awoke with a feeling of alarm! She hated to disturb anyone, but at last something was happening. Her water had broken and she called softly for

Edwina. Without further ado, brother Arnie quietly slipped into the world. Frances knew by his lusty cry that it was another boy! Edwina quickly came to her aid, and aroused her little sister Tootsie, who also lived with her. "You stay here with Frances and hold the baby, Toots. I'm going down the street to get the doctor!"

The young girl was half-drowsy from her interrupted sleep, but quickly woke herself up enough to respond with authority. "No way! I don't know what to do with new babies! You *stay*! I'll go fetch the doctor!" She was off in a flash, before her older sister could argue. The doctor soon arrived and declared both mother and son to be in fine shape. Thus, Brother Arnie joined the ranks of the Spielbauer clan.

* * *

The seasons continued, another long cold winter, another ray of warm sunshine promising spring, and once again lengthening into hazy hot summer days, changing into cool crisp fall evenings, back again to the stark, frigid white form of Old Man Winter with his sharp winds blowing over snow-covered fields. And yet another child, Helen Mae, arrived in late March of 1931. Her birth was one for the history books, for unfortunately the month of March had arrived as "meek as a little lamb" and was now taking its leave "like a raging lion!" Frances remained at the farm for this delivery and once again, the aid of young Tootsie was called upon.

It was the very end of March and the worst snowstorm had left these hills and valleys of the surrounding countryside almost totally isolated from any communication or contact with the outside world. Every farmhouse for miles around was iced-in, snowed-in, and drifted-in. George had been trying to get through to the doctor for hours, but all the county roads and side lanes were impassable with huge mountains of snow and not even the most daring of travelers could venture forth.

This baby was undaunted, however, and they tell me there is no dissuading a redhead! Now, I believe it! Helen was determined to be born *now*;—and so, she was, with George and Toots doing the best they could to bring her into this world. The usually very placid and calm father had become an absolute "nervous-wreck." He was on the phone frantically trying to get advice, all the while fumbling through the pages of the "doctor book"—and at the same time, rapidly praying his rosary beads! He at last succeeded in making contact with his younger brother, Jack, and ordered him to go after the doctor. After waiting an unreasonably long time, he decided to fetch the doctor himself, but soon realized the uselessness of his efforts and returned to help with the birth as much as he could.

In the meantime, thanks to the buzzing of the rural "party line," help as last did arrive in the form of close neighbors who traveled by bobsled across the open fields of snow. Thank God, this marvelous "angel of mercy" had some experience in nurse's training. She expertly took over the care of the new baby and saw to the mother's comfort—to the vast relief of the harried father and young Aunt Tootsie, who needless to say could do nothing much more in a crisis like this, except to boil water. Between the two of them, they had enough buckets of water bubbling away on the old cook stove—enough for triplets!

The good doctor finally showed up at the farmhouse a full day and a half later. All was well. Yes, Frances smiled to herself; the good Lord had always been there, in her hour of need—and for sure, he always would! She knew!

Kathy, the oldest daughter, was at this time staying in Guttenberg with her "white grandma" and attending the grade school at St. Mary's. She loved going to school and got along very well with the nuns who wore those long, black dresses and veils and a "rosary belt" around their waists; but she was often homesick for the companionship of her brothers and now, two little sisters. Weather permitting, she often came home for the weekends to be with her family.

On one of these occasions, she overheard Mama and Papa talking about moving from the farm. She didn't understand what the conversation was all about, but she heard them talking about things like "mortgage balance" and "selling the land" and "renting" and a place called "Petsche." None of this made any sense to the little girl. She just knew that something was amiss. And she was worried.

At long last, the pieces of the puzzle fell into place and it was made clear to Kathy that her Beunie home was no longer to belong to them. Papa was going to move all his animals and machinery to a new place, but this time, he would be "renting" the land and the house from a man named Mr. Petsche (who turned out to be a person and not a place as the little girl had first thought). This change took place on March 1, 1932.

Chapter II

Petscheland

Mr. Petsche actually owned two farms and our family lived on both of them. They spent only a short time on the first one, which was located around the Guttenberg Hill near Miner's Creek. My older brothers and sisters were still quite young at that time and their recollections not very clear; but they all remember that the house sat very close to the road. The second farm house was in the other direction just past the Guttenberg City Cemetery. That house was situated on the right side of the road as you come out from town. It was not very well constructed and the second story was left unfinished. It did not have any plaster on the walls, just the bare studs showing. During the winter months, the drafty old house was always cold and damp and yet summertime found it hot and humid. This old building has since been torn down and replaced by a newer, more modern structure on the same site.

The surrounding landscape was much like the Buenie farmland with its beautiful panorama of hills and valleys, natural springs, and running creeks that tumbled down hillsides and meandered aimlessly and without direction into the lowlands. In the fall of each year, usually peaking in late September to mid October, the area attracted the tourists who came in droves from miles around to view the brilliant red, gold, yellow, green, and bronze display of colorama that Mother Nature so lavishly spread over this land. The Guttenberg Hill seemed to serve as a vivid, hand-painted backdrop curtain for a stage performance that was being daily enacted by the inhabitants of the little town nestled at its base, as they went about their private businesses and lived out their routine lives.

The town itself was a picturesque community that boasted of the Catholic Church and school, a railroad station, a Lutheran Church, Public School, a few small factories, grocery stores, and a Main Street known as "uptown." Uptown was in reality, a line of buildings that stretched about three blocks in length and ran north and south in a parallel with The Mighty Mississippi River, which is the eastern border of the state of Iowa. The highway also traversed in a north and south direction following the traffic pattern previously established by both the river and the railroad tracks, which ran in north and south directions right through the center of the town.

During the two-year time period that the family lived on the Petsche land, not many noteworthy incidents occurred. However, there was one highlight that, for the sake of posterity must be recorded, November of 1932 brought another new baby into the family. By this time, Frances had a "hired girl," who lived in and helped take care of the small children. But with the new baby about to arrive, she would be in need of more mature help. This time, it was Aunt Louise (another sister of George's) and her husband, Arnie Hutter, who came from Dubuque and stayed at the farm for a couple of weeks. Uncle Arnie helped George in the fields and Aunt Louise took over the household operation while Frances was confined to her bed.

Fortunately, this time there were no adverse elements of nature at work creating havoc as was the case with Helen's birth. However, Dr. Beyer was a little late getting out to the country and just as he walked through the front door of the farmhouse, baby Frankie loudly announced his presence by greeting the good doctor with his very first sound—a very loud and lusty cry of life! And, once again, Frances smiled, for she already knew by the baby's cry that this was another boy! And once again, the continuity of the girl-boy lineage lives on!

On nice days, the older children, Kathy, Joe, and Rosy walked to and from the Catholic School in the town. When weather was disagreeable, they were allowed to stay overnight in town with Grandma Rohner.

One such morning, on a very cold and blustery day, Papa had to take a wagon load of wood into town to Grandma's house, so the school children rode along with him. Frances was worried the girls were not dressed warm enough for a wagon ride in their skimpy school dresses and insisted that both Kathy and Rosy put on bib overalls that belonged to their brothers. Now, mind you, this would have been the winter of 1933, and a great many years prior to Women's Lib and the "jeans scene" that is so popular in today's society. This was an age when little girls would not dare to be caught "dead" in boy's pants, no less! How embarrassing! What if they were seen by some of their friends?

However, back in 1933, little girls were yet dutiful daughters and never would have dreamt of arguing with their mamas. So, our sisters most disgustedly pulled on those horrid britches over top of their detested "long stockings," which in turn had been pulled over top of yet another disgusting female undergarment, something called "snuggies." Snuggies were similar in mission to a man's pair of "longjohns." By this time, even the skinniest of children took on an overweight appearance. With their lower appendages now triple-layered against the cold wind, our sisters climbed up on top of the wood with Joe and hung their faces in abject shame as they rode into town behind Papa's team of horses.

As soon as they came to a halt in the alley behind Gram's house, both Kathy and Rosy grabbed the sack that held their school dresses and quickly dashed into the house and changed into their more feminine attire.

Papa winked at Joe as they unloaded and stacked the wood and said, "Silly little girls!" But, to Kathy and Rosy, it was no laughing matter!

Another recollection of the Petsche farm, which is well remembered by my older siblings, is that of "butchering." Mother Frances would not allow her young children to watch the actual killing of the animals as she was of the opinion that the "letting of blood" was much too gory a sight for their young eyes to view. So their first sight of this ritual was the body of the animal being suspended from a tripod. The little ones huddled about the window and observed Papa and whoever happened to be assisting him carefully dissect the carcass into its various cuts of meat.

However, I am certain that our Mother was never aware of this, and perhaps I am tattling. But, Brother Arnie has confidentially told me that there was at least one occasion when he and Joe hid in the back seat of Dad's old Model T and observed the ritual of the killing by peeking through the curtained window of the car. They secretly watched Papa and his friend Matt Duehr (Matt and his wife, Maggie, lived on the next farm toward the town) strip away the hide and make the meat cuts. They would catch some of the blood in a large container. This was set aside and later used in the making of a certain type of sausage, which Papa would prepare from an old family recipe. It was called "Blutwurst." Our father's strong German heritage not only introduced us to this rare dish but to another German delicacy called "head cheese," which was not a cheese at all, but another type of cold cut, utilizing parts of the hog's head that oftentimes are discarded today. Waste not—want not!

Now, there are some amongst us who would turn their noses up at these very definitely German dishes; but I, for one think they are very delicious! (It would, of course, be quite a few years before I would be sampling my father's culinary talents, as I was yet to be born), but I must truly be my "father's daughter" for it appears that I have inherited all those German taste buds for that rare ethnic food.

It was not often that our mother relinquished her position of authority in the kitchen, but at these times, she more than willingly allowed George to take over. For years, I had thought this culinary art and old German recipes had died out with my father. But it is now, my understanding that Aunt Martha's oldest son, Bill Duehr still carries on the traditional preparation of these "old world" specialties, the likes of which you'd probably never find in today's grocery stores.

Hog butchering also brought forth a lot of smoked hams, bacon, and salt pork. Gram Rohner had a smokehouse in her backyard and the men would hang large hams from ceiling hooks and lay bacon on iron racks. A smoldering fire was built in the base of the small concrete structure. The smoke would work its way upward, slowly penetrating the meat and finally escaping through a very small aperture at the top. This process was very long and slow, but the results were wonderful.

Meanwhile, the ladies would fry down skillet after skillet of salt pork. This was stored in huge crocks. The rendered fat was poured over the pork slices and since the crockery was always kept in a cool place, it soon congealed, preserving the meat for a long time.

The animal fat was fried down and stored in wide-mouthed jars to be later used for piecrusts and other cooking needs. The leftover "cracklings" were delicious when baked in corn bread or just nibbled on for snacks. Mama also used cracklings to actually make her piecrust for apple pie! Yummy!

When a cow was butchered, Gram and Mama would can much of the meat. This was a time, of course, prior to our modern day refrigeration and freezing methods. Canning beef was a great deal of work and one had to be exceedingly careful to prevent spoilage, but the finished product proved to be a most delicious entrée. The meat was usually canned in its own gravy and simply reheated before serving.

I, of course, was too young to remember any of this myself. However, in later years, a very dear friend and next door neighbor, Mrs. Ed (Evelyn) Kempker from Osage Beach, MO, was kind enough to introduce me and my young family to this rare delicacy. Even though she had all the modern household conveniences at her disposal, she still resorted to this old-fashioned method of preservation only because her family was extremely fond of canned beef. And, dear reader, I am here to tell you, it is very delicious!

* * *

Arnie was bored and restless—he'd watched Papa as he carried the basket of fresh eggs from the hen house, placing it on the floor of the car, and loudly honking for the older kids to hurry up and get into the car. Kathy, Joe, and Rosy rushed out of the house with their books and pencils and climbed into the back seat of the car. The little boy sighed deeply. He was envious of the older kids, who were allowed to go to school all day and he sure wished that he had been big enough to join them.

He was only five years old and would have to wait another year, at least. Mama kept saying it would be "someday," but that someday seemed to take forever! It was so boring when you were just a little kid and didn't know how to read or write or do numbers even. He was just starting to learn some of his A-B-Cs, thanks to his older sisters who loved to "play" schoolteacher and were more than willing to share their newly discovered knowledge with the little kids.

Papa was driving out of the yard now, heading toward the bridge and when he got to the other side, he again honked and waved to Arnie. He could at least have taken me along for the ride, thought Arnie. He knew his dad had planned to stop at Gram's house to drop off the eggs, which were meant for her. The little boy loved to visit his Grandmother in town and was certain she would offer him a snack of cookies and milk, if only he could have gone along.

Mama now called to him from the back door, "I've finished cleaning out the bread box, Arnie. I have a whole pan of crumbs here for the birds. Come and get it." She understood how the little boy felt—she knew he was eager to learn and couldn't wait to attend school. "Come on, the birds must be hungry," she encouraged.

He shuffled back to the house and took the pan from his mom. He carried it to the edge of the yard where the ground was hard and it sort of ran into the pastureland behind the house and carelessly scattered the breadcrumbs onto the bare ground. The birds must have indeed been hungry for they quickly landed at his feet and noisily pecked in the dirt. The big fat blue jays were *very* bold and bossy and tried to hog all the crumbs, scolding and chasing the smaller and less aggressive birds away. Arnie shooed the rude birds off and made sure the little sparrows and wrens got their fair share and then dutifully returned the pan to his mother's kitchen.

He plopped down on the wooden steps on the back porch where he spotted Old Sport snoring away under the stairs and thought, that dog is getting lazier and lazier. All he ever wants to do anymore is sleep, 'cept when it looked like Papa was going to go hunting. The minute Papa took down his gun, the dog would become excited and start to sniff around him and head out across the pasture toward the woods as though he was afraid he'd been left behind, but the dog was always lucky. Sport was a "good hunting dog" and our dad never went hunting without the animal. Lately, Joe was allowed to join them on some of the hunting trips. Alas! Never Arnie! Papa still thought he was too little.

Yep, Sport and Joe were the lucky ones. Arnie had recently noticed that ever since Joe had started going to the town school, he'd begun to call Papa "pa." Maybe Papa liked that, and from now on, Arnie vowed he would call his Papa "pa," as well. Maybe then, Papa (he quickly corrected himself), Pa, would invite him along, too!

What a dull morning, this was. Nothing was fun for the small boy. He wandered aimlessly out to the big tree and played a while on the swing. But, he soon tired of swinging back and forth—he tried going 'round and 'round, twisting the rope around itself into a tight coil and then quickly reversing his direction; but, as he unwound, he became very dizzy. That was not much fun either. Besides, it made him sick to his stomach!

Soon he heard the sound of Papa's—whoops—Pa's old car chugging back over the bridge. He pulled to a stop almost in front of Arnie. As he got out, he said, "Well son, what are you doing to keep busy this morning?"

"Nothin," replied Arnie. "I'm just bored."

"Bored?" Papa gave him a quizzical look. "What does that mean?" His father teased.

"Well-l," Arnie thought for a while. "I guess it means, kind of like you can't think of anything that's fun to do."

"Well, guess I'm kind of bored myself, today. Why don't you and me just take us a little hike down toward the creek this morning. You better put on a jacket because it'll be chillier in the woods. Go on now and I'll tell your ma you're with me." The young boy grinned up at his dad and then quickly ran into the house. *Wow*! This was going to be a fun day after all!

They headed across the pasture to the creek with Sport at their heels. By the time they reached their destination, both of them had worked up a thirst and Pa showed the young child how to squat down on his haunches really close to the edge of the stream that flowed into the creek. They leaned over the cool water and scooped up a refreshing drink from the clear bubbling spring by cupping both hands together to form a container. Of course, the little boy dribbled more water down the front of his jacket than he actually consumed, but what fun he was having with his Pa!

Pa stood up and looked around at the silent beauty of these woods. The trees were barren of all their summer foliage that now lay in clustered heaps upon the cold hard ground. "Yup," Pa said. "Winter's comin' on all right. Won't be long before this old creek is froze over." "Hey, lookie there—up in that tree. See that brown squirrel? He's a perfect target! Just waitin' to be picked off. Wish I had my rifle. We could have us a good old "fried-squirrel" supper tonight. Why didn't I think to bring my gun along?" Pa watched that squirrel for a long time. Arnie remained silent. He could see that Pa was thinking *real* hard.

At long last, his father broke the silence. "Arnie, now you listen to me. I want you to go back to the house and tell your ma to give you my rifle and one bullet. The bullets are on the top shelf in our big closet. Bring 'em both to me. Hurry now, but mind you, I want you to be very careful coming back down, you hear?"

The little boy's feet were rooted to the spot. He couldn't believe what he was hearing! "Go on, son. You're big enough," he urged. "You can handle the gun—just remember to be very careful coming down the hill."

Wow! The lad took off like a "bat outta hell!" He had long legs and was a fast runner. Faster than his big brother, even. Wow! He was going hunting with his Pa! "Mama, Mama," he started yelling as soon as he sighted the back door. "Pa's 'tree-ed' a squirrel and we need his gun and one bullet, 'cause me and my Pa are hunting! Hurry up, Mama!"

Mama started to frown. She did not approve of this at all. "No, Arnie, you go back and tell your papa to come and get that gun himself. What is he thinking of? I will not have a child of such a young age carrying a gun! I just won't hear of it and that's that!" Mama could be awful stubborn!

"But, Mama, I got to do it—Pa said I had to be careful and I will be! I just got to do it! Pa is waiting. He trusts me. Please!"

Frances shook her head in desperation. "Darn that George," she muttered. What was a mother to do? "Well," she seemed to relent, just a little. "Maybe you could carry the gun—but, Helen must go with you and she will carry the bullet in her jacket pocket. I won't let you have both of those things. It is far too dangerous. And you will have to help your sister down the hillside. Hold her hand and don't let her fall. And *do not* touch that bullet!" She carefully wrapped the bullet inside an old hankie, shoving it deep down inside the pocket of Helen's red coat, and then pinned the pocket shut so no one could get to it except Pa.

She then handed the gun to the little boy. *Wow*! It was even heavier than he had anticipated. As Mama helped Helen get into her coat and button it up, she gave careful instructions to her little daughter, "Now, Helen, you be sure and hold onto Arnie's hand and don't let anyone touch that bullet except your Papa!"

The mother stood in the doorway of the small house and watched with worried apprehension as the two children headed out across the field, hand in hand with Old Sport faithfully trailing behind them. Arnie struggled with the weight of the heavy gun and Helen obediently clutched the pocket that contained the bullet with her free hand. "Darn that George," she spoke again. But, no one could hear her—no one that is, except the new baby that stirred within her body. She gently patted the unborn child and hurried back into the kitchen to pull the loaves of hot bread out of the oven.

Brother and sister wended their way across the pasture and down the hill to where Pa was patiently waiting. Helen started to call out to her daddy, but her older brother, suddenly very grown up with his newly acquired responsibility quickly "shushed" the little girl into silence. "You'll scare the squirrel," he admonished.

Arnie was certain that he stood much taller than he'd ever stood before, as he proudly handed the gun to his Pa! He watched with fascination as his father took the bullet from Helen's pocket, loaded the rifle and placed it against his shoulder. He sighted the squirrel, took careful aim, and then a loud *bang* echoed through the silent woods—as the squirrel fell to the ground.

Wow! Pa was a good shot! Sport, without waiting for the command from his master, quickly retrieved the small game and brought the dead animal right to George's feet. "Go on, son. Pick it up. You can carry him home," Pa grinned down at Arnie, who, needless to say, was more than thrilled with his first experience at hunting.

It was obvious that little Helen was too softhearted for this game. One glance at the small animal dangling from Sport's mouth brought forth a torrent of tears! And no amount of persuasion on anyone's part (not even her mother's) would convince the child to eat a piece of this unfortunate creature for supper. The very sight of that tiny portion of squirrel meat on her plate only served to initiate another onslaught of tearful anger and rage directed toward her Papa and her brother, and she vowed *never* to go hunting again!

On the other hand, a whole new vista had opened up for our brother, for this was only the first of many hunting expeditions that the son, in years to come, would be undertaking with his "Pa"!

Old Sport

Somewhere an old dog is seen
His nose, two shaggy paws between,
Flat on his stomach, one eye shut,
Held fast in dreamy slumber, but
The other open, ready for
His master coming through the door.

—John Greenleaf Whittier

* * *

It must have been about this time that our old dog, Sport, "sported" his new tail. As the story goes, Fritz Brimeyer had driven up from Buenie one Saturday afternoon to help Dad saw and chop the dead timber that would be used for firewood during the cold winter months that were fast approaching. The two men oftentimes took turns helping each other at this tedious task as the strength of both men proved to be more productive than when each man worked alone.

It was late in the afternoon and they had brought the final load of wood up close to the house where the older children were busy stacking it into neat rows against the outside wall close to the back door. Kathy, Joe, Rosie, and even little Arnie worked diligently under the supervision of the older men. Even though they could only handle the smaller pieces of wood and only one at a time, their small contributions were greatly appreciated.

Fritz, in an endeavor to make the task a little easier and save many steps for the small children, backed the wagon up closer to the house. But, alas! In his haste, he had not noticed that Sport had taken advantage of the soft comfort provided by a pile of fallen leaves, and was now comfortably napping in the warm sunshine. As he backed up, he suddenly felt a heavy "thud" against some seemingly inert object. Silently, he prayed that it was just a piece of firewood that had fallen in his pathway. One quick backward glance assured him that all four of the children were safely accounted for; but, almost simultaneously with the thump of impact, he heard the yelping, crying, and pained whimpering of the dog!

He jumped out of the car and began "cussing" in self-reproach! Why on earth was that danged-fool, blamed dog taking a nap, for crying out loud, right behind his wagon? Poor old Sport "slunk" away with his tail between his hind legs, as though he was guilty of some grave misdemeanor and crawled under the back porch, which was his own private sanctuary, still whining plaintively, as only a wounded animal can do.

The children were greatly alarmed and quite angry with Fritz. Papa at last had been able to coax his dog into trusting him enough to come out from underneath the porch, and after carefully examining the animal it was assured that little harm had been done. Sport was much more frightened than actually hurt, for the metal rim of the wagon wheel had run over just the tip of the dog's tail.

Fritz was very apologetic, but as he looked deep into the eyes of the four children, who stared back at him with most accusing and glum expressions, he knew it would be quite some time before they would forgive him. And deep down, inside his heart, this man also knew it would be quite some time before he could forgive himself!

Now, Sport was no "fool" dog, you know. He quickly seized this opportunity and was soon basking contentedly in the loving care and lavish attention that the children eagerly bestowed upon him during the next few weeks of his recovery. He was most willingly pampered and waited upon to the extent of becoming one very spoiled family pet.

The tip of his injured tail dried up and eventually dropped completely off. Sport was most reluctant, however, to give up any portion of his beautiful "orange" body, no matter how insignificant. He possessively carried this tiny piece of his anatomy around between his teeth for many weeks—a very dirty habit that utterly disgusted Gram on the occasions that she came to visit. On one such visit, the dog's prized possession suddenly disappeared off the face of the earth, or, in this case, "Petsche Land." Grandma Rohner walked around with a satisfied smirk upon her face, but refused to talk about the incident!

Well, dear reader this, like most stories, does, indeed, have a happy ending! Eventually, old Sport's tail did grow back in. Only this time the very tip of his tail sprouted a new fur that was silky soft to the touch and—would you believe—snowy white in color! This stark white was a vivid contrast to the rest of his orange body and Sport was very proud of his new and handsome appearance. From that day forth, he stood a bit straighter and walked a bit taller and carried himself with a pompous majesty that heretofore has been known only to the "king of beasts!"

* * *

Even though the children of George and Frances were relatively young, they had already been introduced to hard work and learned to accept their responsibilities at a very early age. Just as they had learned to stack the firewood into neat rows, they soon became adept at performing other tasks. Kathy and Rosy were already experienced in drying dishes, dusting furniture, sweeping floors, and together they hung up the laundry on outside clotheslines. Rosy was still so small that she could only handle the small items such as socks and underwear on the part of the clothesline that sagged toward the ground in the center of the line.

Both little girls spent many a summer afternoon sitting on the back steps snapping green beans and shelling peas in preparation for the canning that was done by Frances and her "hired" girl. Every afternoon, Kathy would take time out to rock Baby Frankie to sleep in the big rocking chair and sing lullabies to her little brother.

Rockabye baby in the tree top,
When the wind blows, the cradle will rock,
When the bough breaks, the cradle will fall
Down will come
Baby
cradle
and
all.

Meanwhile, our older brothers were not allowed to shirk their duties. They worked outdoors with Papa, feeding the chickens and hogs, gathering eggs from the hen house, leading the cows out to pasture in the morning and rounding them up at night. They spent endless hours in the vegetable gardens pulling weeds, hoeing, picking peas and beans, and digging potatoes.

In the winter months, they shoveled snow, carried in heavy armloads of fire wood and just as often carried out pans full of dead ashes from both Mama's cook stove in the kitchen and the big round potbelly stove in the living room. Seems as though they would just get curled up with a good story book or engaged in a rousing wrestling match with old Sport when Mama would say, "You boys, get your jackets on and bring in some firewood before it gets too dark."

Or Papa would say, "Joe, you best empty out that ash pan in the living room." Joe despised having to carry out the ash pan, especially on windy days. The dirty ashes would always blow right back into his face. Oh, yes! It's a dirty job, but somebody's got to do it.

* * *

Well, all work and no play does, indeed, leave much to be desired in anyone's world. And this family did make time for play. They often met with neighbors and relatives for good times, and good food and good drink. One of these occasions of merriment was New Year's Eve in 1934. Hard times had already set in, and George and Frances, like many of their close neighbors had for some time, now been feeling the "pinch," but it was the beginning of a New Year and their newly proclaimed president-elect, Mr. FDR, had given them high hopes. It was, indeed, a cause for celebration!

Everyone in the area was invited to Matt Duehr's for a big party—the social event of the year! Joe and Kathy vividly recall all the kids squeezing into the back of Papa's Model T with Mama holding Frankie on her lap in the front as Dad drove slowly down the hill in the dark to the Duehr farm. Many people were already there—grown-ups and children alike.

Tables were laden with delicious smelling foods, mountains of sandwiches stacked neatly on trays, platters of fried chicken and baked hams, bowls of baked beans and potato salad and coleslaw, pies and cakes and cookies of all kinds! There was beer and whiskey for the men. Some of the more daring ladies sipped daintily on a glass of homemade wine and the children indulged in a very rare treat—homebrewed Root Beer! It was mostly "suds," but to these very juvenile palates, it was finer than the finest of champagnes!

One of the men played an accordion, while another fiddled on a violin. Somewhere, in the shadows, a plaintive voice began to sing:

"Beautiful, beautiful brown eyes,

I'll never love blue eyes again" he hummed.

"Tomorrow, we would have married" his voice slowed.

"But, likker has kept us apart" he forgot the rest of the song.

Truly, it was a night of merriment and everyone cast aside their worries and frustrations of the times and indulged themselves in love and laughter and gaiety!

The children were allowed to stay up much later than usual and indulged in their own little games of fun and frolic. But eventually, stifled yawns and droopy eyelids warned the mothers that it was way past bedtime!

They spread thick warm quilts on the bare wood floor and put the small children to sleep at one end of the big living room. The makeshift bedroom was barricaded by chairs with more blankets and quilts draped over the chair backs to filter out both the light and the whispered noises of the adults. One after another, the little ones reluctantly gave into sleep as the quiet voices of the grown-ups droned on and on, discussing the various problems of these troubled times.

Many of these farm folk were now desperately aware that they might be forced to seek another livelihood, and George Spielbauer was one of these men. He had already convinced himself and Frances that it was time for him to "throw in the towel," so to speak, at least as far as farming went. He had reluctantly realized that in spite of his long hours and hard work, he was not gaining any ground and it was becoming more and more difficult to make a living from the land.

He informed his friends that this very week, he was going into town to talk to those government men and sign up for one of those WPA jobs that were being offered. The new government had big plans to build a series of locks and dams up and down the length of the Mississippi in an effort to control the flooding as well as to facilitate the navigation on the inland waterway.

The party goers suddenly became silent and there was not a man amongst them who did not know how it felt to be in George's shoes. They both admired his courage to begin anew, and yet, they poignantly felt his defeat. But what was this man to do? With already six growing children to feed and clothe, not to mention the doctor bills and a once again pregnant wife, and the fact that good-paying jobs were almost nonexistent; he did not have much to hope for.

There was one blessing. The grandmother in town had a big house and was willing to have her daughter, son-in-law, and their growing family move in with her. She also had an extra plot of land across the alley behind her house, where George could plant a huge vegetable garden this spring. That would surely keep the grocery bill down.

A few hours later, the younger children were awakened from their sound sleep and once again piled into the back seat of Papa's car for the short ride home. As Kathy climbed in behind her little brothers and sisters, she heard Matt Duehr talking to her daddy. "I tell you, George, you'd be a lot better off if you tried to find work at a carpenter's job. You're just as good—maybe even better than most of those town guys. You settle for one of the helper guys and you won't earn near the money. They'll never pay you what you're worth. Tell em you're experienced. Take my advice—for once!"

Papa grinned down at his good friend, who was a short, round, roly-poly, and very likeable man. "Well-l, mebbe you are right, Matt. But, I gotta be honest with 'em. You can't brag on yourself too much, you know. Goodnite now, you hear? Thanks for everything and Happy New Year!"

* * *

The time had come. The family was leaving the Petsche Farm. The big, old truck loaded down with all the furniture had just been driven over the bridge and headed into town. Mom was helping the kids into the car and Pa had ordered Joe to get the cow out of the barn.

Joe had been dreading it all morning and as he entered the barn and looked at Bossie, he felt that somehow this bovine animal knew exactly what was going on and she did not like it one bit. She balked stubbornly, as he led her out to the automobile. She did not particularly care for that noisy, stinking, sputtering, old rattletrap. She was actually afraid of the danged fool thing! The loud honking horn made her nervous, and its manners were atrocious. The engine kept backfiring, spewing its guts, exhaust, smoke, gas fumes, and whatever right in her face!

Young Joe eyed the sad-looking milk cow and sensed her confusion and wonder. He placed a gentle hand on her backside and patted her comfortingly on the rump, as he observed his Pa looking forlornly around the yard, the empty house, barns, and the land.

Young Joe made himself a solemn vow! He was only eight years old, but today, he had become a man! He had truly loved the farm and the animals, especially old Bossie. He was very grateful that Pa had been able to keep her even though he knew her days were numbered. They couldn't keep a cow very long in town. It just was not the thing to do! And come the day her milk dried up, they would have to butcher her for the meat. He closed his eyes and shuddered. He did not want to think about that day!

Joe understood more than his parents realized, certainly much more than his little brothers and sisters (they were just dumb little kids and didn't know anything about life). Even Kathy, though older didn't know. Girls did not understand about farms, banks, and stuff like that. That was only for the menfolk to worry about.

Well, maybe some ladies did worry, like his mom for instance. And another thing, Joe knew she was going to have a baby again—real soon. His ma and pa tried to keep it quiet, but he knew—he wasn't dumb, you know!

He remembered a year ago when the herd of cows had all come down with TB. He was not quite sure what that was, but he remembered it spread like wildfire from cow to cow. Pa even had the animal "doc" come out to the farm and administer medicine, and shots and stuff. But, in the end, at least six cows and two horses had died.

And, at the same time, Pa had to borrow $450.00 from that bank in town. He did not have the money to pay it off in the allotted time, and those rich and greedy men became upset. They did not care about a man's feelings, pride, and family. They couldn't, they said, wait for the money, and so Pa was forced to sell out!

Eight years of hard work and sweat, tears, hopes, and dreams are all gone. But they, those banker men, were happy. They came out to the farm in their white shirts and ties, expensive suits, and wide-brimmed hats and eagerly watched the proceedings of the sale—and watched a man's dream die.

As soon as it was over, Pa (in his bib overalls) counted out the money and one man signed a paper that said "Paid in Full." The bank men got their money and left. And Pa? Well, Pa still owned old Bossie, his Model T, and the responsibility of his wife, Francie, and their growing family.

Joe was wearing his striped "bib overalls," just like Pa's. Only the boy's one pant leg was cuffed higher than the other. He could never get them cuffed evenly. He looked down at the hard, rich earth beneath his feet and stubbornly dug his booted toes into the soil and solemnly swore to himself! He spat onto the earth, just like he'd seen his Pa and lots of other grown up men do. He'd make this old dirt work for him someday and he would own acres and acres of it. And he'd make darn sure that he always had enough money or assets or whatever those big words were to pay back some crummy old bank debt of $450.00—you bet he would! Even $4500.00! even $45,000.00!

Joe knew this was not his Pa's fault—he had worked so hard, this tiller of the soil. But times were tough for everyone. Damn the Depression, anyway. Why did it have to come along and mess up their lives? The boy spat again: and his father, sensing the lad's bitterness placed his hand on Joe's shoulder and said, "Come, son. I don't like this any more than you do. But, a man's *got* to do what a man's got to do."

Joe squared his shoulders to the world, stuck out his lower lip in defiance, and silently promised the earth he would conquer it one day; he furtively wiped away the tear that had begun to trickle down his cheek. The father wisely averted his face so as not to notice this emotion—or perhaps to hide his own.

The two "men" climbed into the car and slowly and silently drove into town. Bossie, who was now securely tethered to the rear bumper followed behind in bovine obedience, at least in body, if not in spirit. The tiny faces of the younger children peered out at the empty outbuildings, the old pump that had provided many a cool and refreshing drink on hot summer days, and the vacant house that once had been "home."

To Grandmother's house we go—over the hill and through the woods, to town. To the tree lined streets, concrete sidewalks, stores, the park along the river, the railroad tracks, schoolhouse, and church—and to Grandma!

Chapter III

Guttenberg

Arnie breathed a deep sigh of relief as he gazed out of the back window of the old car and could see the creaky old wooden bridge was behind them. They had actually made it safely across without mishap. He had been fearful that all of them, including his mama and papa, the cow and even the car would surely end up in the creek.

He had been so sure that the old rickety bridge would be weakened with the heavy weight of the big truck compounded by the additional weight of its immensely fat driver. The driver was a friend of his dad's and he was so fat he could not fit behind the steering wheel of the truck. He had to completely remove the door on the driver's side in order to squeeze into the cab.

Arnie was fascinated and watched with awe as big Art huffed and puffed his way up and into the driver's seat. The fleshy parts of his body hung over the side of the seat, jiggling and jouncing up and down as the truck sputtered into motion and laboriously lumbered along, slowly bumping its way across the bridge to the road on the other side that curved around the Guttenberg Hill.

He was only five years old, but already his young and active mind was leaning toward the analytical and methodical manner of thinking, which is typical of the engineer he was later to become. Surely it would have made much more sense and also serve as an added precaution if papa had driven the family across first. And the truck should have followed them. They were doing everything backward. Sometimes, grown-ups could be so "dumb"!

Now that they were safely over that hurdle of the bridge, Arnie was able to relax and he began to get caught up in the excitement of their new adventure. He was even able to laugh at the ridiculous sight they created as they wended their way around the hill, onto the Highway, and then across the railroad tracks. The fat man was leading the parade with all their worldly possessions piled onto the flat bed truck—the old Model T with Papa and Mama in the front seat with baby Frankie on Mama's lap. All the rest of the kids piled on top of each other, packed like sardines in the back seat—the milk cow still snarling contemptuously tied to the tail end and last but not least, Old Sport bringing up the rear!

Thus it was, that the Spielbauer family made their grand and glorious entrance into Guttenberg and pulled to a stop in front of the two-story, white frame building that was Grandma's house and now to become their new home. Gram welcomed the children with open arms, as they eagerly shoved and spilled their way out of the back seat in much the same fashion that they had so recently entered it a short time ago.

They were shy and timid at first, these little country mice. And their new surroundings would be difficult for some of them; but as children everywhere in this world must learn to adjust, so would these little ones. That adjustment must come later. However, for now, even the smallest amongst them was put to work, unloading and carrying the many boxes and beginning the task of unpacking and settling in.

By nightfall, all the sleeping accommodations had been set up and the beds freshly made with clean sheets and blankets. One by one, the exhausted children tumbled into bed and instantly dozed off. Tonight, the children of George and Frances would dream the dreams of childhood—tomorrow, they would face a new and challenging world.

George sat alone on the back steps of his mother-in-law's house and silently puffed on his last cigarette of the evening. He reflected on the day's long and hectic pace, which at last was drawing to its close. His mood was at first pensive, as he looked back on the years that had transpired—each year bringing a new mouth for him to feed—but it quickly changed to one of apprehension, as he thought of what the morrow would bring.

This country was in a sad state of affairs and the future did not look bright to the young father. Times were tough and George knew they could only get tougher! His body was tired. He went inside and laid his body down beside his sleeping wife. Tonight, this man would dream the dreams of a broken man, and tomorrow, this man (not unlike his children) too would face a new world—a new job—and a new beginning! Thanks be to God!

* * *

Let us now take leave of George, Frances, and the grandmother (white-haired Juliana) and let us say "good night" to these children: Kathy, Joe, Rosy, Arnie, Helen, and to Baby Frankie. Permit these folks for a little while, at least, to find relief from the worries of their world. Allow them to cast aside the tension and the strife of this long day—to find solace in dreams of hope that will dominate those sleeping hours. Come, oh dark of night and provide a respite to these tired bodies and exhausted minds. This is an excellent moment for you and I, dear reader, to quietly slip away. It is a moment to seriously consider the times and tribulations that by now have become a strong influence and will have a lasting effect on the lives of these once simple peasant farm folk as they begin a new life style in the little town of Guttenberg, Iowa.

Earlier today, you all witnessed the heartache of young Joe as he silently "cursed" these times—this "damned Depression" that had so shattered the small world of the Spielbauer family. Not having appeared on the scene as yet, I was not an eyewitness to the incidents that have been described thus far. I can only attempt to repeat as accurately as possible that which has been related to me by those who were alive at the time this new decade began its devastating journey through time.

It has all been said before (via the written word and verbal expression) much, much more eloquently and in a much more profound manner than I could ever hope to achieve, but in the interest of my story, it must be brought to light again. So, please bear with me.

You are all well aware of the much-publicized "bread lines" and "soup kitchens" that had been a commonplace scene during the 30s, as was that endless parade of men in search of jobs that stretched across this vast expanse of land and reached from coast to coast. They stood in line—their foggy breaths visible in the cold air. They were young and they were old—they were black men and they were white men as they stood with frigid fingers jammed into threadbare pockets, searching for warmth that was not there. They waited despairingly for whatever jobs they could find. They found none.

Poverty prevailed in every city, hamlet, and small town, and eventually reached its long tentacles into the rural areas of this great nation. There was no escape anywhere—no one person or race or region was immune. Rich men became poor men. Proud men became beggars. The strong became weak. Heads of households were forced to resort to begging, borrowing, and yes, even stealing in order to provide for the needs of their families.

Aah! The words have, indeed, all been said before, time and time again. "The Great American Depression," "the crash era," the "lean years," the "hard times," and the "hungry years." But, in truth, these names could only, at best, be but a feeble attempt to describe the misery and despair that existed for almost a full decade. In 1929, banks all over our country had failed. That crash that had broken many a man and many a business and destroyed many a dream was followed by severe unemployment in all the major cities. This reached a staggering total of fifteen million (more than one-fourth of the American labor force) by the year 1933. In addition to this national disaster, our country had experienced severe droughts in 1930 and again in 1931 that destroyed winter wheat crops and resulted in devastating dust storms in the midwestern region—America's Heartland!

America was hurting from deep inside. A great cry rose up from the very vital organs of our Mother Nation, crying for her huddled masses—her children! It was time for a new leader—a new hero! And on March 4, 1933, that hero, in the guise of one Franklin Delano Roosevelt, was inaugurated as the thirty-second president of the United States of America. This man soon became the symbol of hope to a despairing nation. He reached out with the helping hands of the government to the working classes.

He was heralded as the "peoples' president" and soon became well known and much revered for his famous fireside chats that transported him by radio into every living room and into every heart in America. FDR, as he was most often called, with the help of Congress created the PWA (Public Works Administration) and the WPA (Works Progress Administration). These two were interrelated. The PWA federally financed the work projects, whereas the WPA oversaw the entire working operation.

One of the off shoots of FDR's so called "alphabet soup" is the CCC (Civilian Conservation Corps) that enlisted 250,000 young able-bodied men for soil conservation, flood controls, and forestry improvement projects under the direction of the WPA. These men were paid $30.00 a month, plus room and board and lived in meager, but adequate camps near their work sites. In addition, the families of these men received $25.00 each month.

This new president provided employment for the down and out; he created a means by which despairing and emotionally dying men were now able to pick themselves up (along with their shattered pride) and start all over again. Armies of workmen joined forces in building water supply systems, flood controls, roads and bridges, new hospitals and health facilities, city halls, courthouses, and public educational buildings among many other projects. Our government did not stop there. It sought out unemployed artists as well as the working classes. It put men to work doing what they do best. Painters were commissioned to paint—sculptures to sculpt and writers to write!

This now takes us to the upper Mississippi River, which was a natural for inland waterway navigation and it was agreed that this region would greatly benefit from the advantages of a low-cost water transportation system. In 1930, Congress authorized the development of a 9-foot channel navigation project on a section of this river between the mouth of the Missouri River and Minneapolis, Minnesota.

Thus, the WPA was welcomed into the Guttenberg area—and the long arm of the Government reaches out its "helping hands" to our young George Spielbauer, father of six, and scores of other men just like him. George has enlisted. He is one of the lucky ones. He has a job!

* * *

This is the time—March 21, 1934. And this is the place—the small river town of Guttenberg, Iowa; in which our thirty-six-year-old father finds himself as he opens his eyes to a new day and a new dawning on this bright sunshiny spring morning. His loving and uncomplaining Frances already has a meager, but nourishing breakfast as he walks into the kitchen. He has to marvel at her patience and long-suffering, as she daily accepts whatever—for better or worse—that is handed out to her. She has never lost faith in God or her husband, and George is grateful for that. He quickly finishes his meal and swallows the last drop of coffee—grabs for his cap and says, "Well, I'll be on my way, then". He sets off, this time on foot as he heads to the northern part of the town in the direction of the River, the future site of Lock and Dam # 10.

George hastened his way through town with long, giant strides as he allowed his thoughts to halfheartedly dwell on the new job. The air was brisk and fresh and even though he was at least two blocks west of it, he could smell the river. Some folks complained they could smell an offending fishy odor, but this did not bother George. It smelled good to his nostrils. He walked past a majestic brick house on a huge corner lot that was beautifully landscaped with its neatly trimmed shrubbery and well-clipped lawn. A tall apple tree to the left of the house was just beginning to "bud out" and soon would be a-bloom with many pale pink, perfumed blossoms. This house was actually part of the Church grounds where Father Dupont, the parish priest, lived.

He walked briskly past the Catholic Church itself, with its duet of gold crosses caressing the skies, and then beyond the school and playground, turning left at the corner where there was another long red brick structure, which was the temporary home of the Franciscan nuns who taught at the Catholic school. Their Mother House was located in La Crosse, Wisconsin.

Kitty corner from the nun's house was a small grocery store operated by Harold Grimes, a man whom George knew slightly. Next to that was a long, lean gray building that was called "The Bee Hive," Guttenberg's answer to an apartment house. The sleepy little town was just beginning to wake up and its early morning stirrings were but an inkling of what the busy day would bring.

A fat lady with metal "curlers" sticking out of her red hair was letting a yipping little dog outside in response to Mother Nature's early call and at the same time partake of a morning exercise. He did not know her name, but nonetheless, he tipped his cap in politeness and said, "Good Morning." She smiled back and greeted him with a friendly "Hello."

He hurried on and soon realized he was "uptown" now and close to his destination. He turned left heading straight north for two more blocks to the Lock and Dam construction site. The side streets of the residential area of Guttenberg might still be quiet and unstirring in their sleep and the main street businesses as yet unopened for the day; but at the banks of the mighty Mississippi, the scene was a hustle and bustle of activity.

Yes, here was a veritable "little town" within a little town. House trailers had been hauled in and temporary shelters established. Tents had been pitched in neatly aligned avenues to accommodate those men who might be too poor or had arrived too late to find what scarce lodging there was within the houses of the townsfolk. Many of the homeowners had opened up their private lives and rented sleeping rooms to the transient workers, thus adding a few pennies to their own weekly coffers.

George could still smell the remains of strong coffee that had been brewed over the now smoldering campfires. Here and there, men hastily dashed buckets of water on the fires to extinguish the remaining flames and grabbed last minute jackets or jammed billed caps jauntily onto their heads as they hurriedly reported for work. Horse drawn wagons were being loaded with heavy machinery and raw materials were transported from the supply area to the working sites.

George looked intently at the gaunt men with their hollow cheeks, sad eyes, and bent shoulders—young men, much like himself—who were beginning to congregate in small groups. Some of them lounged indolently against the old cars, some with hands jammed in their pants pockets, others puffing hastily on one last cigarette to get them through the morning, yet all of them indicating in some fashion or another their reluctance to begin their appointed tasks of the day. It wouldn't be long, George knew, before they would all be called to order and to labor by the big bosses who were government employees. These supervisors were overseeing the construction of this concrete dam that was designed to span the entire width of the Mississippi River between Guttenberg on this Iowa side and the small Wisconsin community of Glen Haven on the opposite shore.

He felt a little lost and useless as he stood isolated from the scene of activity and silently observed the pandemonium around him. Everyone appeared to be in a great hurry to get somewhere, but didn't seem to know just where that was or just what it was that they were supposed to be doing.

He noticed a young lad about fourteen years old on his two-wheeled bike also observing the chaos around him. The boy had parked his bicycle close to a team of horses and was standing astride his vehicle, but holding it stationary with his two feet planted firmly on the ground. A stray dog dashed through the melee of activity and frightened the horses who "on cue" took two giant steps backward and pushed the wagon heavily laden with a load of 2 × 4s into the boy's bike, toppling both boy and bike to the dusty earth! George quickly ran behind the wagon and helped the lad to his feet. His right arm was skinned pretty badly where it had landed on the bicycle chain, but other than that, he was unhurt.

"Danged fool kid!" What was he doing up here, anyway? Just gawkin' and in the way! They should not allow kids to be near all this dangerous equipment—and so close to the river. That was even more dangerous. But, he smiled down at the young boy and asked, "Are you hurt anywhere, son?"

"Naw, I'm OK," the boy replied in embarrassment. "You took quite a jolt. Those horses look harmless—but they are very strong. What's your name?"

"Really, mister, I'm OK. My name's Lowell. Lowell Eilers. I'll be all right."

"Well, you best pick up that bike and git it on out of here 'fore those horses stomp it to pieces. Best git on home and have your "ma" wash the dirt off those scrapes on your elbow. You're bleeding there—clean that out real good and put some Watkins salve on it. That's good stuff. Now, go on, git out of here, before you git hurt worse."

Again, George thought to himself, "Dang fool kid. This is no place for kids to be hangin' around." He made a mental note to caution Frances to keep a close eye on his own boys. And he would have a good talk with those older ones—he surely did not want Joe and Arnie up here on this riverbank—no telling what could happen to them.

A stern looking, unsmiling, and obviously unfriendly, middle-aged man approached George and spoke, "Are you looking for work here today?"

"Yes sir," said George. "But, I'm not sure where to go or what to do." The man responded with a "Come, then. Follow me. What did you say your name was?"

"George Spielbauer," said our father. The stern man did not respond. He simply motioned for George to follow him in a dead silence . . . thus, our father began his new job.

Chapter IV

Settling In

Let us return to Grandma's house and the rest of the family. Kathy, Joe, and Rosy awoke early and followed in their father's footsteps as far as St. Mary's Grade School, just two and one-half blocks to the north. They were considered "town kids" now and this meant they would be able to come home during their lunch break. They were all looking forward to becoming better acquainted with their classmates, at least the ones who lived on the same block.

Mom and Dad were very strict with their little ones and had already laid down the "ground rules" as to where they could and could not go. They had to stay within the limits of Grandma's block unless they had special permission from their parents. Even though Gram's house was surrounded more or less by the dear, little "granny" ladies who kept to themselves, there were many other children living on the same street. It was only a matter of days before the Spielbauer children would be involved in softball games on the south-end corner lot, close to the railroad tracks. There were also endless games of Red Rover-Red Rover, Kick the Can, Jacks and Marbles, and many others. Hide and Seek and Run-Sheep-Run were the most fun, especially in the twilight hours, just before dark.

Kathy and Rosy soon became friends with the girls next door (Meralda and Rita Frommelt) as well as Lillian Connelly whose family lived down around the corner on toward the River. This family also had older boys who played with Joe and Arnie, and soon both the Spielbauer and Connelly families became good friends. Our parents and older brothers went there often to listen to the radio, as we did not have one of our own.

It soon became a nightly ritual for Joe and Arnie to rush through their evening meal, ask to be excused from table, dash out the door, and arrive at the Connelly household just in time to listen to Tom Mix at six thirty. Papa and Mr. Connelly preferred to listen to the President FDR speak on Sunday nights, and, of course, the boxing matches preempted everything else. Mr. and Mrs. (Hattie) Kipper lived just two houses south of Gram, and they too would invite our parents to visit and listen to their radio. All in all, it was a very nice neighborhood and they welcomed our family warmly.

Mrs. Schutte, one of the "grannies" lived right next door to Gram. She was slight of form and wore dresses with long sleeves and long skirts (even during the very "hot heat" of summer). Her raiment was usually dark and somber in color, perhaps a tiny floral design, polka dot, or pinstripe pattern. She always wore a white, pinafore apron over top of the dress, its shoulder straps crisscrossing in the back—and, would you believe high-buttoned shoes? She even wore this while hoeing and weeding in her garden. But, most characteristic of her entire attire was that ever-present sunbonnet, tied beneath her chin in a big bow. This bonnet was of course the most colorful part of her costume! And naturally, it was homemade!

She was an exact replica of the little Sunbonnet Sue girls that were so artistically appliqued onto many hand-stitched quilts and embroidered on dishtowels of this same era. Truly she was a picture of nostalgia, as she stooped over in her garden, tippling her sprinkling can above the brightly colored zinnias, marigolds, and nasturtiums that bloomed profusely under the control of this little lady's green thumb!

Directly across the street from Mrs. Schutte lived Mrs. Kregel, another widow lady. And right next to her, lived still another granny, Mrs. Petsche. She was even tinier in stature than Mrs. Schutte if that was possible.

All three were rarely seen outdoors unless it was in the very early hours of the morning or later at the end of day working in their vegetable gardens and flowerbeds. If seen at all during the day, it would be at the clothesline, or perhaps walking uptown to pick up their mail. On these occasions, they shielded themselves from the heat of a summer's day with very feminine old-fashioned parasols.

Our family, of course, had the most contact with Mrs. Schutte, as she was Gram's closest neighbor. Mrs. Schutte also owned a very large plot of land across the alley behind her house that ran clear down to the end of the block. Dad rented this land from her and planted a huge vegetable garden. He always claimed that the reason he planted so many gardens was to keep his boys busy with weeding and hoeing. That way they wouldn't have any time left—and, even if they did, they would be too tired to get into trouble.

Grandma took charge of the first garden right behind her house where they planted onions, radishes, lettuce, carrots, endive, cabbages, etc. Mrs. Schutte's land soon became home to rows of sweet corn, potatoes, squash, pickles, and whatever else my father chose to experiment with. He always planted much more than he needed with the intention of sharing the harvest with whomsoever needed it.

The year 1934 was a particularly dry summer and this created a slight problem for George's gardens. He was able to water the backyard plot with the garden hoses but Mrs. Schutte's land was impossible to reach. Here, he had to rely on Mother Nature and her rainfall to make things grow. Gram's pickle patch was located in that garden and its under developed fruit had literally "shriveled on the vine."

Even though, our gram's hair was now "snow white," she, in her youth, had once been a flaming redhead and we all know what that means, right? Determined and gutsy, our Gram commandeered every available child in the neighborhood, grandkids, neighbor kids, stray kids, and even kids from the north end of town—most of whom she didn't even know, and she put them to work!

She grabbed them by their hair, shirt collars, ear lobes, and whatever else she could latch onto and equipped each child with a bucket, pail, pot or pan, sprinkling cans, and even assigned a huge rinse tub to the two biggest boys. She herself manned the pump handle. A steady stream of kids now lined up in a row that went from the pump, out into the alley, and all the way down to her pickle patch, dispatching containers of water from hand to hand and eventually dumping it upon the thirsty garden plot.

Of course, Gram's inexperienced "pickle brigade" spilled more water on each other and onto the dry dusty alleyway and most of the containers were only half full by the time they reached their destination, but Hallelujah! Our once redheaded grandmother had defied Mother Nature and not only did her pickle patch survive, but it flourished, as well!

A summertime highlight was the 4th of July! Small towns all across the land have always found this holiday a cause for lavish celebrations and fireworks and Guttenberg was no exception. Nor was the Spielbauer family. Even though they could not afford an elaborate party back in '34, they managed to have a good time with what little they had.

Relatives on both sides of the family had begun to arrive very early in the morning. The men had already gone to their fishing boats, hoping for a "good catch" to add to the day's feast. The women all pitched in and helped with the food, some bringing dishes already prepared and the kitchen was now filled to overflowing with all the aunts, Gram, and Mama. By mid-morning, they had huge bowls of potato salad and coleslaw ready to serve. These dishes had been placed in a large tub with a secure handle and carefully lowered down into the pump well on a rope in order to keep them cold until mealtime.

Frances had boiled a big ham the night before. With the addition of fresh vegetables, green salads, and that prized Mississippi channel catfish (which would be dredged in corn meal and flour, and crisply fried in hot, spitting lard), it would, indeed, be food fit for the Gods!

George already had filled Mama's copper boiler with big chunks of ice floating in water, which now contained bottled beer for the men and soda pop for the children. This was the only day in the entire year that the Spielbauer children were allowed the luxury of drinking pop. Papa would send the two oldest brothers uptown to "Johnny Pop's" to buy a whole case (twenty-four bottles) of his special recipe. Johnny Pop offered many different flavors: orange, strawberry, cherry, root beer, and cream "sody," which was our black Grandma's favorite.

Johnny Pop's real name was Mr. Wolter, but every kid in town and most of the grown-ups too, for that matter, knew him as Johnny Pop. He was quite a legend and I am certain there is not a single boy or girl who attended school in Guttenberg who does not remember Johnny Pop. Our school held an annual Picnic at the close of each year. The entire school along with teachers (and yes, they even wore their long black nun's dresses and veils) would hike or ride bicycles out to Petsche's Grove, or Lakeside or Ceres Church with a sack lunch to spend the entire day. And always just before lunchtime, Johnny Pop would show up with cases of his wonderful thirst-quenching brew, which we could buy for a nickel a bottle!

This also brings to mind our milkman, Lewis Carrier. He too would drive his vehicle to the picnic site with an ample supply of Dixie cups and wooden spoons shortly after our lunch and we could also purchase his ice cream for the same price of one nickel.

Needless to say, both of these men were destined to become friends with every kid in town! But, speaking of ice cream, I must return to the 4th of July! That homemade strawberry ice cream had by now become a family tradition for the Spielbauer children. Our frugal mother, for weeks prior, had been scraping pennies together and at last had enough money to purchase the necessary ingredients for her own special recipe. She'd managed to retain enough fresh eggs from the laying hens and always had a big jar of homemade strawberry jam on hand for this special day. I never knew her exact recipe (I don't think my sisters did, either). I do know she whipped together a custard-like mix of beaten eggs, milk, vanilla, and the strawberry jam, which turned everything pink. I think she referred to it as the "junket."

The making of this frozen treat began early in the morning as soon as the men returned from their fishing expedition. The ice cream freezer was a large wooden staved bucket that housed a smaller metal canister into which a set of beaters fit snugly and the whole contraption was then connected to the lid. There was a crank attached to the outside of the bucket. This was also connected to the inside canister. Mom's ice cream junket was poured into the canister, the lid securely sealed and the container immersed into the wooden bucket and tightly packed with salted ice chunks all the way around it. It took a strong and steady arm to turn that crank.

Each of the children clamored for their turn to crank the handle. Alas—one by one, they soon tired of the hard work and quietly disappeared. Only the very little ones who were allowed to lick the beaters remained to the bitter end. Of course, it was Papa George whose strength endured long enough to complete the job. At this point, the wooden bucket was repacked with ice surrounding the cylinder inside, and the entire container submerged into a huge tub of more ice. Tub and all was then completely covered with a heavy quilt and placed somewhere in the shade where the process of freezing was left to itself.

Our Aunt Louise and Uncle Arnie Hutter were always the first to arrive and the last of the relatives to leave. They did not have any children of their own and soon became the favored aunt and uncle of the Spielbauer kids. Aunt Louise, without fail, would always have a big bag of store-bought candy for the children. Most of the time, she would tease us into thinking she had forgotten to buy it, but we were never disappointed. Store-bought candy was a rare treat and Aunt Louise never let us down. She always had a sack of jellybeans, circus peanuts, licorice, gumdrops, occasionally chocolate stars, or malted milk balls stashed in her purse.

When it was time to serve the ice cream, Uncle Arnie assembled all the children from Kathy on down to the baby and lined us up on the back porch steps. In his loud singsong voice, he began to chant

I scream—you scream!
We all scream
For Ice Cream!

He would emphasize louder and louder each "scream" until the final "Ice Cream" became a deafening shout. The children loved it of course, and more than willingly added their own musical voices to the chorus, over and over, and over again!

Mom always said that once the Fourth of July was celebrated, the summer itself was over with. I think what she meant was the leisure part of summer, for by now the backyard gardens were rapidly producing their yield of fresh fruits and veggies at a much faster pace than she and Gram could keep up with. All of July and August were spent canning, preserving, and preparing for the long cold winter that lay ahead. Potatoes were stored in raised bins with slatted flooring so air could circulate around the produce. Carrots were buried in sand in the cellar to keep them fresh and crisp. Onions were tied into bundles and hung from the ceiling rafters in the basement.

The first week in September sends the older Spielbauer children back to school to begin a new term and Frances once again to her birthing bed to bring forth a new child. And true to everyone's expectations, this one turned out to be another girl born on September 4, 1934. She was a sickly babe and Frances recalls that she cried constantly. The doctors explained to the new mother that the child was suffering from a great internal pain. She was afflicted with some sort of rare blood disease that left black and blue bruises all over her tiny body, wherever she was touched.

This baby demanded constant care and attention from both mother and father as each parent took their turns watching over her throughout the long nights. She had to be held around the clock. And dear Gram Rohner did double duty during the daytime hours. The illness was treated with a twice-daily shot (each day for the duration of ten days), which had as its healing powers the venom of the poisonous Water Moccasin snake. The shots were then reduced to once a day, eventually every other day, and finally down to once a week until such time as the infant was a few months old.

I have researched this particular illness and the only reference I can find in the medical books is "hemorrhagic disease of the newborn." Basically, what it amounts to is the inability of the blood cells in the baby's body to coagulate. It is my understanding that a newly born infant relies on the blood cells developed within the mother's womb for approximately the first month of its life. On rare occasions, a freakish thing occurs and the baby suffers from an adverse reaction to its mother's cells. This results in an internal bleeding, which would explain the black and blue marks all over the new baby of Frances and George. Now if the child is fortunate enough to survive the first crucial weeks of its life, the danger point is past, as at that time, the baby begins to develop its own blood cells and no longer is dependent on those formed by the mother.

At this point, I should like to bow my head in reverend gratitude, for a moment here, as I extend a most sincere thank-you to all the young children in attendance at St. Mary's Grade School in that early fall of 1934. I wish to thank them for the many prayers that wended their way heavenward in my behalf. For, yes, dear reader, that sickly little babe was none other than "yours truly." My sister Kathy tells me that as all the school children arose from their benches each morning, they stood beside their desks to recite first in tribute to the State, The Allegiance to the Flag. Then, in equal obeisance to their God, they prayed The Morning Offering and dedicated these prayers to "the sick baby in the parish." I am, indeed, most grateful.

Fritz and Hilda Brimeyer became my baptismal parents and in the ensuing years would always be my special friends and would hold a place of endearment within my heart. Yes, I did recover and I was most fortunate for the doctors say, back in those days, only about one-half of its victims survived this disease. As Frances was later to say, "that Hildagarde became the fattest (I think in those olden days, fat was synonymous with healthy) of all her babies." However, our mother was also known to have added to that statement "and the ugliest." This latter literally destroyed my ego.

My only saving grace was my Aunt Tootsie's explanation that is an old adage of sorts and was intended to console me. It went something like this, "Ugly in the cradle—pretty at the table." Well, I am still waiting for that pretty part to happen, but, at least, I am not *fat* anymore. And I do recall with great detail, however, that my Uncle Arnie used to tease me without mercy and call me "skinny little Hildagarde." I was devastated! I'd run upstairs to the girls' room and crawl under my bed and cry. Now, I don't mind being called skinny or little at all. These days, Uncle Arnie, I rather like it.

Dear reader, let us now leave this fattest, but healthy baby as she lay cooing and gurgling in her crib, contented and happy in her own existence, trusting herself into the hands of her mama, her papa, grandma and all of her big brothers and sisters. Even though she lives in troubled times, this little tyke has not a care in the world! Her needs are simple: a dry diaper, a warm bottle of milk, a hug, and a kiss. She truly wants for nothing!

Interlude

Alas, the needs of the Spielbauer Family, as an entity are, indeed, tantamount.

The next ten to fifteen years undoubtedly constitute the very heart and soul of my story. These are the years that give us a deep insight into the moral character and inner strength of George and Frances. These are the years of a struggle, both financial and emotional—the years of back breaking labor and the years of a lost pride. At last and most reluctantly, our mother and father were forced to concede to that loss of pride. They accepted it and learned to cope with it. This was not easy for they both came from a strong and proudful German heritage and losing what they had fought and struggled to gain for so many years was difficult for the two of them to face.

The responsibilities of providing their growing family with food, clothing, health care, and education must have at times seemed like an insurmountable task to our parents. But their faith and strength endured. It was this very endurance that gave them the courage to face the daily adversities of their lives, surviving for the next few years as best they could—just one day at a time.

My older brothers and sisters relate to me that during this period in our lives, we were one of Guttenberg's poorest families and without a doubt, its largest in number. In plain truth, we were the "poor kids" of the town. We were well aware of this fact. We couldn't hide it nor could we deny it. We had no choice but to learn to accept it and face up to the harsh realism of its existence.

Ah, yes! We may have been poor by society's standards, but were also a proud breed. Our clothing may have been well worn and obviously handed down from child to child, but it was always freshly laundered and neatly pressed. The colors may have become slightly faded (after so many washings), but we were *never* tattered or torn. For our mother and grandmother were both able seamstresses and as quickly as a worn-out seam would give way to its ordinary wear and tear or the stress of a growing body, it would be reinforced on Mom's treadle operated Singer sewing machine. Overalls and underwear were patched and re-patched to the point of no return, and socks were darned and darned again—beyond original recognition.

For the most part, we were all well-mannered kids—a little shy, perhaps. Our parents and our gram were strict in their disciplinary actions and our behavior was impeccable. Well almost! We were raised in a devout and Catholic religious environment and very early in our lives were taught the Fear of God and held dutiful regard for anyone in authority. We treated our elders with respect and were soon considered by others in the community as polite and well-behaved children. Most of us were reasonably good students in school and learned our lessons well.

All of this was under the guidance and watchful eyes of our parents who constantly worked hard and continued to worry equally as hard. However, they were determined to overcome, or at the very least survive, the obstacles of these tough times. George and Frances were forced to become an ingenious, innovative, and inventive pair—and our gram was no slouch either. For, she labored right along beside them—in the kitchen, bending over the washboard or ironing board, alongside a sickbed, or out in the garden wherever her help was best utilized during these most trying and difficult years.

Personally, I look upon these next few chapters as sort of self-made "survival kit" of the Depression years. I shall try to depict how one family, large in number, poor in its worldly possessions, but rich in its togetherness and determination (which is characteristic of our German bloodline) managed to procure the very basics necessary for its survival—food, shelter, clothing, and medical care. As a guideline for these next chapters, I can think of nothing more appropriate than The Corporal Works of Mercy. These cover a lot of territory and take into consideration all of the demands of the human body.

Feed the Hungry
Give Drink to the Thirsty
Clothe the Naked
Shelter the Homeless
Visit the Sick
Bury the Dead

These merciful works can best be described as acts of the virtue of Charity. This virtue is or should be practiced by all good God-fearing Christians for the benefit and betterment of their fellow man. And, indeed, these acts of Charity were daily performed by our self-sacrificing parents, by our loving grandmothers (both "black" and "white"), numerous aunts and uncles who cared about our large family, and all those countless kindhearted neighbor ladies and thoughtful townsfolk who took us under their wings. And lastly, each of us children in turn soon learned to help one another where ever that help was needed and to share what little materialism we possessed with whomsoever was in need of same.

Many of our good and generous benefactors still walk along the streets of the little town of Guttenberg and many others amongst them now "rest in peace" within the cemeteries located just outside the town and south around the Guttenberg Hill. But, our grateful hearts have never forgotten their indulgences in practicing The Corporal Works of Mercy for our behalf in our growing up years. May God bless each and every one of *you*!

Chapter V

Feed the Hungry Give Drink to the Thirsty

Feeding the hungry and giving drink to the thirsty was placed at top priority within this household, which now came to a total head count of ten—ten hungry mouths to feed. Our father's job at the Lock and Dam allowed him to work for only five hours each day. He was certainly eager for more and would have liked to put in longer days in order to bring home more pay; but there were so many men in need of jobs—and so few jobs available. The government divided the daylight hours amongst them and hired the men into two daily shifts, each shift working only five hours max.

However, our energetic George was not a wastrel, even with (or perhaps, I should say), particularly with his time. Most of his free hours were spent in his garden plots, hunched over rake, hoe, or shovel, incessantly chopping away at those "damnable weeds" that, like the plague, had followed him from those Buenie hills just such a few years ago.

George, you know, never really gave up being a farmer even though he was considered town folk now. His heart was still in the land, so to speak and always would be. In addition to his job at the Dam, he worked part-time for his old friends and neighbors, Andy Elsinger and Norbie Nieland, who farmed their lands just south and around the Guttenberg Hill. He assisted both men during the peak seasons of farming—never accepting a cash payment for his wages, but bartering his labor for fresh eggs, milk, chickens, beef, and pork during the butchering times.

Thus, he was still able to make the blood sausages, headcheese, and homemade pork sausage that he enjoyed so much. He would grind up the pork meat and mix it with his special blend of spices and seasonings in Mom's big wash tub. Of course, it goes without saying that prior to this use, that container was thoroughly scrubbed out with a strong disinfectant bar soap (Proctor and Gamble), carefully rinsed, and then scalded with boiling water to properly sanitize it for the meat preparation. It was the only container large enough to hold all the ingredients and still have room to blend in the seasonings that were added according to George's taste buds.

My sister, Rosy, particularly recalls one of these incidents. Before I begin, I should once again remind the reader of that very Catholic environment in which we were being brought up. For we strictly adhered to the rules and regulations of our Mother Church and there was *never* ever any meat consumed within the Spielbauer household on Fridays. Just at the moment when George was inclined to taste test his recipe, in walks Mama. She observes him stirring and mixing, first adding one spice and then another blending all ingredients en masse in the big tub. Mama says, "I sure hope you know what you are doing. Now don't be putting in too much of that sage. Grandma will complain and won't eat any of it, if you over season it."

"I know what I am doing," replied George. "I'll be tasting it in a second here, as soon as I get it blended well. Then, we can stuff it into the casings."

"Best trust to your judgement, then," cautioned Mama again. "Because you don't dare taste it today. Did you forget that it is Friday?"

"Dang," responded George under his breath. Frances did not approve of cussing especially in front of the children. "We'll just see about that," said George and quickly dispatched his young son Joe (rather reluctantly on Joe's part) on a hasty mission to Father Dupont's house in order to request a special dispensation from that "no meat on Friday" regulation.

The amused Father Dupont (he knew our father well for he was a captive audience to George's weekly confessions each and every Saturday) politely listened with a somewhat controlled chuckle to Joe's rendition of Papa's dilemma and finally nodded his head in agreement to this unusual request.

Joe hurried home and informed his dad (who was still bent over the large tub, still stirring the sausage—still in the exact same spot where Joe had left him. Permission granted! George tasted and added a dab of this and a dash of that—and voila! Perfection! The sausage was stuffed into its casings, sealed into fruit jars, and cold packed by Gram and Mama. It was by far the very best batch that George had ever made—undoubtedly due to a certain priestly, if not, saintly blessing!

And those two aforementioned cooks, Gram and Mama worked daily, side by side over a huge, six-burner, wood-burning, cast iron stove that took up almost one entire wall in the kitchen. The first two burners on the left side were located directly above the firebox and this is where the main cooking occurred. The second two in the center of the stove were used for simmering and slow cooking. The last two on the right kept the finished dishes warm until serving time.

Attached to the right side of the stove was a reservoir that contained approximately ten gallons of water, which of course, was always hot and readily available for quick premeal clean-ups and those inevitable after dinner dishwashing rituals. This nasty job was assigned to Kathy and Rosy and would eventually be handed down to each girl in turn. The girls also were responsible for keeping the reservoir filled with water.

There were also two smaller ovens called warming ovens located at eye level that hung like cabinets from the back splash of the stove. Directly beneath the two hottest burners was a very small square opening that looked like a miniature oven door and it was through this aperture that the fire was fed and controlled. Below that was a long slender drawer that held the ashes as they dropped through the grating just above it. This ash pan of course had to be emptied often, especially in the winter months.

By this time, Mama was mixing a batch of bread every other day in order to keep a steady supply available for her large family. It took a lot of bread to feed this family. She always bought flour in increments of twenty-five pound bags. These bags were made of colorful printed cotton material that was a prized item in this family. Most of the clothing worn by the female members in our family was made out of these flour sacks.

One batch of bread would usually make about four to five loaves along with one huge pan of hot rolls that somehow always managed to pop out of the oven just in time for the evening meal. On Saturdays, mom would add sugar and honey to her bread dough. As a special treat for the family she would bake a pan of cinnamon rolls covered with a sugar and nut glaze, a couple loaves of raisin, nut bread, and two or three coffeecakes topped with brown sugar and hickory nuts.

These treats were always saved for Sunday morning breakfast after Mass and savored by the entire family and whatever friends and relatives just happened to drop by. There was always someone dropping by because Mama was famous for her sweet rolls and coffeecakes. To this day, I am totally amazed at how everything baked in that oven turned out so marvelously delicious and baked to perfection when the only control of the temperature was Mom's own careful and constant tending of the flames that spread the heat throughout the stove.

Mom was proud of this kitchen appliance and kept it immaculately clean at all times. If anything accidentally spilled over in the process of cooking or canning, it oftentimes would hit the hot cast iron and immediately burst into flames. She would quickly smother that flame with a generous application of salt—the salt box was always within ready grasp on top of the warming oven.

After each meal, the stove top itself was first wiped clean with a dampened cloth and then rubbed down with a coating of paraffin wax and polished to a high gloss with an old soft rag, usually an old worn-out diaper and Mama had an ample supply of these. She always said they made the best cleaning cloths. How well my sisters and I remember Mama's wrath when we failed to perform this particular task to her demanding specifications. I can assure you that we did it over and over, again. Until we got it right! At least, I did! Helen, of course, managed to always do it right, the first time.

Both of our parents worked very hard at providing their family with nourishing meals, but in spite of their dedication, it was an insurmountable task and at times, they were forced to accept food supplements provided by the government. Many of you, I'm certain recall the Relief Trucks that were now as commonplace in small towns and rural communities as were the breadlines in our bigger cities. The amount of food commodities that a family was entitled to receive was based on the number of dependents within the household. The recipients of this program would receive an advance notification card in the mail advising them of the date and an approximate time when the truck would be expected to arrive in their town.

Once a month, it showed up in Guttenberg and always parked on the main street near the Post Office. My older brothers, Arnie and Joe borrowed a wagon from one of the neighbors and would pick up the food staples for our family. They both detested having to do this and were extremely embarrassed to be seen by anyone who might recognize them. They made a special effort to travel through the back alleys and side streets of the town, en route to and from their destination in order to avoid a chance meeting with anyone of their friends or classmates from school. They were ashamed to be seen pulling their wagon filled with "charity"—the free hand-out of dry cereal, corn meal, prunes, raisins, dried navy beans, sometimes margarine and peanut butter, and on rare occasions a slab of salt pork.

Picture for a moment, these two little depression era brothers, one pulling and the other pushing a coaster wagon laden with food. They are obviously blood-related—both a little on the skinny side, freckle faced with very dark (almost black) hair, shy, and brown eyes downcast now to avoid recognition. They are wearing faded and patched-upon-patches bib overalls and colorless chambray shirts (on a really hot summer day no shirt at all, just overall straps covering their thin shoulder blades, and of course are barefooted. They do own a pair of shoes, but in the summertime, these are only worn for church and school.

We all know that little boys are notorious for dawdling along the way at whatever errand their mothers may send them on. Joe and Arnie were known to dawdle on many occasions, but never on this mission. They always hastened homeward as quickly as possible with their shamed eyes glued to the ground in hopes that by avoiding visible contact, they might camouflage, for a brief moment at least, their true identify—the poor kids of the town.

Shortly after the family moved into town, the old milk cow dried up and it was time to butcher her. She had but one purpose left in her life and that final duty was to now provide meat for this needy family. Old Bossie's days had finally come to a halt. She had always been a country cow, anyway, and had never adjusted to life in town. The tiny barn and the vacant lot down on the corner where she was let out to graze were much too confining for her.

Mama did not want the children to know about the butchering, so she contrived to have Gram take all of them into her big bedroom upstairs. The only windows looked out one to the north of town and the other to the front street. No one was allowed to go into the backyard. Kathy and Rosy played school with the younger children, while Gram entertained the older ones by teaching them string games. She made a circle of cord string and intricately twisting and entwining it in and around, and about one's fingers formed an inanimate object such as a baby cradle or hangman's noose, etc. It was rather boring, or so thought Joe, who had an inkling of what was going on in the backyard. He quietly slipped out of the room and made his way down the hall to the bathroom where he had a good view of the backyard and the barn.

He could clearly see everything that was going on. The wide barn door was completely opened. He knew he wasn't supposed to view this, but he couldn't help himself. Some uncontrollable force rooted him to this spot. He watched as his dad took the heavy mallet in both of his strong hands. He swung it hard, with all his might into the side of the cow's head. Joe couldn't hear the sound of the thud, he didn't have to, for he felt it—a dull heavy impact—right over the spot where his own heart was rapidly pounding. The boy's nose was pressed against the windowpane and his hands were dropped to his sides, both fists clenched tightly in apprehension. He sadly watched as his old friend, now stunned by the heavy force staggered to the ground. Her legs buckled beneath her own weight and there she lay, inert upon the dusty barn floor.

Joe didn't cry this time. Only his heart was heavy and his brown eyes very sad. He felt a numbness and an emptiness which he could not understand. Mama came into the room and put her arm around his shoulder, One glance out of the window and she knew her son had seen everything. "I had hoped you would not see this, Joe. Why didn't you stay in Grandma's room with the other children?"

"It's OK, Mama," Joe assured her. "I know Papa has to do this. But, she was a good old girl. Wasn't she"?

"Yes, she was all of that," answered his mother. "Come now, Joe. I want you to take a cup of hot tea up to Grandma. Those stair steps are too much for me these days. I just took some frosted graham crackers in there for the kids. Gram said she'd save you one."

Mother and son slowly descended the stairs—Frances sadly noted the look of resignation and silent acceptance (one of life's bitter lessons) etched upon the fine features of her young son's almost manly face. He was yet such a child, she reflected, and children should never have to suffer heartaches like this. But young Joe was already years ahead of his mother, more of a man than she realized. For he knew that butchering this cow was just another part of living and it had to be this way.

The following July was a beast of a hot month. And wouldn't you know, it was on the hottest day of summer that our first (of two) redheaded brothers decided to join forces with our world. July 17, 1936, welcomed little Lawrence Robert into our family. He had no trouble arriving and soon warmed his way into our lives and into our hearts as well, with his winsome baby smile and delightful baby ways. He was a chubby, happy, and healthy addition into this ever-growing "playfarmer" family.

Larry was also a very sociable little boy and as soon as he learned to walk he ran everywhere. He was all over the neighborhood, making friends wherever he went. His older sisters were constantly chasing after him and dragging him back home, kicking and screaming for his freedom. At about this time a newly married couple moved into the neighborhood just two houses up the street—Mike and Eunice Vorwald. Mike was a Captain on one of the Mississippi River barges that traveled up and down the River, and of course would be away from home for weeks at a time. Eunice, as I recall was the youngest married lady living on our street and therefore, the prettiest and, in my own estimation, the nicest. She also made very good cookies.

Eunice had red hair and lots of freckles and quickly fell in love with our redheaded little brother, who looked so much like her that they were often assumed to be mother and son. Larry idolized her and followed her everywhere. She rewarded him with cookies and milk. She did not have children of her own, as yet, and more or less, adopted our little brother. This mutual admiration between the two of them has stood the test of time and in later years, Larry always made a special effort to stop at Eunice and Mike's whenever he came home to visit the family.

Our father's crew had finished their job at the dam site in Guttenberg and had now been transferred to Le Claire, Iowa, which was further south on the Mississippi River. This was Lock and Dam #14. It was simply too far to commute, so he and a fellow worker, Matt Duehr, rented a small kitchenette apartment where they slept and cooked their own meals during the week. They returned home to their families only on weekends, riding back and forth with another worker from Guttenberg, a man by name of Clifford Noggle.

On one particular weekend toward the end of August, Dad arrived home late on a Friday evening. He had already planned to make sauerkraut this weekend and asked mom how the cabbages were doing. Mama did not answer him right away. She just gave our Grandma a very ominous look, as though to say, "Go ahead! You'd better tell him?"

Dad looked back and forth at both women. His male instinct warned him that something was amiss. “Tell me what? What’s going on here?”

Grandma looking rather proud of herself now quickly replied, “Well, I already made the cabbages into kraut, George. We have that huge thirty-gallon crock of it brining in the cellar right now. Go on down and see for yourself.”

Now, our white-haired grandmother did have the best of intentions at heart. She knew how hard my dad worked and had witnessed for herself that the cabbages had already developed to the point of bursting their heads and that they were ready to be harvested right away. And since Gram was an old hand at kraut making, she could easily have it all done by the time George came home and that way he could relax over the weekend. She knew she had done a good job and was sure that her grateful son-in-law would highly praise her efforts.

But, alas! She was in *no way* prepared for the anger that exploded from our father as he dashed up the cellar steps, taking them two at a time and brandishing his old oaken grape stomper on high—cussing and swearing a blue streak! George never got around to examining the kraut—he never got past the sight of his prized tool (which was to be used only in his wine making) and for no other purpose! He took great pride in the making of his wines—and even though he could not afford such a luxury these days, it didn’t mean that the tools of his trade could be used so carelessly.

And Gram had been careless. In her eagerness to do her job well, she had used the cube of heavy oak to tamp down the layers of shredded cabbage and coarse salt as she firmly packed it into the crock. Worse yet, she had left it there—had forgotten it, actually. She could see for herself that it was all encrusted with brine and salt that by now had begun to crystallize. George was fit to be tied! No one—not even his mother-in-law messed with his winemaking equipment!

But, Gram (remember she was once a redhead and still had that feisty temperament to match) took a back seat to no man. If George was capable of cussing up a storm (we children rarely heard him do so), so could she. An outright swearing match ensued! Our father lost!

However, Gram and Dad actually held a mutual respect for each other and soon, the aforementioned incident became just another laughing matter. Most of the time, Gram was on Dad's side. She highly regarded his conscientiousness and his devotion to hard work. He of course respected his mother-in-law and forever owed her a debt of gratitude.

This was not the last time we would be exposed to our dear grandmother's wicked tongue. One hot summer afternoon, one of the many transient bums in search of a friendly handout unsuspectedly walked into a "buzz-saw"—our dear sweet little Gram!

The frequent appearance of these bums was not an uncommon occurrence as the railroad tracks were almost in our backyard. From early spring into late fall, as long as weather permitted, we had a steady stream of those transient men, who too were victims of the depression. They couldn't (and I suspect, in some cases, wouldn't) find regular paying jobs and took to the road to bum their way through life. They hitched rides on the freight cars, having no definite destination and lived off the generosity of small town folks along the way.

Gram did not have much time for most of these "free loaders" as she liked to call them. But one day, she was approached by a nice-looking young man who offered to chop some firewood for the kitchen stove in exchange for a little lunch and something to drink. She took pity on the young man and went inside to fix him a light lunch, which he would have to eat outside under the plum tree. For she was not about to open her door to any stranger.

The young man worked hard and had already stacked a neat pile of wood near the back door when she returned with a plate filled with fried catfish, fried potatoes, homemade bread, and the very first ripened tomato she had picked from her garden. He was famished and ate heartily. Gram went back to the kitchen and when she returned with a tin cup of steaming coffee, she caught him throwing the tomato slices over the fence to the chickens she raised in her backyard. She threw a fit! "You wasteful little ingrate!" she yelled at him.

The young man, not much more than a boy, tried to explain to our Gram that his mother always peeled the skins off of his tomatoes as that was the only way he liked them. Grandma had not peeled them, therefore he couldn't eat them. Gram was not accepting any explanations. She threw his coffee onto the ground—cup and all and grabbed a broom off the back porch. She let fly a string of cuss words that shocked the entire neighborhood as well as her grandchildren and literally chased this frightened dastardly derelict off her property! This poor man took off on a run barely catching the last freight car as it chugged its way out of town. Nobody messed around with our Gram!

* * *

A change of season—Frances was feeling poorly—she wasn't sure if it was actually her body that was feeling poorly these days or her spirit—probably a little bit of both. But she was tired of trying to put good and nourishing and satisfying meals on the table when in actuality, they were always the same old thing—monotonous and boring. Like last night's supper had been a big pot of navy beans and boiled potatoes with the jackets on. Tonight it would have to be the same thing. But even white beans tasted pretty good to her hungry brood. She seasoned them with a bit of catsup, salt, and pepper. Salt pork or bacon rind would be good, but she didn't have any of that. Maybe she'd have the time to mix up a big batch of corn bread to go along with the beans. That always was a big hit with the youngsters.

Frances allowed her thoughts to ramble and hoped that George would remember to check with Andy Elsinger about getting a few more chickens from him for Sunday dinner. We could have chicken soup on Monday and . . . Oh, gosh! Here I am planning meals way in advance when I don't even know what I am going to feed the kids for lunch! What is wrong with me?

She was, indeed, having a very bad day. It was bitter cold out—twenty degrees below zero, and the wind was whipping about the outside of the house, and even in here with both fires blazing away, it was cold. During the daylight hours she and Gram used as little of their wood and coal as possible—because their supply was running low, and it would take more fuel to keep the fires going throughout the night hours. They all wore sweaters and long-sleeved shirts in the house to thwart off the chill; even the little toddlers as they played at her feet.

But quickly to the kitchen, now. She glanced at the clock. The older kids would be coming home for lunch and she must hurry to fix something. She grabbed some farina left from last month's Relief Rations—at least it would be nourishing and warm on such a cold day.

Automatically, like a well-programmed robot, Frances set out bowls and spoons on the kitchen table. The baby crawling on the floor—chubby little Larry—began to fuss. She picked him up and placed him in the high chair and pulled him closer to the stove where he could feel the warmth. Frankie and Hildi came in thinking it was lunchtime and climbed up to their accustomed places at the table. She knew they were hungry, but lunch wasn't ready so she handed each child a crust of bread to chew on while she cooked.

She sipped on her coffee and stirred the bubbling cereal at the same time. She moved the pan to the side of the stove where it would cook more slowly. The front door banged open. That would be the boys—they always ran home and arrived much sooner than their sisters. She carried the pan of hot cereal directly to the table and began doling it into the bowls. Gram came into the room and began to cut thick slices of homemade bread to add to the meal. She said, "No cereal for me, Francie. I just want coffee and some of this bread, as I am not very hungry right now."

Mama finished serving while Joe proceeded with The Sign of The Cross and rushed through his "Bless us, Oh Lord." Frances could barely understand his muffled "Amen" as he was already spooning the cereal into his mouth. She automatically poured sugar over her own bowl and glanced down at what she was doing. "Oh My God," she cried and threw her spoon down on the table!

"Children," she commanded. "Stop eating this. Don't take another bite! This cereal has bugs in it!" The children looked into their bowls—sure enough, there were tiny black specks dotting the thick, creamy white cereal. They obediently laid the spoons on the table and looked at their mother with dismay. Mama shoved her bowl away. Her glance traveled around the table and looked deeply into the eyes of each of her children in turn. "I am so sorry," she whispered helplessly. She put her head down on the table—and she cried. Our mama cried!

Gram came over and put her hand on Mama's black hair. "Frances, why don't you go to your room and lay down a bit? You've been working too hard, lately. (Mama was going to have another baby.) I'll fix some lunch for these kids. Go on, now," said Gram gently. Mama obeyed her mother, for she, too was a dutiful daughter.

Once again, as she left the room, she said, "I am so sorry." Gram came to the rescue. She quickly stirred up a big pan of hot cocoa made with canned milk, and ordered Joe to go down to the cellar and bring up a small jar of Elderberry jelly and a big jar of canned applesauce. The Elderberry jelly was a special treat as it was rarely used to spread on bread. It had a far better purpose, and was normally saved to make a medicinal soothing tea for sore throats and coughs; but maybe its healing power might do these dejected little ones some good on this very cold and bitterest of winter days. If not for their bodies, at least for their spirits.

* * *

The following week was Thanksgiving. Papa came home from Le Claire on Wednesday evening. It was very late, and the little ones were already in their pajamas and Kathy was reading bedtime stories to them. Frances had kept her husband's supper warm on the back burner, and as he was washing up at the kitchen sink, she ladled out a big bowl of thick potato soup and cut off a big slab of bread for him. She joined him at the table with a hot cup of tea for herself. This was their time to talk.

"Soup's good," said George. "What are you planning for Thanksgiving Dinner?"

Mama sighed. "I tried to get some chickens from that Lucille Jaeger over on the hill, but she doesn't have any to spare right now. The only other thing I have is some canned beef that we put up last fall. I've been trying to hang onto that for a long time. But it looks like we'll have to use that tomorrow."

"I don't think you'll have to do that," replied Dad. "I'll get up early in the morning and go out to Norb's timberland. I should be able to bag a couple of rabbits or a coon, maybe. I'll find something that you can cook with dressing. It won't be a Thanksgiving dinner without dressing and pumpkin pie," he added. The pie was easy to come by, Frances assured him. As a matter of fact, she already had two big pies freshly baked and cooling out in the summer kitchen. She offered him a piece for dessert, but he declined. "I'll just have a little more soup right now. If the kids have to wait 'til tomorrow for pie, so can I."

True to our father's promise, bright and early the next morning, he arose from his warm bed and laced up his high-top boots that went half way to his knees, donned his old hunting jacket, and put on his black and red woolen cap with the ear flaps. He slung his rifle over his shoulder and called to his old dog, Sport. Together, they trudged out to Norbert Nieland's land where our father was allowed to hunt at will.

And once again, true to his promise, George returned home a few hours later with success—a groundhog! "How on earth do I cook this thing," Frances wondered to herself. She had *never* prepared a groundhog before—nor had her family *ever* eaten one.

Well, there is a first time for everything. Nothing ventured—nothing gained. While George and the two older boys went out to the shed to skin and dress the animal, Mom and Gram busied themselves in the kitchen. The pieces of meat were first par-boiled in a salt solution to remove any trace of its wild gamy taste. The meat was dredged in flour and seasonings, and browned in a hot skillet. It was then layered into the big roasting pan, covered with bread stuffing mixed with raisins, and shoved into the oven to roast very slowly the rest of the day.

This special meal was delayed until the evening this year and served in the formal dining room instead of the kitchen. Mama's place was at the end of the table closest to the kitchen door, and Papa sat at the opposite end. Baby Larry was seated in his high chair right next to Mom. Hildi was perched on her little green high chair on the opposite side next to Grandma. The rest of the children lined up on both sides of the table. The steaming platter of roasted groundhog was placed center stage within easy reach of everyone.

"Bless us, Oh Lord, and these, thy gifts
Which we are about to receive—
Through thy bounty—
Through Christ, our Lord. Amen.
And a special prayer
Thank you, God for keeping us together, well and happy!"

Our brother, Joe, without fail, at the close of every "before-meal" prayer always added, "The one who eats the fastest gets the most!" "Amen!"

This was not the first time, and certainly not the only time, our father came through in a pinch and provided his family with meat for the table through his hunting prowess. His hunting endeavors were as equally important in "feeding the hungry" as were those huge gardens that he planted every spring.

One of our father's hunting expeditions resulted in a terrible tragedy for our family. It was the early fall of 1937. Dad and Sport took off to an unfamiliar area. They'd been gone for an awfully long time, and Mama and Gram were scared that something had happened to Dad. They reluctantly put our supper on the table as it was already getting dark outside. None of us felt much like eating, because we too were apprehensive.

At last, we heard our father's heavy footsteps at the back door, and we all breathed a deep sigh of relief; however, we still sensed something was terribly wrong. We were happy to see our dad, but, we all shouted, "Where's Sport?" in great alarm!

The dog had always announced the return of the hunter with a very loud bark at the back door, and on this occasion failed to do so.

Papa was very sad and told us that he and the dog had somehow separated, and no matter how hard he tried, he could not find the dog or any trace of him. He'd searched everywhere and retraced his steps deep into the woods—to no avail! It was getting so dark in the woods, he could no longer see and at last, he came home—alone.

Everyone cried that night, and very little supper was consumed. We all waited hopefully for the dog to find his way home. For days and weeks, we waited. But, he seemed to be gone for good. We were sad for a long, long time.

* * *

Christmas 1937.

Jolly old St. Nicholas
Lean your ear this way.
Don't you tell a single soul
What I'm going to say.

Christmas Eve is coming soon.
And, now you dear old man
Whisper what you'll bring to me.
Tell me if you can.

All the stockings you will find
Hanging in a row.
Mine will be the shortest one
Mended at the toe.

Frankie wants some 'navy' beans.
Hildi wants a dolly.
Helen wants a storybook.
She thinks dolls are folly.

But, as for Larry's little brain.
It's not yet very bright.
Choose for him, Dear Santa Claus,
What you think is right.

Yes, Christmas was coming soon and Frances, mother of eight and "one on the way" was beside herself with worry and frustration. I wish, she thought to herself, that I were able to work outside the home and earn a little extra money. Lord knows George does the best he can, but that paycheck barely keeps us in food and the barest of necessities. How can I possibly buy any toys for these children?

In desperation, she'd gone uptown, early this morning, and tried in vain to hock her wedding rings to Mr. Purnhage at the jewelry store. But that nice man just shook his head negatively and said, "Mrs. Spielbauer, I don't want to take your rings. They'll mean much more to you in the years to come—much more than I could ever pay you for them." He shoved the rings across the glass counter and gave them to her. "You don't really want to sell these," he sort of scolded her.

"No, I don't want to sell them, but, I do want my children to have Christmas presents," she stubbornly insisted. "What do I need with jewelry? My babies are more important."

"Go home, Mrs. Spielbauer," insisted the kind man. "Go on home and put your rings back on your finger where they belong. You'll think of something. Do some sewing for the little girls—your husband maybe could make wooden toys for the boys. I can't buy your rings."

Frances was sad. She was in her final month of pregnancy, and she was tired. She walked home with a heavy heart—a heart that was much heavier than her body right now, even though she had the extra weight of this new baby.

It was the littlest ones she worried the most about. She knew the older ones, Kathy, Joe, Rosy, and Arnie would all understand, but it was the younger ones who talked of nothing except of what Santa might bring them. She smiled sadly to herself when she thought of Frankie's wish. All he wanted for Christmas was a big bag of navy beans. He really loved baked beans—it was his favorite dish and his only wish for Christmas.

And then, there was Helen. Her only wish was to have her eye patch taken off permanently. They tried to tell her she would have to wear that patch for a very long time, until the vision in one improved. The eye doctor in Dubuque couldn't offer much hope at this time. Frances worried a lot about that child's eyesight.

The baby Larry was too young to really want for anything, but Hildagarde was already certain that Santa would be bringing her that "pretty dolly" she'd seen on display in Kuempel & Lake's Hardware store. The price tag read $5.00. And, there was just no way!

Frances spent the next few days preparing as best she could for the Holiday. At least, this time she did not have to think about the meal, for George had already bartered some of his working hours with Norb for a goose that, at this very moment, was being "fatted up" for their dinner.

She had taken Mr. Purnhage's advice and had been sewing up a storm. She had just completed a set of new pajamas for each of the children—thanks to her mother's help. Yes, Gram Rohner had paid for yards and yards of flannel material, which she ordered out of the Sears and Roebuck catalog. Frances had also made some new blouses for Kathy and Rosy out of flour sacks.

Frank Rohner (our mother's older brother) often had Joe and Arnie stay at his farm near Garnavillo, and they loved to help our uncle with the daily chores when they visited. Uncle Frank knew his sister was concerned about Christmas gifts for the children, and had bought each of the oldest boys a shiny new pocket knife. "Don't tell them, the knives are from me, Francie," he said. "Let those youngsters think they came from Santa Claus." Uncle Frank always called Mama, "Francie," just as he did when she was little. He was very good to his little sister.

Someone, I am not for certain if the donor was Gram or again it may have been Uncle Frank, bought a small toy gun and holster for Frankie. Frances knew he would love that because he liked to play "Cowboys and Indians" with his friends Roger Ferris and Warren Swartz. Until now, he had always used a clothespin gun. Grandma also bought a book of paper dolls for the girls to share and coloring books for the little ones.

At last, Christmas Eve Day rolled around. George and the oldest son headed out to the Nieland farm to chop down the Christmas Tree and pick up the goose for the holiday meal. Meanwhile, Frances and the older girls busied themselves with scrubbing and waxing the kitchen floor and thoroughly cleaning the rest of the downstairs. They would be setting the tree up in the corner of Mom and Dad's big bedroom.

After lunch, Kathy and Rosy gathered all the children around the kitchen table and everyone was soon deeply involved in decorating the cutout cookies. Frances was grateful for this diversion, because by now, she was feeling a little fluttery in her abdominal area and had *such* a backache! She should not have scrubbed that floor. Maybe she should lie down a bit.

By early evening, she realized she was not just tired—she was in labor—and thoroughly disgusted with herself. After eight kids, you would think you'd know the signs by now. Right after supper, Gram hurried the children through their baths and sent them off to bed very early, threatening them with "Santa won't come down the chimney unless you are all sound asleep!"

Even the older ones retired to their rooms earlier than usual, and a few hours later, Dr. Beyer showed up with his ever-present black doctor's bag! And, sometime before midnight, on Christmas Eve, the very heavens opened up! Lo and behold! A beautiful baby girl made her appearance at the Spielbauer household. Merry Christmas, one and all! And welcome, little Cecilia Margaret! Frances laughingly commented, "Now, Hilda will be happy. For she has received her new dolly!"

Somehow, magically in the middle of the night, someone (could it be Santa?) decorated the tall cedar tree that now graced the corner of our parents' bedroom. And magically, in the middle of the night or early dawn, the meager gifts for each child were placed under the tree—yes, dear reader—even a very large bag of "navy" beans for young Francis George. This package was placed right out in front, where the little boy could easily spot it.

And sometime in the wee small hours of the morning, when the exhausted new parents were in a deep sound sleep, our white-haired grandmother (by this time, equally as exhausted) tiptoed into their bedroom. In the darkness, she slipped a Chinese checker game, two hardback storybooks, and a furry brown Teddy Bear (for Larry) under the tree. It seems as though some of the uptown merchants had heard of Mama's plight and her desperate attempt to pawn the wedding rings, and very late last night a huge box of groceries along with these "toys" were anonymously delivered to our house. See, I told you, Guttenberg is the best place to live!

Soon the upstairs was alive with the pitter-patter of bare feet on the wooden floors overhead and the sound of children dashing down the stairs—two at a time! Papa George was ready for them. He had already spread a thick warm quilt underneath the

Christmas tree, and that tree itself was now glowing brilliantly with all its shimmering lights. He placed his tiny baby daughter on the blanket as though she was the most precious gem in the world. Grandma was sitting beside the bed and had Mama propped up against the pillows so she could see the excitement. The older children burst into the room—and screeched to a halt! They stood in awe and reverence as they stared down at their new baby sister—their very own Holy Child!

One and all, they cleared a path for the sleepy little Hildi, as she walked into the room still rubbing her eyes. She searched all around the tree, totally ignoring that tiny wriggling, squirming bundle on the floor. She frowned. "Where's the dolly?" She was very puzzled. "Didn't Santa Claus bring me a dolly? I can't find her!" Surely Santa had made a mistake. He was not supposed to forget. And she had tried to be so good for days!

Papa motioned for her to come forward. He was grinning from ear to ear! He pointed to that wriggling little bundle on the floor. "Here is your dolly, Hildi. She is your new baby sister and she is your real dolly! Santa Claus brought her just for you!"

"*No*, that's not my dolly! I don't want her! Take her back!" She shook her head vehemently! "I just want that dolly in the window with the yellow dress. Take her back!"

The older children laughed but this disappointed three-year-old child did not. Even the paper dolls failed to console her. The rest of the family was very happy with their gifts, and when Gram with a lot of help from Kathy and Rosy served them a delicious roast goose dinner, complete with all the trimmings, they one and all agreed this was the *Best Christmas* ever! Everyone—but Hildi! She was very disgruntled and much disillusioned with Jolly Old St. Nicholas!

Well, Papa had had enough! And he made the cranky little girl take a nap. She awoke a few hours later and found her sister, Helen, sitting at the foot of the bed, hugging a real dolly with black hair! Her eyes opened wide. She smiled—for the first time, that day! "Is that my dolly?" she asked hopefully.

"No," said Helen. "It's mine. Isn't she beautiful?" Hildi was really ready to cry now. Helen continued, "Santa Claus came back while you were sleeping. He brought something for you, too! Come on, Hildi, I'll show you." She took her little sister by the hand and pulled her over to the tree.

Hildi's heart jumped for joy! For not only was there a beautiful china doll with black hair and, yes, a yellow dress under the tree, but that dolly was tucked into a shiny blue cradle with tiny pink and white flowers and green leaves painted on the headboard!

Well, dear reader, may I now confess that I have never lost my fondness for beautiful little dollies—in yellow dresses. However, I have truly grown to *love* my new beautiful baby sister of so many Christmases ago!

I must, in all justification, give thanks—where thanks is due. Mrs. Alfred Frommelt, who lived a few houses to the north of us made the blue cradle from a wooden apple crate. She painted and decorated it and made blankets and pillows with scraps from her sewing basket. She salvaged two dollies that had been discarded long ago by our older sisters and refurbished them to look brand new. The black hair on both dolls, in actuality, was our mother's own real hair that had been saved from a recent hair cut. Thus, one creative, talented, and very kind lady "made" a Christmas for two little girls who have never forgotten her thoughtfulness! May God Bless You, Mrs. Frommelt—and Thank You for our very special Christmas 1937!

A very dear friend, Margaret Connelly (she was the reason for my baby sister's middle name), came to our house each day to help take care of Mama and the baby during this most recent convalescent period of childbirth. She was young and very pretty and we all liked her immensely. With Margaret's help, our family soon settled back into its routine of daily living, and our baby sister steadily grew more beautiful and more endearing to each and every one of us. Margaret kept in contact with our family for many years and always had a special interest in little Cecilia Margaret, the child she helped bring into the world. She became my sister's Godmother. Andy Elsinger Sr. was her Godfather.

The exact date is not known, but it is approximately around this time that our father changed jobs. He worked for The Enderes Plant in Guttenberg and also for a man named Billy Vogt, who was a cement contractor. Both of these jobs were of short duration and eventually, our dad (through the assistance of Uncle Arnie Hutter) got a better-paying position at The Northhome Furniture factory in Dubuque.

Of course, our dad could never afford to buy another car (after the old Model T conked out), so he rode back and forth to his job with his old and dear friend, Matt Duehr. George's new job offered longer hours and thus, more pay. But all that extra money was never noticed, as by now, our parents had equally increased the number of their children. The extra income was quickly absorbed into the daily costs of living. At this point in my narrative, the family is still struggling to make it through another long cold winter 1937-1938. And upon one such cold and dreary winter's night . . .

"Once upon a midnight dreary
While I pondered weak and weary
Over many a quaint and curious
Volume of forgotten lore;
Suddenly there came a tapping
As of someone gently rapping
Rapping at my chamber door!"

Edgar A. Poe

It was not exactly midnight, albeit dreary. I might have been only a tad tuckered out—by no means weak and weary; my quaint and curious lore was no more than the daily funny papers, which I could not read, as yet, I looked and laughed at the pictures. In truth, the sound was not a tapping—or even a rapping. It seemed to possess more of a scratching singularity. It was a sound that alerted every ear in the household!

Papa had been poring over the daily Telegraph-Herald (newspaper from Dubuque). Mama was doing some sort of magical thing with her fingers and a bit of thin thread and a shuttle. I think she called it "tatting." Gram was sitting in her rocking chair, hand stitching tiny diamond-shaped pieces of fabric together to form a quilt top. Some of the conscientious older siblings were doing their homework. Others were concentrating on a homemade board game called "MILL," which was a by-product of our mother's imagination—the poor man's answer to checkers. The game pieces were usually dried navy beans or kernels of corn. If these were not readily available, we used two sets of different colored buttons from Gram's button jar.

This remembering can certainly run into a bit of rambling; and before I completely lose my train of thought, I must now hie back to my "midnight dreary." Dreary it was. Not cold enough for snow, mind you, but a damp chilling rain and sleet type of night that penetrated into the very marrow of one's bones. The entire family, as they indulged in their various forms of evening entertainment, huddled around the potbellied stove, basking in its warmth.

But, hark! Once again they hear this same puzzling noise—at the outside door—on the front porch. Who—or what could it be? I must interrupt my story here, and interject that today was Helen's seventh birthday. She, of course being of a most curious nature, was second only to my father in reaching the front door. Feeling safe in the security of his close presence, she pushed her way forward and displayed little fear of the unknown as she dashed out onto the front porch and boldly threw the door wide open!

It was dark and damp out there and a blast of cold air rushed in. And then, we heard Helen gasp in surprise, cry out in happiness, and squeal with delight! Our father, in stunned disbelief, could only utter the following words, "Well, I'll be danged!" He repeated himself, "Well, I'll be—if it isn't Old Sport! Come on in, old boy!" Dad and Helen were both grinning from ear to ear! And so were we all!

For, there on the stoop, hardly able to stand on all fours—skinny, shivering, bedraggled, half-frozen, and dripping wet—not to mention, starving, thirsty, and very mangy-looking—was our own "old yellow Sport!"

A most welcome reunion ensued. The entire family had rushed to the door at the sound of Helen's excitement and now, as if on practiced cue, they parted as the Red Sea. They formed a pathway of welcome for their pet, as he limped and dragged his exhausted and filthily matted body from the cold and damp to his very own warm spot between the wall and the potbellied stove, a spot he well remembered as being exceptionally cozy and comfortable.

He lay his aching and ailing bones down to rest as his sad, but now much wiser in the ways of the world, eyes glanced gratefully from one family member to another. He was so worn out he could not even whimper. His eyelids drooped downward. It was—oh, so good to be home.

The younger children were openly crying from sheer joy—the older ones were bravely attempting to hide their tears; but when they noticed the moist eyes of both Frances and George, and actually saw a wayward tear or two escape down Gram's face, they, too, released their joyful tears!

Joe quickly rustled up a plate of table scraps and a bowl of fresh water, and poor old Sport knew for sure, he was home! Arnie quietly disappeared into the cellar, where he, after much rummaging around in a box of junk, dragged out Sport's old favorite—the doggy-smelling worn-out woolen sweater that used to be worn by Dad and later served as a sleeping pad for the pet. Sport was indeed in "dog heaven"! For no prodigal son has ever received such a warm welcome. This welcome was made complete when the little red-haired birthday girl cuddled up beside the dog and hugged him "good-night." Old Sport yawned. Tomorrow is another day. First things, first. First to sleep—and then perchance to dream.

Moving right along with my story, it is time to bring yet another Spielbauer child into our world. Actually, I think I shall make it two, as both of these babes came so close together and have something in common. They are unique in the fact that they are the only two children who had the luxury of being born in a hospital. Dr. Beyer was concerned about our mother's health and wanted her to be hospitalized for the birth of this next child.

He was well aware of our financial situation at this time, because our dad had been, for the past several years, working part-time on weekends for the Doctor. He did both yard and maintenance work at the Beyer residence in town and also worked as a hired hand on the Doctor's farm just south of town. This was our father's way of making sure our family's medical expenses were covered, as he never accepted cash for his labor, but received a credit on the "doctor bill." With all of these children, that "doctor bill" was an ongoing as well as an on-growing thing.

Dr. Beyer contacted the county health officials, and not only were they willing to provide financial assistance to cover the hospital expenses but insisted on paying for a child-care person to come into our home while our mother was confined. This person would be in charge of the cooking, cleaning, and child care. Dad tried to argue with them. He said Grandma Rohner was more than capable of handling this household while he was at work. Besides, Kathy was already close to fifteen years old and was a tremendous help with the children. "They will be just fine," our father insisted.

The Dept of Health deemed our most capable grandmother too old to be in charge of nine children under age fifteen. Thus, they made arrangements to have a licensed caretaker come to our home during Dad's working hours. So, we now had a stranger in our midst! Her name was Mrs. Ed (Helen) Krogman. Actually, she was not exactly a stranger, for she was distantly related to Mom, a second cousin or some such thing.

Now, this lady, bless her heart tried very hard to efficiently run the household, but heretofore, she had been accustomed to raising daughters—two of them, who were delicate, decorous, and dutiful and always well behaved. They wore white gloves and beautiful "picture hats" to church on Sundays. These young ladies were in direct contrast to the passel of noisy, rambunctious, rough, and tumble Spielbauer kids who seemed to be hanging out in every nook and cranny and would suddenly appear out of the very woodwork of our grandmother's house.

To make matters worse, Grandma Rohner was more than upset by the state's declaring her incapable of handling so many children. She decided to give Mrs. Krogman a very cold shoulder. She remained in her room most of the next week and was of little, if any, help to our new caretaker. On the very first day, Mrs. K decided to make "scalloped potatoes" for the evening meal. We had never heard of them, but she immediately put Kathy and Rosy in charge of peeling and thinly slicing the potatoes. She asked Kathy how many potatoes Mom cooked for one meal, and Kathy grabbed the big huge pot that Mom always used when she made "boiled potatoes with the jackets," and said, "Well, she always fills this pan way to the top and then just boils 'em until they're done."

"Well, girls, today we are going to serve your family scalloped potatoes. They are very good. You girls go fill that pan with potatoes and then the two of you will peel and slice while I put this dish together. Quickly, now get to peeling and remember very thin slices."

The girls peeled—and peeled—and peeled—a mountain of potatoes! Mrs. K lavishly buttered the bottom and sides of a big cake pan, and layer after layer of sliced potatoes, seasonings and flour, pats of butter, and chunks of cheese went into the pan. Mrs. Krogman did not really understand that we were quite poor, and from the looks of what went into this scalloped potato dish, it would appear, thought Kathy, that this was a dish way beyond our food budget.

The next day, our surrogate mom asked Grandma where the grocery money was kept because she needed to send one of the kids uptown to buy some bread. Gram, still giving her the "cold shoulder treatment" replied, "We don't eat store bread. It's too expensive. Frances always makes homemade." Mrs. Krogman was trying very hard not to be upset and sweetly smiled at Grandma as she spoke, "Very well, then I too shall make some homemade bread for this family."

Mrs. Krogman had just finished kneading the dough for one last time and was now rolling it out on the floured table, shaping it into loaves, then into the pans, and generously brushing the tops with melted butter when Papa walked in. He smiled at her and said, "I did not realize that you could bake bread, Helen. That's real good because these kids go through a lot of it. My wife usually makes a batch three to four times a week." Then our father took a good look around him and noticed the entire kitchen table was covered in a layer of flour—flour was all down the front of Mrs. K's apron, covering her arms up to her elbows, and even in her hair. A layer of flour resembling dust lay all over the kitchen floor linoleum around the table. Papa hurriedly left the room and did not say another word. But at a much later date, he was overheard saying, "That woman could throw away more food with a teaspoon, than a man could bring home with a shovel!"

At last, word came from Iowa City, and we were now informed that our mother had delivered another baby boy on January 29, 1940. She had already named him Loras John, but to his older brothers and sisters, he was immediately known as Johnnie. And, he has remained "Johnnie" to this very day. Once again, the "battle of the sexes" is tied; the score is now five to five—five girls and five boys!

Baby John, I am sorry to report, at a very early age, developed an addictive taste for that loathsome tobacco leaf. He was left momentarily unattended, seated in his high chair, while Kathy went into the kitchen to prepare his dinner. It would seem as though the chair was just a tad too close to the dining room buffet, and the top drawer (where our dad stored his cigarette papers and can of tobacco) was for some unknown reason left slightly ajar. Little John, of course, was attracted to the brightly colored can of Red Velvet and promptly proceeded to help himself to its contents.

After all, the little tyke was hungry, and if this food tasted as good as it looked, go for it! When his older sister returned with his plate, she found Johnnie already feeding his face with Papa's "roll your own" tobacco! Not only was his mouth full, but the tobacco juice was dribbling from his drooling lips, all over his hair, his clothing, his high chair tray as well as the floor beneath him!

It is not known for sure, just how much tobacco had actually been consumed by our baby, but from the looks of the small bit remaining in the can, it appeared to be a generous amount. We were all certain the little boy would become deathly ill, however, his innards (a Grandma expression) must have been made of steel, for the child never once, even burped. Alas, to this very day, Brother John still possesses an insatiable craving for this noxious weed.

When Johnnie was approximately a year and a half, Mama made another trip to Iowa City, and once again, our friend, Mrs. Krogman, showed up at our front door. This time, however, our Grandma Rohner was very, very sick, and was totally confined to her upstairs bedroom as an invalid. And I feel compelled to inform you that Mrs. Krogman must have long ago forgiven Gram for that "cold shoulder treatment" during her last visit, because she was the most patient with our grandmother's demanding ways and willingly responded to her every need.

Kathy was considered a young adult now, and willingly or not, had taken over most of the kitchen chores—even the baking of the bread. She had carefully mixed up the dough very early in the day, but for some unknown reason, it would not rise. Perhaps it was the cooling breezes that wafted through the open window, or a misinterpretation of Mrs. K's instructions, or whatever, but that lump of dough refused to do anything. Mrs. Krogman returned to her own home. Papa came home from work and supper was served. The dishes were washed and the kitchen floor swept clean. Finally, George, in exasperated impatience, told Kathy to bake it anyway or they would have to throw it out.

By the time she pulled the pitiful loaves out of the oven it was way past her bedtime and she was very tired. Poor Kathy's first attempt at homemade bread turned out to be a real disaster—the dough was heavy and tasted like paste and the loaves remained small and flat and hard as a rock. Kathy cried at her first failure. We ate it anyway. We told our sister, it was "delicious"—just as good as Mama's—but, she cried even harder, for she knew we were all fibbing!

On June 4, 1941, Frances gave birth to her new baby—*not* the girl we all expected—but another baby boy! Yes, indeed the girl's team was a bit disappointed, at first, but it wasn't long before our new little brother tugged at our heartstrings. Danny Lee was such a dear and delightful baby. When he was but a few weeks old, he developed an allergic reaction to cow's milk. This resulted in an eczema that spread all over his tiny body. He was subjected to much pain and discomfort and cried a lot.

In an attempt to prevent him from scratching and further irritating this rash, Mama encased his entire body in white clothing throughout those first humid, hot summer months of his babyhood. Long white baby stockings were pulled on over his hands and arms much like a pair of gloves and pinned to the sleeves of his undershirt. Another pair covered his feet and lower limbs and was attached to his diaper with safety pins. She would generously pat cornstarch all over his skin prior to dressing him, hoping that this might prevent the itching. I doubt if any of these precautions were of much comfort to our little brother, but he always managed to maintain a grinning smile on his face and just a hint of deviltry in his laughing eyes.

Secondary to Danny's birth was the arrival of our goats. Since our brother's digestive system was unable to tolerate the milk from cows, Dr. Beyer strongly recommended milk from another ruminant animal—the goat. Goat's milk was more than difficult to come by in the small community of Guttenberg. First of all, it was not readily available in the grocery stores, and even if it were, its cost would have been prohibitive. The only solution was to raise our own!

The first "nanny" was purchased from Charlie Hess, a man who farmed in the Buenie area, I believe. Dad paid $12.00 for her, and she soon proved to be worth her weight in gold. At least, that is what Papa said. Ordinarily, goats are not known to produce a generous supply, usually only about one quart per milking, if the owner is lucky. But Dad referred to her as an "excellent milker" (dairy farmer terminology) because this first member of our goatherd was able to fill two full-quart containers at each milking session!

Of course, he had to scrimp and save and sacrifice, but it wasn't long before Billy Goat Gruff came to live with our "Nanny." This happy goat couple soon became established in the now-abandoned chicken coop with its attached fenced-in front yard. Well, nature taking its course and all, it was inevitable that Billy and Nanny soon became the parents of twin babies. We called them "the kids."

In all honesty, I must admit that the adults of this animal species—at least in my estimation—are far from beautiful creatures. Their newly born offspring on the other hand are absolutely adorable. They resemble little lambkins and are totally irresistible. Three-year-old Celie was particularly delighted with this first set of twin babies, identical in every respect except for their color and sex. One was black and male. The other was white and female. Their short hair was soft and curly. And best of all, they were not ornery or smelly or mean like both their parents.

Little Celie wanted to lead them around the backyard, but the frisky little animals refused to cooperate—they had a mind of their own and that was to follow the mother goat not our little "Bopsy." She struggled and pulled on the leashes, one for each goat, clutched tightly within her chubby baby hands. But they proved to be too much for the little girl to control, and soon they were the ones doing the tugging and pulling and leading—right through Papa's garden, tearing up the tomato plants and ripping through rows of beans and peas! She hung on for dear life—somebody was being taken for a walk, but it obviously was *not* the baby goats!

Our goat family nimbly mastered climbing the three steps that led to the entrance of their home—after all, they were originally mountain creatures, you know. But, once again, Bopsy became the center of attention. Still being a little unsteady on her feet, she found it a bit awkward to ascend the stairs to the goat house. Not yet being trained in the art of climbing, she was forced to crawl her way up the three risers in order to gain entrance. She was so persevering in her efforts and so very proud of her success, that she, upon reaching the top step of her destination, would turn her entire little person around and smile with smug satisfaction and clap her baby hands together in applause to herself.

Alas, that nasty old nanny goat was laying in wait—just inside the doorway with head lowered in ready anticipation—and just as our sister presented her little backside to the old cantankerous goat, she would be butted right back down those steps, landing spread-eagled on the dusty ground. Somewhere, in the recesses of my mind, I hear the words of an old refrain that keeps coming back to haunt me . . .

"Pick yourself up—
Dust yourself—
And, start all over again."

These words must have been written with little Bopsy in mind, for that is exactly what she did. Undaunted and without shedding a single tear, she'd stand up, brush the dirt from her little red dress, and hustle right back up those steps—once again, a ready and willing victim for the ire of that mean old nanny. She was right there waiting to "butt" the little girl right back down again—and again!

Sad to say, one of these adorable little goats did not live very long. I am quite sure it was the black one. Joe and Arnie had to take turns every other morning to make sure the goats were fed and watered before they went to school. And Dad had been kind of worried over the black one for sometime now. At first, Joe thought the little goat was not awake yet, but when he looked again at the inert animal, he realized that it was dead. Dad explained to us that this was a common occurrence in multiple births within the goat family. Usually the last one born was the weaker and its survival was pretty iffy. We all felt bad, however, because, especially to the younger children, these little animals had already become family pets.

Joe went to school that morning and made a formal announcement to his teachers and classmates. "One of the kids died last night," he said, very sadly.

Everyone just stood there and gaped at him—even the teachers. Then, an onslaught of questions followed from every person in the room. "Oh, my gosh! Which one? Was it an accident? Was it the baby?" "Oh, your poor Mother and Father," from one of the kind-hearted teachers. "Tell us the child's name! Does Father Dupont know? Was the doctor there? When will the funeral be?"

Joe hung his head in shame, as he patiently explained to everyone that no, it was not one of his siblings that had passed away, but one of the baby goats. Doesn't everyone know that baby goats are referred to as "kids?" Apparently not—for even the teacher did *not* know!

* * *

Kids and cookies go hand in hand. Rarely do you see one without the other, right? Well, with the large number of children that Frances had, you can well imagine the dozens upon dozens of cookies that this lady had baked throughout the years. Basic ingredients were quite easy to come by, and it was then, and today it is much cheaper to make cookies as to buy them. In spite of our mother's busy work schedule, she managed to always have a ready supply of cookies on hand. Of course, she now had Kathy and Rosy assisting with the kitchen chores, and they both loved to make cookies.

Let us forget about the cookie baking for just a moment here. Much was going on in the world that these young Spielbauer children were not aware of. They and their friends were too young to be concerned or to worry over affairs of state or nation. Their elders worried and had just reason to do so. Uncontrollable forces were at work creating havoc in many areas, and what the people feared most came to pass. On December 7, 1941, on a quiet and lazy Sunday afternoon, the Japanese Nation declared war on our very own United States of America!

In a sneak attack, they dropped their vicious bombs on Pearl Harbor, our nation's greatest stronghold located in the Hawaiian Islands. A chagrinned and angry America stood up in unison and shouted! Our young men were summoned to do battle! Just yesterday, they were but boys—today, however, they cast aside their High-School Band and Boy Scouts of America uniforms. Yesterday they marched in Fourth of July and Armistice Day Parades, and today, they donned another and more realistic uniform and marched to the cadence of a different drum!

These young men stood straight and tall, and they responded to their Uncle's call! You have all seen the characterized likeness of Uncle Sam, dressed in his bright blue top hat, red and white striped tuxedo jacket with his flowing white beard and hypnotic eyes. When he flashed his "*all*-American" smile upon these young men, and pointed his elongated bony index finger straight at them and commanded, "*I want you*," they responded.

Believe me, they responded! Young men from all across this nation marched in unison—from the Midwestern farmlands and small communities, from the college campuses, from the wide open plains and prairies, from the ghettos, and the factories (those steamy and scorching furnaces of the metropolitan cities) they responded. One and all, they came—in answer to the Uncle's call!

I am six years old—much too young to comprehend the true meaning of war. But, as I listen to the grown up conversations around me and struggle to separate the war news broadcast from those screeching static sounds emanating from the radio (our one contact with the outside world), I soon become educated and familiar with the terminology of war. Words like "bombings," "infantry," "destroyer ships," "fighter planes," and many others would literally send chills up and down my spine. I remember how frightened I was when the "blackout" sirens sounded, and all the townsfolk sought shelter within their homes, locking the doors and turning out the lights, as well as pulling down the shades. Within seconds the entire town would be engulfed in total blackness. I did not realize that these were simply practice sessions and immediately my very active imagination would picture an enemy bomber circling overhead, zeroing in on the rooftop of our house with one of its deadly bombs.

My mind is filled with many thoughts of that war, but without a doubt my one outstanding recollection is that of the troop trains. These trains were the Army's passenger trains with cars that were drab, olive green in color. They were used to transport soldiers from one training base to another, most of who were in their late teens and early twenties and leaving their homes and their hearths, their mothers and their sweethearts for the very first time in their lives. These homesick young men eagerly responded to the warm welcome of the loyal citizens who turned out in droves to greet them as the train engine idled at the railroad station.

My family saw a lot of these troop trains as the railroad tracks ran right through the center of town and bordered on the back edge of my dad's vegetable garden. Late one Sunday morning, right after Mass, one such train shrilly whistled its arrival into the sleepy quiet of our small Iowa town. "It's a troop train," someone shouted! This was a signal to which we all immediately reacted. Even our mama left the Sunday dinner unattended on the back stove and with the youngest baby in her arms ran out to greet the soldiers. Our father as well dropped his hoe on the ground and meandered toward the tracks, asking the boys their destination and wishing them well.

Mom's "mother love" at once went out to these homesick travelers and promptly ordered Kathy to go back to the house and bring out her huge roasting pan that was filled with dozens of homemade oatmeal and raisin cookies that the girls had baked the previous day. Well, as soon as that mountain of cookies appeared on the scene, a loud cheer went up for our mom! A pair of eager outstretched hands reached through an open window and quickly grabbed the roaster. We lost sight of Mama's pan as it disappeared inside the train, and it goes without saying that when it finally reappeared at the other end of the car, not one visible cookie crumb remained. Boys of all sizes and shapes—short ones and tall ones, black hair, brown hair, blondes, and redheads, freckled faces, bold grins, and shy smiles—all waved their cookies on high and cheered!

But, alas! Mama was quick to observe that there had not been enough cookies to go around. Once again, she sent our sister back to the kitchen to refill that roasting pan with our Sunday dinner cinnamon rolls! Another shout of joy—and once again, another empty pan! As that Sunday morning troop train chugged its way out of the station, a multitude of "Thank

You" shouts, fond farewells, and best wishes bounced off the steel rims of those railroad tracks and echoed throughout the surrounding hills.

Our mother, indeed, had taught us a lesson that morning—one that would never be forgotten. "It is truly more blessed to give than to receive." And who could have been more deserving recipients than these brave young men en route to battle?

Well you have seen how our parents "fed the hungry." Let us now give drink to the thirsty. One of the "relief truck" staples was a generous supply of dried raisins. Our frugal mother utilized them in every form of cooking imaginable. She stuffed them into her dressing, stirred them into rice pudding, cooked them with hot cereal, mixed them into bread pudding, made raisin pie, and baked them in bread and cookies. And still we had raisins. Mama had truly exhausted her imagination and had used the raisins in every way she could think of. She even tried sharing them with neighbors and relatives but we still had an over abundance. At last, our Papa had a solution.

Papa and his conscience had indulged in a severe battle. He did not want the raisins to go to waste. So why not put them to some practical use? Such, as in the making of a raisin wine. He hadn't been able to make wine for sometime now, and with this ample supply of dried fruit, the idea of raisin wine was very tempting. On the other hand, what would people think? After much belaboring on his part, our father decided to make the wine. It would be better than *not* using the raisins at all; and besides, the wine could be used for medicinal purposes of sorts. Raisin wine was known to serve as a soothing cough syrup as well as a painkiller for those frequent sore throats that kids were always coming down with. Yes, indeed, it would be very useful to have on hand!

Papa's wine as I recall was the most delicious. It was secretly hidden away in a crock that sat on the bottom shelf of

Grandma's chimney closet in the kitchen. This container was camouflaged with an old white linen tablecloth draped over its top and sides. I recall that it was only served to relatives and a few of Papa's very close and trusted friends. Yes, it is true that it did ease the pain of many a sore throat, toothache, or upset tummy—at least, we thought it did. One would be surprised at what miraculous cures were wrought with but one tablespoon of Papa's medication. One thing always puzzled me, though. I noticed that our father and other grownups usually had a much larger dosage before this "wonder drug" had any effect on them. Hmm!

While on this subject of "giving drink" we, as a family, were indeed a thirsty group. However, satisfying that quench was at times difficult to achieve. Soda pop was a rarity in this family—I have already told you that we were only allowed to drink pop once a year on July 4. On other special occasions, we enjoyed the luxury of Kool-Aid and lemonade. The few quarts of milk delivered daily by Mr. Carrier were to be utilized only by the newest baby and perhaps the next two older siblings.

Once a child reached the status of being the fourth youngest, the said child automatically graduated to the next stage in life, where he or she now drank "canned milk" mixed "half and half" with water. This is also what we used at meal times and on our cereal in the mornings. Of course, we could not afford to purchase boxed cereal such as Corn Flakes, Wheaties, or Puffed Wheat. Our "cereal" consisted of oatmeal, cream of wheat, or, most mornings, day-old bread torn into chunks with a little sugar sprinkled on top, and of course the diluted milk. Actually it was very good. When each of us reached this milestone in our life, we knew for certain that we had now achieved the status of being one of the "older kids." It was like our first step in growing up—our rite of passage, so to speak. We did not mind this passage, however. I personally recall sipping on a cup of hot coffee early in the morning when I could not have been more than twelve years old. I must confess I don't think my mother ever caught me at it, however.

It is about time to introduce another new baby (boy, again) into our family. On July 15, 1942, James Leonard was born. Mr. and Mrs. Leonard (Ella) Mikota had moved into the neighborhood about a year before and had become good friends with our parents. Actually, Mom and Ella had been childhood friends. This couple became our new little brother's godparents. Mr. Mikota seemed to be a grumpy man, but Ella was the *best* lady in the world—at least to my brother, Larry, and myself. We loved to "visit" her because she had this wonderful, most delicious bottled drink that we had ever tasted! She called it "root beer"! She and her husband made a batch of it every winter, and she often invited Larry and me into her home to share a glass with her. The very first time she uncapped the bottle, there was a very loud popping noise, and then the foam exploded all over her kitchen table, floor, and ceiling. After that initial unhappy and messy experience, Mrs. Mikota always insisted on opening the bottles down in her cellar.

My little brother and I soon figured out that if we offered to help her pull some weeds in her garden, it would not be long before this kind lady retaliated with her suggestion of "a nice cool drink." Once in a while we might have to prod her into remembering her good manners. We'd say things like "Whew! It sure is hot today" or "I'm getting kinda thirsty—a cold drink would sure taste good." Mrs. Mikota caught on very quickly. She would smile tolerantly at us and say, "You kids have been working hard—how about a glass of root beer? Come on in the house." She'd then disappear down her cellar steps and we would soon hear that loud pop and she'd come hustling up those steps again and pour the liquid into two glasses. It always "foamed up" and gushed down the sides of the glass—and it was delicious!

Now, back to our new baby—he was exceptionally beautiful and truly did look like the angels delivered him at our doorstep. Each of us kids, in turn, had spent the greater part of our babyhood in what we called a "jumping chair," and little Jimmy loved to sit in it. This was a contraption of sorts that was suspended by a large hook from the top jamb of an open doorway. It had a bucket seat made out of heavy canvas cloth that had two circular holes for the baby's legs to slip through and barely touch the floor. At the top was a strong spring that allowed the infant to bounce up and down with his own weight; or swing to and fro; and exercise his feet and legs by walking on his "tippy toes." Jimmy played in it for hours and would invariably jump, swing, or "walk" himself to sleep. He'd slump over to one side and blissfully fall into a deep sleep. We soon learned not to move him to a more comfortable bed as this would immediately alert him and he would become wide awake and ready for more "bounce"!

Chapter VI

Clothe the Naked
Shelter the Homeless

Clothing and sheltering were two responsibilities that were seemingly an endless responsibility for our parents; and I know for certain they could never have accomplished this great task had it not been for the many helping hands—and hearts that reached out to our large family. Shoes, socks, and underwear were, no doubt, the most difficult to come by—and the fastest to show signs of wear and tear. Let us just start with shoes, for example. Shoes were a constant headache to George and Frances, and a constant drain on their purse strings as well. At least once a month one of Dad's paychecks had to be set aside to accommodate the purchase of a new pair of shoes or boots for one member of the family or another; or at the very least, some sort of repair work on the family's existing footwear.

We were trained at an early age to give careful consideration to our shoes, as they, like all other items of our clothing, were handed down from one child to the next, whenever possible. If the "next" had not quite grown into the shoes of his or her older sibling, we'd simply stuff wads of cotton batting or crumpled paper into the toe of the shoe to help the foot fit more comfortably.

Many times, we traced the outline of our foot onto a piece of corrugated cardboard. We would cut these out and slip the makeshift innersoles inside of our shoes to protect the feet from nature's more rugged elements of cold, snow, rain, and mud that often seeped through the thin soles and worn-out heels. Of course, this cardboard prevention rarely survived a single day of severe Iowa weather and the rough graveled alleys that we trod upon. Fortunately, this was something that we could readily replace many times, and thus made our shoes last until papa's next paycheck, at which time we could afford to take them to Joe Wach's shoe repair shop.

Papa often patched our galoshes and knee-high winter snow boots himself. Many a winter's night found him sitting on a straight-back wooden chair by the kitchen stove in front of another chair, on which was mounted his "iron shoe." This served as his cobbler's bench. He was able to purchase "patch kits" from the hardware store or more often than not, he'd simply cut his own patches from old inner tubes. Using a rubber cement type of glue and a tiny metal scraper to roughen up the surface, so the glue would adhere to the patch, he repaired the holes and slashes in our footwear.

But, in all honesty, I don't know what we would have done without Joe Wach. I vividly recall my very first visit to Joe's Shoe Shop as if it were yesterday. I could not have been more than five years old, but each and every detail is deeply imbedded within the recesses of my mind. The walls were stacked from floor to ceiling with boxes of shoes, hundreds and hundreds of them in all sizes, colors, and styles. He worked behind a glass-topped showcase counter that held various and sundry displays of polishes, shoe dyes, belt buckles, and much more. At one end of this counter was a shiny black old-fashioned cash register—a large spool of cord string dangled from a hook in the ceiling—and attached to the counter was the biggest roll of wrapping paper I'd ever seen. There was a distinct aroma to the shop itself—a unique blend consisting of new shoe leather, shoe paste, and the strong chemical smell of rubber cement. Last, but not least, was the "shoe man," himself.

I first spotted him laboriously guiding a strip of leather through the foot feed of his sewing machine. He was so deeply engrossed in his work that he did not even notice our entrance. He looked just like the pictures in my fairy tale books—the ones that showed the shoemaker wearing a long leather apron, shirt sleeves rolled up to the elbows, wire-rimmed glasses sliding down, and perching precariously on the very tip of his nose.

Mother cleared her throat in an effort to attract his attention. He turned in our direction and I couldn't help but notice a pair of brown eyes twinkling merrily as he warmly greeted us with, "Well, well, well! Look here—what the cat drug in! How are you? What can I get for you?"

"This one starts school next week and needs a new pair of shoes. Something sturdy," my mother said.

The shoe man rambled on, "A little girlie like you should have herself some fancy-dancy slippers. You don't want that sturdy stuff, now do ya?" He smiled and winked at me. I liked him right off, for indeed, I had been eyeing a pair of white, shiny, patent leather slippers in the window, but alas, my mother had other ideas. She wanted something that would withstand a lot of rough wear and tear.

The shoe man sensed this age-old conflict between mother and daughter, and tactfully talked her into purchasing a then-popular brown and white saddle shoe that not only satisfied the practicality of my mother, but also pleased my own inimitable sense of style as well. These were not exactly the pearly white, shiny slippers that my heart desired, but I was still delighted with their newness and vowed I would keep them shiny clean forever!

During the ensuing years I would come to know the interior of that shop as well as my own home, for it housed at least one pair of my family's well-worn shoes at all times. The shelves in the back repair shop had weeks of work stacked up patiently awaiting the skillful handiwork of old Joe, whose days were spent hunched over his sewing machine or metal shoe form, stitching or tacking or gluing. His workmanship was in great demand, for he was the master at his trade.

I often suspected that he reserved Saturday afternoons strictly for fixing my family's footwear, just so we kids would have something to wear to church on Sunday morning. Joe always displayed a great pretense at grumbling and griping and impatiently mumbling under his breath, all the while plying his skilled fingers over the leather. He'd say, "Why, these old shoes aren't worth fixin' up. Throw 'em out! Buy some new ones." But, by the time he finished with them, our shoes would look brand new.

His fee was ten cents or a quarter at the most. While I'd fish through my pockets for the money, he'd quickly work some sleight of hand magic, deftly wrapping the shoes in paper and securing the parcel with cord string. "Here you go. Now, git on outta here, before I raise my price. Cost goes up in five seconds! Now git!" Frightened child that I was, I'd quickly grab my package and my change and dash out of the door.

In later years, I became a close friend with his daughter, Dorothy. I enjoyed many Sunday dinners with the Wach family. Verna soon became a second mother to me. She was determined to "fatten me up," and often took the liberty of scolding me when she thought I needed it. Dorothy and her brother, Jerry, always took turns at saying Grace. As soon as that final "Amen" was spoken, Verna would say, "Well, this meal does look pretty good—even if I *do* have to say so myself! Now, pass me the potatoes, please!"

This command not only served as the official opening of the meal, but was also a subtle reminder for those of us who were not smart enough to figure it out for ourselves that we now owed a vote of thanks to the cook. Let's all hear it for the cook! I am certain that on this very day, Verna is happily preparing the very best pot roast in the holy Kingdom of Heaven—even if she does have to say so herself.

When Kathy was about sixteen years old, white majorette boots were the high fashion of the day. They were "all the rage," and Kathy desired a pair of her very own. Papa thought they were ridiculous. He didn't have much time for so-called "glamour"; and even though Kathy was in need of a new pair of shoes, Papa said, "Not that kind! I am not spending my hard-earned money on such foolishness!"

So, our sister scrimped and saved every penny of her babysitting money for what seemed like forever. Papa was very disgusted with his daughter at such an impractical purchase, but the rest of the family was happy for Kathy. She was very proud of her new boots and a good thing, too. As she had to wear them everywhere; church on Sunday, to school, even out to hang up the laundry in the backyard, for you see, they were the only pair of shoes she had. Faithfully, every night just before her bedtime, Kathy would painstakingly apply a coat of white shoe polish to the boots and buff them into a brilliant glossy shine and always place them directly beneath the kitchen sink, all ready for her to slip into first thing each morning. Gram's kitchen sink was one of those old-fashioned wall-hung basins. The unsightly plumbing pipes and curved gooseneck were openly exposed underneath—not exactly a pretty sight.

Just as faithfully, every night, the last thing Mama would do before she went to bed was to place underneath the same sink (as a convenience to the little brothers who slept downstairs on the davenport), a white-enameled chamber pot, more often referred to as "slop jar." This eliminated many nocturnal trips up the long flight of stairs to the bathroom. Well, in all truth, it really was not a bathroom because it didn't have a regular built-in bathtub. The bathtub actually was nothing more than a very large oval-shaped enameled tub that hung on the wall when not in use. This was fine for little children, but grown-ups and some of the bigger kids were forced to become expert contortionists in order to fit their bodies into the tub. We considered ourselves lucky, however, just to have the convenience of an indoor toilet.

Let's get back to my story. It seems as though one of the little brothers was urgently awakened in the middle of the night by that customary call from Mother Nature, and as he had done many times before hurried out to the kitchen to relieve himself. He wasn't quite tall enough to use the light switch, so he found his way by the light of the moon that filtered through the curtained windows.

Are you still with me? I think by now you've got the picture. In his half-drowsy, semi-somnambulistic state, this unknown little boy took careful aim at what he thought was the white chamber pot—and let go. Alas, Kathy's beautiful boot and the chamber pot took on an identical appearance in the false light of the waning moon, and the following morning when our sister slips her dainty little female foot into the boot—*yuck*! Oh no! Remember this was her only pair of shoes. Yes, she had to scrub the boot out with soap and bleach and dry its insides as best she could—and wear it! She wore two pairs of socks in the one boot that day.

Now, which little brother did I say this was? Sorry, I didn't say—I do not know—Kathy does not know (although she tried hard to find out)—the guilty little brother does not know (he was much too young to even realize what derelict deed he had committed). Alas, only Mama Frances knew for certain who he was—and Mama said, "I will never tell! I shall carry this knowledge to my grave!" And so she did!

Same boots—different story. Kathy eventually got a new pair of shoes (more sensible ones, thought Papa), and these boots became a secondary item in her wardrobe. There was already a small hole in one of them (no doubt the one that had been subjected to uric acid so long ago), and so they eventually lay discarded on the closet floor. However, Rosy's only pair of shoes had to make a trip to the repair shop one day, and rather than miss a day of school for lack of footwear, she decided to wear the boots, hole and all.

During the course of the day, one of the nuns caustically made a crude comment about the "odd shoes" Rosy had on; which just goes to show you that even grown-ups and even godly nuns can be unthinkingly cruel at times. Our sister was too embarrassed and too ashamed to bother with explaining the extenuating circumstances. She wisely chose to ignore the comment and hurried away.

Socks and underwear always wore out way too fast. Even though Mama patched and darned for hours at a time, these items had to be frequently replaced. The "mending" was separated from the rest of the laundry at the time the clean clothes were being folded and put away. We had two lined bushel baskets—into one was placed all the clothes that needed to be mended and into the other all the clothes that needed to be ironed. Trust me, both of them were always full. I don't guess we ever saw the bottoms of either one. My sisters and I learned to darn socks as soon as we learned how to hold and thread a needle. To make the job easier, we stretched the "hole" part of the sock, usually the heel or toe over an old doorknob, a light bulb, or sometimes the open end of a drinking glass. This enabled us to manipulate the intricate in and out weaving action of the needle and thread.

Patching overalls was a nightmare for all of us. First of all, the rough denim material was very thick, and it was most difficult to push the needle through (it actually poked holes in our fingers and drew blood before it dented the fabric), and then, too, our mama, alias teacher, was *so* very fussy! First we would have to sew a square patch to the inside of the garment larger than the hole with very tiny stitches all around the perimeter of that patch. Then the entire garment (usually overalls) was turned right side out. The hole was neatly trimmed into a circle with its raw edges folded under and then carefully hand-stitched onto the new patch. Of course, each stitch had to be very tiny, and the thread not visible to the naked eye. It was a tedious task, and I am embarrassed to admit that I was never able to master the art of "patching overalls." At least not well enough to please the discerning eye of my mother.

And yes, even our underwear was often subjected to the needle and thread treatment. Elastic waistbands oftentimes would have to be completely replaced, loose seams re-stitched, and holes darned much like we did the socks. I must confess that occasionally we actually had to wear "holey underwear"! And I certainly don't mean to imply that our undergarments were laundered in "Holy Water" or anything like that. It's just that they had holes in them.

Speaking of underwear, I cannot help but recall one of my most embarrassing moments as a child. Actually, I committed the sin of telling my very first lie, at least the first one I remember! Worse yet, I lied to a nun! How bad is that?

I was in the third grade, and my teacher's name was Sister Mary Amelia. The whole class loved Sister Amelia because she made going to school *fun*! It was the first day back after a very lengthy Christmas vacation, and of course all the children were excited to see each other and talk about their Christmas presents. So, Sister announces that it is now time for Roll Call. "Since you all want to talk about Christmas, instead of responding with 'Here' when I call out your name, each of you may stand up and tell the class what your favorite Christmas present was and who gave it to you." Everyone in the room clapped their hands and shouted with glee—everyone but me.

I broke out in a cold sweat! You see the only present I received that year was a small package that contained two pairs of pink cotton underpants. I was mortified! And I immediately knew there was absolutely *no* way I would ever disclose this piece of information to my classmates—particularly when over two-thirds of the classroom was represented by the male species! Already, I could hear their taunting, singsong voices chanting.

"I see London—I see France!
I see Hildagarde's underpants!"

My desk was the fourth one in the first row, which made me number four on Sister's list. I was desperate! Don't you see? I had no choice.

Patricia Carrier had received a pink sweater and a plaid skirt to match. And she had it on that day. She looked lovely—she always did. Duane Frommelt proudly announced that he had received a brand new sled. The boys all thought that was a great present. I really began fidgeting in my seat. My turn was getting closer. Mary Rhomberg was now telling everyone about the "paint-by-number" canvas of a horse's head that she had received. It came with all the paint as well as several different brushes that she would need to complete it; she was already half-finished with it and promised to bring it to school when she was done. Mary's dad was a doctor and she actually owned her very own horse. Mary loved horses, and I was grateful that she was taking such a long time to talk about her present. The longer it took Mary to finish, the longer I could keep from telling my lie.

"That sounds lovely, Mary, but we have to move along now." Sister said. Then I heard it, "Hildagarde, it's your turn."

I wanted the floor to reach up and grab me out of her sight! I wanted to disappear into thin air! Desperately, I wanted to become invisible! Of course, none of my wishes came true. I abjectly hung my head, and in a muffled voice spoke, "My present was a dolly."

There, I had done it. I had told a falsehood! I was a sinner! Now Sister would call on Andrew Elsinger. It was over. But Sister was still looking right at me, and then I realized that she was still talking to me. "Speak up, Hildagarde. Class can't hear you."

Curses! Now I'd have to do it all over again! That's the trouble with telling lies. Once you start, you just can't stop! This time I looked Sister Amelia straight in the eye and boldly spoke, "A dolly. Santa Claus brought me a dolly." There, I had done it again—my second deliberate lie! I hated myself! My teacher was satisfied, however, and calmly called out the next name, "Andrew."

I do not recall what Andy received for Christmas—for I was still too much involved with my own self-hatred. I bore my guilt for five more days until such time as I could attend Confession and tell our parish priest exactly what I had done. In the meantime, I stopped every day in the church basement and lavishly splashed "Holy Water" upon my person in a circular motion (sprinkling the floor more than myself, I'm sure). I faithfully made "The Sign of The Cross" in a childish, yet valiant, effort to rid myself of this terrible transgression. But it was not until the following Saturday at Confession when I had at last fulfilled my justly deserved Penance of three Our Fathers and three Hail Marys assigned to me by my confessor, Father Dupont, that I felt truly cleansed. I breathed a deep sigh of relief, when he said, "Go in Peace, my child! Your sins are forgiven."

This is another underwear story—this one involves our father. Late morning on a hot, humid August Saturday, Dad and Joe were working in the back alley garden, tilling the loose soil up and around the potato plants. This is a dirty, beastly hot, and very dusty job. Dad was wearing only his overalls, and his shoes and socks; he was sans shirt and yes, even his underwear as he slavered in the noon day sun. Remember these were tough times and he only had two pair of undershorts to his name. On Saturday mornings, our mother always did the largest heavy-duty loads (mostly overalls and work shirts) that included all of the working clothes worn by our dad and brothers. More than likely, by now, both sets of Dad's underwear were freely blowing in the breeze on the backyard clothesline.

George looked forward to his noonday break when he would at last be allowed to rest on the back porch steps and indulge in an eagerly anticipated cigarette, while Frances prepared lunch. He was running low on tobacco and had to ration his meager supply in order to make it last until next payday. This, of course, would make Dr. Beyer very happy, he reflected, as his friend was constantly nagging at him to quit smoking. "Every cigarette you smoke is another nail in your coffin," the good doctor often admonished our father. But alas, George did not want to give up his one luxury in life, and now that addiction was calling to him. "Quittin' time, Joe. Let's go in and have some lunch."

Joe pushed back the shock of black hair that had fallen over his eyes (he liked to think of that mop of hair as his "pompadour"), and pointed his index finger in the direction behind George. "There's some guy headed this way—coming from the tracks. He looks like a bum. He's waving at you, Dad. Wanna wait and see what he wants?"

"Yep, guess I'd better. You go on and get washed up. Tell your Ma I'll be right in." Our father was ordinarily an easy-going man of even temperament, but he found this interruption extremely annoying, especially when he noticed this approaching stranger showing little regard for the tender young plants growing at his feet. He was oblivious to the tidy footpaths between the neatly aligned rows and trod carelessly wherever he pleased.

As the stranger neared, George noticed that he was quite well dressed, albeit a bit dirty and unkempt. He wore a dark suit, carrying the jacket over his arm, and a disheveled white shirt with the sleeves rolled up to his elbows; rather unusual attire for a "man of the road." His suit was rumpled and baggy, and the shirt could certainly have stood a good go-round with Frances and her washboard, but George thought the man was quite well dressed, even though his shoes showed the dust and grime of travel. George looked down at his own worn and scuffed-up shoes and was embarrassed.

Now, our father, you understand, was the most kind and generous man and rarely objected to helping the "down and out." People often said of him, "George Spielbauer would give you the shirt off his back, if you needed it." And that is very true! He was now expecting this man to ask for a "bite to eat" and maybe a "glass of cold water" or perhaps a "cuppa coffee." The man spoke, "Hey, Mister, I was just—ah, wondering if maybe, you might have an extra pair of underwear that you could spare. It's kind of well, embarrassing, but I really need some."

George's mouth gaped wide open! He wiped the noonday sweat from his brow with the back of his hand and stared at the bum in disbelief! He was a silent man and rarely spoke his piece of mind unnecessarily, but this day, as he rested his weight upon the handle of the hoe, he slowly and deliberately spoke in a very controlled voice. "Mister, I've been working in this sun all day and it is damn hot out here. That young boy (he pointed toward Joe, heading up the alley) is my oldest son. I got seven more kids younger than him to feed and clothe! And another one on the way! And that boy, walkin' yonder on the hard gravel isn't going barefoot because he likes to! He's going barefoot because I can't buy shoes for him. Even my little girls have to go barefoot. And, my missus ain't had a new dress—since I can't remember when!"

Dad stopped to catch his breath and again wiped the sweat from his brow. He slowly walked toward the man, who appeared nervous and frightened. Dad, in a now quiet and gentler voice continued, "Now, as for underwear," our father, without shame, boldly unbuttoned the side flap at the waist of his overalls, and openly exposed the naked skin of his bare buttocks. "My only underwear is pinned to that clothesline over there trying to dry out. My missus just washed them today. I only own two pairs—sorry Mister, I have no underwear to spare!"

This railroad bum hung his head in abject shame. In a quiet voice, he said, "Sorry, sir, I just didn't know!" He turned quickly away and headed back toward the tracks that unfortunately had become a "home" to him. George returned to his home for that longed-for cigarette and his lunch. A short time later, as he was relaxing on the back porch steps, calmly inhaling his cigarette, he couldn't help but chuckle at the irony of it all.

Now, that I look back, our mom, to my knowledge *never* had a new dress. Actually, she owned very few dresses. There was her "good dress" for church on Sunday, her "nice dress" when she went up town or to the doctor's office, and only two "house dresses" that she wore every day. While one was on her back, the other was in the wash or the ironing basket. Of course, her meager wardrobe was all homemade.

I can truly speak with open honesty when I say that all my sisters and myself hated "wash day" with an open passion! Of course, the "wash on Monday" rule never was sufficient for this family. Not only did we wash on Monday and iron on Tuesday, we washed on Wednesday and Saturday—and ironed on Thursday and Saturday as well. Thank God, Sunday was a day of rest. We deserved it!

Mama's washing machine was an old-fashioned wringer type that was very ugly in appearance. It was a Maytag brand, and my mother deemed it most beautiful! According to her, "Maytag is the *best* there is!" Our mother was, indeed, a living "walkin'-talkin'" commercial for The Maytag Corporation! This machine had little wheels on four legs, and when not in use was rolled behind the kitchen door in Gram's house and hidden from view by an old worn-out blanket. On wash day, it took center stage in the middle of the kitchen with two very large, circular, galvanized rinse tubs flanked like bridesmaids on opposite sides. The wringer rollers themselves swung freely from side to side.

We did have inside plumbing in Gram's house, but no hot water heater. So, all the water for laundry (and that was a tremendous amount) had to be heated in a copper boiler that fit perfectly over the two hottest burners on the cook stove. This boiler was always filled with water the night before and when Dad left for work in the morning—usually around 5:00 a.m., he would build the fire underneath the boiler. By the time the rest of the family was up and running, the water would be steaming hot and ready to be transferred to the machine. The laundry was separated by color and sorted into as many loads as necessary. The "whites" had been put to soak in a bleach and water solution the night before. These now had to be wrung out by hand prior to dropping them into the hot sudsy water as the first load.

Mama had a routine that never varied from the first load of "whites," to the sheets and pillowcases, towels and wash cloths and undergarments, baby diapers, pastels, coloreds, and finally the work shirts and overalls for Dad and the boys.

The soap that she used was usually P&G (Proctor & Gamble), Fels Naptha or sometimes a homemade concoction that Gram had cooked up. It was formed into bars that had to be shaved into a pan of boiling hot water to dissolve and then added to the heated water. The agitator inside the washing machine whipped this now-liquid soap into a mass of bubbling, scrubbing suds that oftentimes flowed over and down the sides of the machine onto the floor itself, which is why we *had* to scrub the floor every time we did laundry! In later years, after Gram died, she used soap in a box such as Oxydol and Rinso.

Another gooey mess that was cooked up on washday was starch. Dress shirts for the guys, ladies dresses, and blouses all were dipped into this solution to keep them fresh and crisp in appearance. The cloth was always 100 percent cotton and often times faded—it shrank and became limp after so many washings. Carefree fabrics, such as nylon, polyester, or any wash-and-wear material were nonexistent. The only stain remover known to our mother, other than bleach, was that very strong lye soap, along with her "washboard" and lots and lots of "elbow grease" for rubbing the dirt out.

Doing the laundry was a long, drawn-out process that took most of the day. And we, as little children, were always under foot. When the weather was nice, Mama always "shooed" us outside. But in the winter or on rainy days, we romped and frolicked amid the piles of dirty laundry sorted out on the floor. We made up our own games. Larry and I loved to tease our older sister, Helen. It was our childish way of getting back at her for tattling on us. She would always warn us with a "I'm tellin'! Your gonna git in trouble! I'm tellin' Mama!"

Larry and I were both quite small. We were able to hang onto the door handles and lift our feet off the floor, swinging our weight from side to side. This action actually made the door swing back and forth. Our big sister was four years older than me, and of course was now too big to perform this feat. In a childish effort to make her "mad," we would chant:

"Fatty, Fatty—two by four
Swingin' on the kitchen door—
When the door began to shake—
Fatty got a belly ache!"

What fun! The two of us delighted in our teasing game, but now that I look back, I doubt very much if we actually succeeded in making our sister angry. I think she just laughed at us.

There were times, however, when Helen and I would really get into it. Mom's favorite punishment was to make each of us sit on a straight-backed chair facing one another, yet far enough apart that we could not possibly have bodily contact with each other, for yes, we were known to lash out with arms and legs. The worst part of this penance was the fact that we had to look at each other and not speak. No sound, whatsoever. For whoever spoke first had to remain on the chair, and the other was granted freedom to run and play.

Of course, neither Helen nor myself was about to provide any escape for the other, so we kept our silence—ah, but we were far from still. We resorted to such delightful childish antics such as "sticking out the tongue," indulging in all sorts of insulting sign language, and making ugly faces at one another when Mom was not looking. The ugly face routine got rid of a lot of hostility, and eventually set us both into a giggling hysteria, which utterly frustrated our mother enough to send us outdoors to give herself some peace and quiet.

Once, Helen and I were punished by Mama Frances in a manner that sort of backfired on our mother. I am not certain what actually caused the punishment, but I vaguely remember our playing on the stairs landing, and suddenly Mom was scolding us because there were dirty footprints on the newly papered walls. Undoubtedly, my sister and I were at fault as those telltale prints perfectly matched our bare feet. When

Mom discovered that there had been dirty work afoot (pardon the pun) here, she immediately banished Helen to the top step and imprisoned me at the bottom, while she commenced to wash away the dirty deed. The stairs sort of angled around the bottom, and in the corner of the curvature was a box of magazines and catalogs. Grandma always kept her parasol there as well.

I could easily reach the magazines from my imprisonment and soon became involved in entertaining myself as I flipped happily through their pages. Of course, my contentment proved to be too much for Helen. Step by step, she gradually inched her way past Mama (who was still scrubbing at the dirty wall) down to my area. Soon we were both giggling and having a grand old time. Mama was not happy, and she proceeded to spank us both. The more she spanked, the more we giggled, and at last, in desperation, she grabbed Gram's parasol from the corner and we knew we were in for it! Both my sister and I nimbly scooted our little butts out of the way, at the exact same time that the parasol came down with full force on the very edge of the step and broke in half! Helen and I were uncontrollable as we broke into peals of laughter! We were hysterical! And, Gram was furious! Poor Mama was in *big* trouble!

Boxes of clothing from our relatives in Dubuque arrived at our front door on a regular basis. These boxes of used clothing were the closest thing to a shopping trip that my sisters and I had ever experienced. We eagerly sorted through the contents, item by item, trying on, what looked as though it might fit—or those items that appealed to our individual taste. We indulged in our little style show and loved every minute of it. For being typically female, we truly loved beautiful clothes and realized that without the generosity of our kindhearted relatives our wardrobes would have been reduced to nothing but the barest essentials.

Our mother was able to make over, redesign, and literally create an entire ensemble from the contents of these boxes. My oldest sister, Kathy, remembers, as a freshman in high school, she had to wash (by hand) her only outfit every night and iron it before school the next morning. It consisted of a yellow blouse and black skirt. "With my black hair, my yellow blouse and my black skirt, I looked just like a bumble bee. And that is exactly what the boys in my class called me. 'Here comes the little Bumble Bee,'" they would tease. It made me feel bad, but I just laughed it off."

Kathy, under the tutelage of Mama Frances, soon became a beautiful seamstress, in her own right. She quickly learned to make over, cut down to size, and literally work magic out of those boxes of second-hand clothing. For example, Uncle Arnie had given a navy-blue full-length woolen long overcoat to our father. However, it was way too small in the shoulders for our dad. Kathy ripped out all the seams, cut the fabric down to size, and designed a lovely cape—complete with an attached hood for herself. The garment was fully lined in a soft blue taffeta, which she herself bought and paid for with her babysitting money. Mrs. Al Lake (Kuemple & Lake Hardware), who was probably the best dressed woman in town as well as an expert seamstress, noticed Kathy's lovely cape at Sunday Mass. She asked Kathy if she could borrow the pattern. Our sister was most embarrassed when she had to tell this fine lady that there was no pattern.

Kathy continued to be a "designing woman," and we all remember her greatest work of art—a very soft blue jumper made out of the damask tablecloth that actually had been a wedding gift to our mom. The tablecloth had originally been creamy white with a damask border on all four sides. Kathy dyed the fabric blue and created a "sweet sixteen masterpiece." The jumper had a square neckline and a fully gathered skirt using the damask border at the hemline to accentuate its intricate design. She wore it with a frilly ruffled blouse that she made out of a white "dotted swiss" curtain. Ms. Scarlet O'Hara had nothing over our sister.

Kathy was indeed a pretty picture when she wore this outfit on the Excursion Boat that came from Dubuque via the Mississippi River on its "last hurrah" voyage. She and her best friend, Lillian Connelly, had managed to save enough money babysitting to pay for the tickets. Dad (after a rather lengthy and tense argument) had finally granted his young daughter permission to attend the evening cruise. Little did he realize that Rosy was now waiting in the very next room—trying to get up enough nerve to also ask his permission for her to attend the afternoon cruise of that same Excursion Boat. Rosy as well had earned enough money babysitting and wanted to go with her best friend, Gwendolyn Beck. What was a father to do? George thanked God that no one under age sixteen was allowed to go on the evening cruise without a chaperone. Once again, he nodded his head and cautioned his second oldest daughter, "Just make sure you come straight home and behave yourself. Like a *lady*! I'll expect you back here by 4:00 p.m. Don't be late!"

Of course Rosy was home on time. And now Kathy and Lillian were in the girls' room preening and primping for their evening cruise. The three youngest girls sat cross-legged on the floor and attentively listened to Rosy and Gwendolyn as they lounged on the bed and glowingly described their wonderful experience on The Mississippi River boat to everyone. "I can't believe that it had had four restrooms. Each one was more luxurious that the other. The dining room was huge and very elegant with white tablecloths on every table." Neither of the girls could afford to actually order any of the very expensive food that was served on board, but the two inquisitive teenagers had taken the liberty of peeking inside.

We were all caught up in the excitement and glamour of our older sisters' adventure, and listened with rapt attention to what Rosy had to say. Of course, Helen and I realized that we were much too young for such a glamorous occasion, but not our three-year-old Bopsy. She ran to the closet and tugged on the hem of a little blue dress and proceeded to preen and primp just like the older girls. She begged Kathy to put a big blue bow in her hair; she even wanted her shoes polished. She cried, "Wait for me! I will hurry." We all indulgently laughed at her baby ways, but felt very bad when the little girl actually cried because she could not "tag along." Kathy promised to take her when she was older, but alas, that promise would be one that could not be kept.

On occasion, one of us would hit the jackpot, and an entire outfit from those boxes of second-hand clothing would just happen to fall into place and fit to perfection. This happened once for Rosy, who, at that time would have been a freshman in high school. Our mother's half-sister, Aunt Annie Bobel, often gave our family the outgrown clothing of her daughters. It so happened that from these hand-me-downs, Rosy received a beige satin dress, a brown cape, a pair of shoes, and a hat that magically went together—and amazingly, the entire ensemble appeared to be brand *new*! Rosy was delighted! This particular windfall had arrived at our house the Sunday before Easter. Easter was that special holiday when young girls and sophisticated ladies everywhere dressed in their finest and most fashionable clothing.

My sister's friends were all discussing their new Easter outfits throughout the week, and for once, Rosy was able to join in the conversation, and she delighted in describing her new clothing in great detail. To Rosy's dismay, one of her "so-called friends" looked scornfully at her and said, "But, those clothes aren't actually new! I saw your relatives carry in that box of clothes last

Sunday. I saw that hat. It was sitting right on top of everything. Your Easter outfit is all 'second hand' stuff!"

Yes, dear reader, this "second-hand Rose" was close to tears! And bitterly ashamed! For indeed, she had been gloating. And now she felt that she deserved this cruel "comeuppance." I do not think so. I am of the opinion that her "friend" was not much of a friend, and she is the one who should have felt the shame!

Of course, Mama sewed for all of us. I vividly recall the pretty little flowered dresses she made for Celie and me out of printed feed sacks and flour bags. Feed sacks were very large, and since Uncle Frank was a farmer, the Rohner family had a goodly supply of these on hand. Aunt Irene lovingly shared them with our mother, and it was amazing how Mom could, with just a touch of lace or rickrack plus a few pretty buttons in addition to the brightly colored feed sack fabric, create a beautiful garment that we were very proud to wear. Celie and I were far more fortunate than our older sisters had been, as we received a lot of clothing from the Rohner family as well.

Uncle Frank and Aunt Irene had six children of their own, and these cousins seemed more like brothers and sisters to us because we saw them often and played with them regularly. Marcella was Rosy's age, and the oldest daughter, followed by Marie was close to Helen in age. Marie has always been my mother's favorite niece, and I think that admiration was mutual. Marie always insisted that she was going to have as many, or maybe even more, babies than her Aunt Francie. I am not certain if this came to pass, but I do know that my cousin had to come very close to reaching her goal!

Their oldest son, Donny, is one year older than I am, and next came Betty Ann, just one year after me. The two youngest Rohners are David, better known as Butch (who now farms on his dad's land), and little Dorothy. Both Uncle Frank and Aunt

Irene were very kind hearted and helped our family in many ways.

One particular Sunday, the Rohner family came to visit us, and Uncle Frank hollered at our dad to come outside, "Give me a hand here, George! We brought you guys our old radio, George. Irene and I bought a brand new one. This one still works pretty good. Thought you and Francie would like to have it."

Papa was thrilled. He did have an old radio that Uncle Albert had given him a while back; but it never produced any real sound—just a lot of static and crackling noises. Even though it possessed a lot of interesting paraphernalia—intricate tubes and transistors—inside "stuff in the back, the darn thing never worked very well." This radio was a huge floor model with round dials and knobs, controlling the volume and stations. It was shaped just like one of the Gothic design arches in many of the churches.

At long last, our father was connected with the outside world. He could now listen to the "war news" (uppermost in everyone's mind at that time), as well as Fulton J. Sheen on Sunday nights! There was also another priest, who was a rather controversial figure at the time. His name was Father Coughlin. I think he was most often referred to as that "infamous radical priest." At least that is what Father Dupont and our dad called him. Now for the first time ever, George was able to relax in his own big, comfortable armchair and listen to the "Joe Louis fights" and FDR's fireside chats. President Roosevelt possessed a magnificent speaking voice that penetrated into every corner of the room. There was absolute silence (not even a baby was allowed to cry) when the President came on the air!

There seemed to be one small problem with that radio, however. Whenever the power was turned on, a little red light appeared from somewhere deep within its infrastructure. This light glowed brightly all the while the radio was in the *on* position.

Ordinarily, this would not have been considered a problem, but remember these were the war years, when we experienced those nocturnal "blackout" sessions. George worried that this very small light could be spotted during a "blackout." These sessions were not a joke. Everyone took them very seriously and everyone had to account for all members of their household. Once all members of each family were safely inside, all the window shades were drawn shut and all lights turned off. Not even flashlights were allowed. After Pearl Harbor, the American Nation, as a whole, became very war conscious and very cautious.

George, along with some of the other men on our street, of course, still wanted to listen to the broadcasts, but became more than concerned about the light that emanated from their radios. After concurring at great length, all the men decided they would continue to listen to the "news." However, they valiantly made an effort to cover up the radio lights with a thick heavy towel. It must have worked—I don't think they ever got in any trouble over it.

Now, back to Uncle Frank. He and my dad always had a great brother-in-law relationship between them. They got along famously. In my own estimation, I always thought that Uncle Frank was the nicest and most generous man I have ever known. I never knew of him to scold or spank his own children, and I never saw him become angry or lose his temper or ever "cuss." He was a few years older than our mom, and the two of them were very close. She always said, "Uncle Frank is the best big brother a girl could ever have!"

All of our many aunts and uncles played an important role in our growing up years; and many of them performed double duty by also serving as Baptismal godparents to some of my brothers and sisters. Aunt Irene and Uncle Frank stood up for my brother Frank when he received Baptism, and once again this couple provided our family with their kindness and generosity.

Our brother had spent many weeks in the summer months up on their farm near Garnavillo, and they treated him as one of their own. No doubt about it, Frankie has always been their favorite nephew, and they proved it by presenting him with that very first "grownup" brand-new suit for his high school graduation in 1950! Wow! He and my parents were flabbergasted!

Aunt Tootsie was Kathy's godmother, and she often bought books of paper dolls for her little godchild to play with. Aunt Martha and Uncle Pete were Rosy's godparents, and they too gave her a gift each year at Christmas time. These gifts were usually of a practical nature. Rose remembers most vividly a yellow knitted parka hat with brown fuzzy trim that circled around her face. It was my sister's favorite—and mine, too. She often let me borrow it.

My own sponsors were Fritz Brimeyer and his wife, Hilda. I shall never forget them. Every year just prior to the Christmas Holiday, I would receive a package or a card in the mail. The package would always contain something like a scarf or mittens or warm winter hat. Hilda always wrote a special little message to me. As I got older, she would include a brand new crisp $1.00 bill in the card. I am now ashamed to admit that I actually came to expect it. When I graduated from high school, both Fritz and Hilda attended my Graduation ceremony and presented me with a very lovely pale blue, satin slip with lace trimming at the bodice and hemline. I had never seen anything so beautiful—I was actually afraid to wear it. I had very special godparents.

Andy Elsinger Sr. became Celie's male sponsor. Her godmother was the young Margaret Connelly who helped take care of the family when Celie was born. They too were wonderful godparents. Andy became as regular a Christmas visitor to our house as that jolly old St. Nicholas, himself! I distinctly recall one particular Christmas when I ran to the front door in response to a very loud and insistent knocking!

Standing on the threshold, literally framed within the doorway stood Mr. Elsinger, laughing boisterously and holding one hand behind his back concealing something. He was a very tall and broad-shouldered man. Grinning from ear to ear, he spoke. "I'm looking for a little Bobsy Playfarmer here. Is 'that little Bopsy' girl at home?" My little sister was so shy and frightened that she timidly tried to hide her face behind Mama's skirts. At last, with Mr. Elsinger's gentle coaxing and Mama's protective arm around her shoulder, Celie shyly stepped forward.

Mr. Elsinger whipped his right hand from behind his back and presented Celie with a very funny-looking, gangly, skinny, long-legged rag doll! This doll was even taller than our three-year-old Bopsy, and had red and green striped arms and legs. The doll looked exactly like Olive Oyl (Popeye's "goil" friend) in the Funny Papers. Mr. Elsinger still stood in the doorway and proceeded to make this caricature doll dance and twirl and turn somersaults in the air! We all laughed and giggled! Even our baby sister soon forgot her shyness and realized the doll was hers—to keep! She loved it, and I know to this very day, Celie holds a special spot in her heart for Mr. Elsinger.

Yes indeed, my family had a lot of "helping hands" in those lean years—this time from Papa's Jewish friend, Mr. Sheeny Ben—Mr. (out of respect for his age)—Sheeny (his first name, I surmised)—and Ben (a surname, I assumed). However, now that I am older and wiser, I honestly do believe the name originally was intended to be an ethical slur in reference to this man's Jewish background. Actually, I was informed in later years, that his name was Hartman or maybe, Ben Hartman (meaning "son of"). Nonetheless, everyone in town called him Sheeny Ben, and he never seemed to take offense at that, and I am certain that my father meant nothing derogatory when he spoke of him. Papa befriended this man when most other people in town would not give him the time of day. Sheeny Ben was Guttenberg's only Hebrew—in fact, he was the town's only minority. He was a junkman by trade, and dealt with old brass, copper, scrap iron, and even glass bottles—swapping, trading, buying, and selling.

Some of the more rambunctious kids in town got their kicks from harassing this lonely old man. They shot out his windows (both house and truck) with slingshots and rocks, even air rifles at times. In retaliation, Sheeny erected a high board fence around his property (no doubt to maintain his privacy). He also owned two big German Shepherds as an added protective measure to keep the vandalism to a minimum. The very loud and threatening barking of these guard dogs was more than enough to deter any potential prankster.

The man was definitely a loner and kept to himself, communicating with others only to buy or sell or trade his wares—with one exception, George Spielbauer. I really think that Sheeny Ben was older than our father, but it seems as though he looked up to Dad—sort of like a father image. During one of the very coldest of Iowa winters, Sheeny Ben became very sick. And our kind-hearted father felt obligated to take care of him. Dad even persuaded Dr. Beyer to visit the man. The doctor diagnosed the illness as pneumonia. Dad checked on his friend as often as he could—at least every other day. To do so was difficult, as we lived on the south side of town and Sheeny Ben lived on the north end. Dad did not get home from work until after 6:00 p.m. He would quickly eat supper with the family, then pack up a meal for the sick man, and walk in spite of the snow and cold temperatures to the other end of town. On one of these evening visits, Dad took two quarts of Mama's homemade vegetable beef soup along with a loaf of freshly baked bread to the sick man. Dad came home and told her that Sheeny Ben devoured a big bowl of the soup and had two slices of bread. It was the first decent meal he had eaten in a long time.

Dr. Beyer also shared our dad's concern, and oftentimes the two men would run into each other as they visited this sick man. Dr. Beyer, on one of those very cold and snowy meetings, insisted on bringing our dad home in his car, which was a great relief to our mother, who was worried that Dad would end up as sick as Sheeny Ben. Between these two "good Samaritans" (the doctor supplying medicine and our dad furnishing the nourishment), Sheeny Ben eventually recovered. He was most grateful to both of his benefactors.

He told our dad that it had only been his kindness that kept him alive during that long cold winter and he wanted to repay him in some way. Dad said, "Forget it. Sheeny. That's what friends are for," but the grateful man bought a warm woolen cap with earflaps for George and two brown heavy-knit sweaters for the two oldest boys. Not having any experience in shopping for children, he had to guess at the sizes. As it turned out, Sheeny was not a good "guesser"! One of the sweaters fit Arnie to perfection, while the other one meant for Joe was way too small, and guess who "got" to wear it?

Once again, Rosy was forced to wear boy's clothing! Yuck! It wasn't so bad wearing it around the house on cold evenings, where no one could see her; however, on one extremely cold "below zero" day, Mama insisted that she wear it to school. Rosy cried and said, "I'd rather freeze to death than wear that ugly sweater! My friends will laugh at me!"

Mama said, "Nonsense!" Rosy wore the sweater. The angels must have smiled on my sister that day, because it was so cold in school (for some reason the furnace was malfunctioning), and all the children were huddled together in the frigid classrooms with their coats *on*. They had only been in school a short time when Father Dupont made his entrance into each classroom and grandly announced that the children were to be sent home. They had been granted a "Free Day" due to the severe temperatures. Rosy sent a silent prayer of gratitude heavenward—a quick and grateful "Thank you, God" for she, indeed had been "saved by the bell," and she smiled all the way home.

Another incident with Sheeny Ben was the day he showed up at our house and tried to talk Frances into selling him her big copper boiler. It was very old, Mama knew, but she refused to part with it as she used it at least two to three times every week to heat the water for her washing machine. Sheeny did not give up easily. Joe and Arnie were still sitting at the kitchen table eating the last of their breakfast. Ordinarily this man did not pay much attention to kids, but he had at one time told Dad he thought the boys were well behaved. When he spoke to our mom, he always addressed her as "Missus."

He now spoke very seriously, "Missus," he said in a broken accent, "I maka deal for dat boy," pointing at Joe. "Such a deal, I giv you! OK, Missus?"

"No deal!" Mama quickly responded. Joe breathed a sigh of relief!

Mr. Ben insisted, "Ya, I giv you ten-cent and a banty rooster to boot—and I taka da boy!" Again, Mama refused. But, my brothers were scared. Back in those days, ten-cent was a lot of money, and even a banty rooster had some meat on its bones—enough to make a pot of soup, anyway.

Before any deal could be consummated, both brothers took off on a fast run, heading for the tall timber across the railroad tracks and HWY 52. At a safe distance from home, they stopped to catch their breath. "Hey, Joe," panted Arnie, "how come I'm running? He only asked for you!" Both boys shrugged their shoulders and began to laugh at one another—but they made darn sure that old Sheeny Ben was long gone before they returned home.

Gram's house had a closed-in back porch attached just off the kitchen. There were two rows of hooks on the longest wall, on which we hung our winter coats, parkas, and scarves. The higher hooks were for the older and tallest children and the lower ones for the little kids. Our boots and galoshes somehow managed to look out for themselves and usually accumulated in a mixed-up pile on the floor. The same went for the mittens, unless you were smart enough to stuff them into your coat pockets. Most of the time these were soaking wet from snowball fights or sledding, and then, we were "supposed" to lay them out flat on the windowsills so they would be dried by the next morning. If they were still wet, it was only due to our own neglect and we would have to wear them in that condition.

I swear our grandma's house was haunted by little gremlins who were always at work in the dark hours of the night, purposely mismatching our boots, shuffling scarves and hats around, and always hiding the one mitten we were looking for. Finding what we needed each morning before school proved to be sheer bedlam and total chaos! I marvel at our mother's patience—and Gram's! How did they ever survive those mornings of hectic pandemonium?

Remember the winter fun we used to have? Sledding downhill at a racing speed? Doing a "belly buster" so you go even faster? The huge snow forts we built out of snow blocks? Those snowmen with clumps of coal for eyes, carrot noses, and corncob pipes? Some kid would always have to "donate" his or her scarf in order to keep the poor fellow from "freezing." And those vicious snowball fights with the Leliefeld girls and the Sassen boys? The Leliefeld family boasted of as many girls as we had boys, and the Spielbauer/Leliefeld feuds soon became as infamous as The Hatfields and The McCoys!

One Sunday afternoon, both families were engaged in heavy battle—the most vicious snowball fight of the year—going at one another "hot and heavy"—my brothers pitted against the daughters of the Leliefeld clan! I was still quite young and wisely chose the protected area behind the fort for my personal safety haven and contentedly manufactured a large supply of snowball ammo needed by my team. The Sassen boys, Jimmy and Bobby, who lived in the next block across the railroad tracks had earlier joined forces with my brothers, and it appeared to be an even match. At least, it did—until our Grandma Rohner decided to storm the fortress.

And storm it, she did! Gram carried a lot of weight! When we saw her feisty figure stomping through the knee-deep mounds of snow with that determined look upon her wrinkled visage, there was no doubt in any one person's mind who was going to win this battle! She minced few words as she read the riot act to the Leliefeld girls. They eventually ran to the safety of their own backyard in escape of our Grandmother's wrath. After all, this was her yard, her grandchildren, and her grandchildren's friends, not to mention "her very own turf."

Well Grandma's ominous presence quickly brought an end to that particular snowball fight—but, only momentarily. For you see, Jimmy Sassen (remember he was on our side) just happened to have this perfectly formed snowball poised in his hand and this mischievous young lad was just itching to throw it! Gram was not exactly what you would call "a petite woman," you know. As she turned to head back up to the house, her backside made the most perfect target—the temptation was too much to resist, and that snowball literally flew out of Jimmy's hand, as if propelled by its own power! With a very loud impacting noise this flying missile went spla-a-t against our grandma's leg as it struck her in the very thickest part of her thigh! She spun about and began to vent her rage on the assailant!

"Who threw that? Jimmy Sassen, was that you? You little traitor!" she screamed! "This is the last time I stick up for you!

You can just fight your own battles, from now on!" Then, she turned to the Leliefeld girls who had been watching all of this from the safety of their own yard, "Go ahead. Get him! Pelt him with snowballs as much as you like! See if I care! He deserves every one that hits him!" Then she ordered her own grandchildren to return to the house with her. Well that pretty much called this battle to an end. Jimmy and his brother, Bobby, took one look at the six or seven Leliefeld girls, who were already prepping themselves for further attack and wisely made the decision to call a "cease fire." They quickly turned tail and made a hasty exit via the railroad tracks that were the shortest route to their home.

Hurling a snowball through the air is something that is not often indulged in these days. And I don't recommend that you attempt to do so—unless you'd like a visit from your local law enforcement officer. It is my understanding that a snowball is now considered a "flying missile," and to actually toss one at another person or property within city limits is in direct violation of an expressly coded city ordinance. Such violation is punishable by law. So much for the joy and fun of snowball fighting!

I must not proceed any further with this narrative without mentioning again those warm, thick, patchwork quilts that Gram and my mom made. We could never have survived those cold Iowa nights without them. Gram used whatever material she could get her hands on. When the Furniture Factory where Dad worked had discontinued samples of upholstery fabric that were now useless to them, he brought them home to Grandma. She cut them into four-inch squares or triangles and stitched them together to form beautiful as well as practical quilt tops. An inner layer of batting and the warm soft cotton flannel that she sewed on the backside made these quilts extra thick and heavy. Indeed, they kept us very warm and cozy on many a cold winter's night.

My mom and grandma even went so far as to make full-size mattresses during the war years. As I recall it was a government project that sponsored this operation. There was no monetary compensation for their labor, however, after they had made so many for military use, they were allowed enough materials to make one for themselves. They made enough of these mattresses to "earn" two for our own household—one for Mom and Dad's bed and the other for our grandma. I well remember this mattress project taking up the entire surface of Mom's huge dining room table for many weeks. They used a special curved bodkin type of needle to "tie" the mattress together. It was a tedious chore to push the needle downward, through the thick padding, and then back upward to the top surface. I used to sit on the floor under the table and let them know when the needle came through the bottom. Then, Mom would kneel down and attach a circle of leather that looked like a button with two tiny holes punched into it (about the size of a quarter) in and out of the holes and push the needle back up, where Gram's fingers will be waiting to pull. Another circle of leather was attached to the upper side, and it was then tied off. It was very labor intensive!

Back to those cold Iowa winters, what a struggle it was to keep that old house warm during the lengthy frigid months. As I mentioned earlier, Gram's house was located very near the railroad tracks. The freight trains transported coal throughout the Midwest on what was known as coal cars. These were flat open cars that carried mounds of the black coal piled high onto each car. Fortunately for my family and many others just like us, the constant movement and lurching of these cars as the train moved along the tracks caused some of the coal chunks to fall off the heap. They, of course, rolled on down the sides and landed in the ditches on both sides of the track.

Our brothers Joe and Arnie were the only children old enough to be trusted near the dangerous tracks. They walked beside the moving train along its track bed, and with buckets in hand gathered the scattered coal as it rolled off the cars. This would be used in both of our stoves throughout the night hours. Coal burned longer and was considered to be safer when unattended than wood. You understand of course that this was never considered to be a stealing act for the coal had already been lost. This was more of a gleaning effort, I should guess.

However, on occasion, my brothers were known to sort of "help" that coal slide off the train. They discovered, quite by accident, that by throwing a rock or two aiming at the very highest peak of the coal pile would always, without fail, result in a small landslide. The clumps of coal then rolled freely off the sides of the car, and they could easily fill their buckets in half the time. This action was never disclosed to our parents.

Clarence Frommelt was our next-door neighbor. He and his brother, Ray (who lived up and over one block to the North), together owned a makeshift portable sawing machine. This apparatus was mounted to the rear of a small trailer that could be hitched to the back of their automobile and be hauled from one location to another. This was a great convenience for the town as most of the families, like ours, had to rely on stacks of firewood to heat their homes. A load of wood was always delivered in huge chunks, and it would have to be chopped by hand, with the use of a sharp axe, into small enough pieces to fit into the stoves. I sort of remember that this "saw machine" was an invention of the Frommelt brothers, and their services were in great demand all over town. So they asked our dad to assist them in their jobs, and in turn, they would saw up our own family's supply of firewood at "no charge." It was a good trade-off.

My memory insistently takes me back to my dear grandmothers—both our black grandmother Spielbauer and our white grandmother Rohner. Mathias Rohner had been a widower with very small children of his own when he first met my gram. His first wife had recently passed away, and he was now desperately looking for a "decent woman" to act as caregiver, housekeeper, and surrogate mother for his children. Juliana Johll applied for this position and was hired. Apparently this arrangement worked out very well, because a short time later, Mathias asked Juliana to become his wife, and she became a stepmother to his children.

This union was soon blessed with children of their own, a second family so to speak. These would be our Aunt Josephine (Scholl), Uncle Tony (Rohner), Uncle Frank (Rohner), our Mother, Frances (Spielbauer), and another little girl child, Magdalena, who died approximately at age three. She had accidentally swallowed a kernel of dried corn and choked to death. After her husband passed away, our Gram Rohner moved to town and lived quite comfortably by herself. She would have been approximately sixty-five years old in 1934, when she opened both her heart and her home to my parents and all of their children. What a drastic change it must have been for her the day we all appeared (bag and baggage) at her doorstep. I guess one can say, she truly "sheltered the homeless" the day she took us in.

The following summer, Papa's younger brother, Uncle Jack, also moved in with us. He worked for a short time with our dad on the Lock and Dam, and stayed with our family during the week. On Friday night he would faithfully return to the little town of Buenie, where he lived with our "black" gram. He was a widower. His wife had died when their little daughter, Velma, was a tiny baby. This is living proof that families back in those olden days really stood by each other and helped one another in times of trouble and hardship.

Papa and Uncle Jack were sitting on the back porch steps one evening after a hard day's work, relaxing with some bottled beer that Uncle Jack had brought home. Papa proceeded to play the role of the older and, therefore, wiser big brother. He tried to convince his brother that he should seek another wife and settle down, because he knew his ma was very concerned for her youngest son. "You need to show a little more respect and concern for your ma. Go to church with her on Sunday every once in a while. You need to treat her real good and don't make her worry so much. After all, she's the *only* ma you'll ever have," scolded George.

Uncle Jack did not respond right away. He just sat in silence and sipped his beer. Finally, he spoke, "And you don't think for one minute that Ma doesn't worry just as much about you—and all those little kids!" He waved his bottle in the direction of the backyard, where we were all playing. "Just where in *hell*, George, do *you* think you're gonna find another Ma. She's the only Mother you'll ever have, as well." Now, it was Papa's turn to be silent—and a little ashamed.

Chapter VII

Visit the Sick Bury the Dead

George and Frances were fortunate in the fact that their children were, for the most part, in excellent health. What I mean to say is that none of us were afflicted with what one might call a dreaded disease. Of course, on a day-to-day basis we certainly had our fair share of sore throats, colds, earaches, flu, and toothaches, not to mention; stubbed toes and slivers in same (we did go barefoot all summer long), and occasionally broken bones, especially Frankie. Immune to childhood diseases we were not. We had done our time, so to speak, with measles, mumps, chickenpox, strep throat, roseola, and everything else that kids come down with.

I must interrupt here and explain to the reader that the following incident is a bit ahead of its time. But please bear with me. After Gram Rohner passed away, we continued to live in her house until it was sold, at which time our parents purchased their own home (located just a block north and between the alley and the railroad tracks). It is currently the home of my brother, John. We have always referred to it as the Alley House. This is the location, and I would guess the time to be approximately 1945. I strongly feel that this story belongs in this chapter.

Our entire family, at least ten out of the fourteen children, came down with scarletina. This is a milder form of scarlet fever, and back in those days, resulted in an immediate quarantine. We were confined within our house as well as our own fenced-in yard for the long duration of one entire winter, beginning in the very first days of January and lasting until the following Easter Sunday in the spring of the year. I rather doubt that any of us actually suffered very much with this illness. But for sure, our sainted mother did, for she of course, was quarantined right along with us—the only adult among us.

Actually, Dr. Beyer (after much persuasion on the part of our mother) did agree to lift this quarantine for a short period of time on Holy Saturday. Mom literally begged him to grant us a short reprieve, an hour or so—just enough time to walk to church and confess our vast supply of this winter's accumulation of venial sins to Father Dupont. Trust me, there were many. Of course, it was clearly understood by every member of the family that we were to return home immediately after completing our penance. We were not to be officially released until the following morning, just in time to attend Mass and receive Holy Communion with a pure and unblemished soul.

During our confinement, Dr. Beyer or his nurse came to the house to check up on us every day or so. The front gate to our yard had now been padlocked as a preventive measure to anyone's entering or leaving. This had been put into place by the local sheriff. We had literally become prisoners in our own home. Dr. Beyer and his nurse were the only people who had the key and the permission to open the gate. Even our father was not allowed to come home. He had moved out of the house during this long winter. After all, he had to maintain his job at the furniture factory in Dubuque. During the week, he lived with Aunt Louise and Uncle Arnie. He faithfully returned to Guttenberg, staying with various friends and neighbors on the weekends. He attended Mass at St. Mary's every Sunday by himself and prayed for us—mostly for Mama, I think.

Without fail, he would show up at the alley in front of our house every Friday evening at approximately six o'clock. Of course, he was unable to enter the house or for that matter, even the yard; but Mom was always happy to see him and hastily tossed on her winter coat and scarf and ran out to meet him at the front gate.

I can still visualize my father's long and lanky frame leaning up against the fence, as he discussed the many weekly problems with my mother. We children took turns standing in front of the kitchen window, so Papa could see each one of us as we waved our greetings back and forth to each other. He made sure Mom had enough money to make it through the following week and always left an endless list of chores for the older brothers to complete by next Friday evening. Of course, as soon as the winter snows disappeared and the early spring weather allowed the ground to become "workable," our father passed on gardening instructions to the boys, much to their disgust. After all, they were supposed to be sick! How could he expect them to work in the garden?

Our father had always without fail, planted his crop of potatoes on Good Friday, and this year was to be no exception. Arnie and Frank too were called out to meet with him, however, they could only communicate with Dad from the porch steps (within hearing range of the gate) to receive his explicit instructions. Dad was very particular with his gardening and told them how deep to dig the hole—how far apart to place the plantings—how many "eyes" to drop into each hole—how often to water, etc, etc, etc.

Mr. Carrier continued to deliver the milk supply on a daily basis. Normally, he would just place it on the top step of the stoop at the front door. But, now he had to lift it over the fence and set it down just inside the gate. At this time, Mom was buying most of her groceries from Carl Kann and Paulie Meier. Both of these grocery store proprietors took turns stopping by two or three times a week. They would honk loudly to announce their arrival, and Mom would run out to the gate and give them a list of what she needed. A few hours later the groceries would be by the gate as well. Lloyd and Donny Meier (sons of Paulie) picked up our daily mail from the Post Office and personally delivered it to our home. It would be quite a number of years yet, before Guttenberg provided a daily door-to-door mail delivery service to its citizens, and my mother always said, "Those Meier boys are such nice young men." A telephone would have been the most convenient at this time, however, that was still a luxury that this family could not afford. It would also take a few years for that to happen.

Now, if anyone is foolish to think that we Spielbauer children were allowed to slack off on our schoolwork during this quarantine—*wrong*! I guess you could say that each and every one of us had now been subjected to the "home-school" method of Education—well before its time. If you recall, our teachers were devout members of the sisterhood of the Holy Order of St. Francis, and these saintly ladies were known to be taskmasters at their trade. Every Friday afternoon two of them (they always traveled in pairs, you know) also showed up at our front gate, which during this period in time was our only communication with the community. We truly missed our teachers and looked forward to their appearance. Once again, we took turns waving to them from the kitchen window.

However, at the very sight of these nuns, we instinctively knew that we were in for it, because their arms were always heavily laden with huge envelopes and folders that contained all of our lessons and assignments for the following week, along with detailed "how-to" instructions. Thus, this makeshift school soon became established on and around the kitchen table, where each child's "desk" was the exact same spot as his or her place at supper time. With pencil and paper before them, along with a huge stack of the daily Monday through Friday homework assignments, these children attempted to become educated. It goes without saying that the older children helped the younger ones with their lessons. And, of course, our mother was also known as a relentless taskmaster, in her own right. She personally saw to it that each child's homework was properly completed by the following Friday—when they would be exchanged for a whole new batch. There seemed to be no end to it. Thanks to the persistence of our Mother and our teachers, every "student" who attended this home-schooled "Spielbauer College of Knowledge" did succeed in "passing" on to the next grade level by the end of the school year, even though we had only attended less than half of it.

This quarantine lasted such a long time due to the fact that we were so many in number. First one child, and then another, and still another came down with the symptoms—never more than one at the same time. One by one, each of us developed the telltale symptoms and eventually broke out in that ugly red itchy rash. We all blamed our oldest brother, Joe, who had returned home for the Holidays on his very first furlough from the Navy. He ended up spending most of his vacation time in bed with high fever, and still was not up to par when it was time for him to return to The Great Lakes Naval Base. Upon his return, he was immediately ordered by his commanding officer to report to "sick bay," where he remained for a few more days. Since he had never actually come down with the illness—that red itchy rash—but had manifested all of its symptoms, the doctors thought he was probably just a "carrier of the germs" and not a real victim.

Now let us step back in time and return to Gram's house. Dr A. E. Beyer was as typical a "good ol' country doctor" as any you'd find in Northeast Iowa in the 1930s and the 1940s. He was truly dedicated to his work and devoted himself freely to the health of the townsfolk and to our family. He was well aware of my family's financial situation and approached my father with the offer of a part-time job on weekends. He needed a handy man to do yard work and maintenance at his residence in town, as well as chores out at the farm that he owned just south and around the Guttenberg Hill. Papa agreed to do this, even though he had to travel by foot to both locations. None of us ever knew what George's hourly wages were for these services, as he insisted at the time that all of his labor would be applied to the medical care of our family. So one more time, our father bartered his hours of labor, not for an exchange of money, but for the cost of those family medical bills that were an on-going challenge.

As soon as each of our older brothers (Joe, Arnie, and Frankie) became old enough and strong enough to do a man's work, they too were hired by Dr. Beyer. They shoveled coal into the basement in the fall and shoveled snow from the sidewalks in the winter. They cleaned, painted, and installed window screens in the spring. In the fall of the year, it was a reverse operation as they replaced the screens with storm windows. Dr. Beyer raised horses on his farm, and the boys liked to take care of them.

They kept track of the hours they worked by recording the dates and times in a little black book. Once a month Dad and Dr. Beyer tallied it together, and payment was credited to the family "doctor bill." The good doctor and our father soon established a lasting friendship between them. Each man respected the other for what he was and what he stood for. Although they came from two different worlds, each learned from the other. Papa taught Dr. Beyer a lot about farming, and he, in turn (even though he did not have much more than a sixth grade education) learned a great deal about medicine from the doctor. Very soon, George was liberally dispensing his own form of medication to his children. In his own way, our father was "tending to the sick." However, in all due respect to Papa, he did know when he was "outsmarted," and whenever any of us showed signs of fever, it was time to stop relying on homemade remedies and hie us to the doctor's office for professional services. George never messed around with a fever.

For many of the minor aches and pains that all children are exposed to, we were subjected to the homemade medications conjured up by both our dad and our "white" gram. If we suffered from the pain of a tooth cavity, we stuffed a whole clove into the cavity itself. I am not certain what that was supposed to accomplish, but do recall that I liked the spicy taste. Another toothache remedy was the little cloth bag (our gram and mom made these out of material scraps or the toes of old socks). The cloth bags were filled with coarse salt and warmed on a rack in the oven. The hot salt bag was placed on the outside of the cheek over the painful area. The heated salt was supposed to "draw out" the infection and thereby relieve the pain. I don't remember that it ever worked.

A family favorite was Dad's homemade cherry bark cough medicine. It was so delicious that, we children oftentimes faked a sore throat along with its accompanying cough, usually giving such a convincing performance that we were immediately treated with this special concoction. The recipe actually came from "The Doctor Book," which was a huge, black, hard-cover volume that was filled with medicinal advice. It was almost as important as The Family Bible was back in those days, especially in the rural areas where doctors were few and far between. In late fall of each year, Dad would make a trip into the woods and strip off small pieces of the thick bark from the black cherry tree. When he was certain he had washed every speck of dirt off, he placed the pieces of bark into Mom's big old stockpot that she used for making soups and stews. He then covered it with water and let it simmer for hours on top of the stove, adding more water as it cooked down. Then he had to strain the syrup like liquid through cheesecloth to remove any residue. He then added sugar, honey, and lemon juice to the strained liquid and allowed it to simmer slowly until it reached a syrup-like consistency. He often dried the pieces of leftover bark and then burned them in either the cook stove or the potbelly stove in the living room. The scent of the cherry wood as it was burning permeated the whole house and it smelled absolutely wonderful.

The cough medicine was wonderful just as it was, but I also recall that sometimes Dad would add a bit of whiskey when he happened to have it on hand. I guess the liquor brought out the healing power. I also recall our dad dipping his finger into the whiskey bottle and rubbing the babies' gums with it when they were fussy from cutting teeth. It must have been soothing to the little ones, because they certainly slept better after that treatment.

Another concoction consisted of a blend of tobacco and onion roasted for a long time in the ash pan of the potbellied stove. This was then wrapped in cheesecloth, and all the liquid squeezed into a small container with a tight lid. This was used for earaches, and was administered by drops one at a time into the infected ear. Thank God we did not have to taste that medication. Gram also made a cold medicine, which was a combination of onion juice and honey. This was very "yucky" tasting, and unfortunately for us, it had to be taken orally.

One of Dad's remedies was "goose grease," which he rendered from chunks of fat that he saved when he dressed the fowl for cooking. This too was used for inner ear infection. Dad would place a very tiny amount of the grease in a teaspoon, hold it over the hot burner until it melted into an oily liquid, and pour one drop of the warm oil into the infected ear. Trust me, this one did work. I know because I had a lot of earaches as a child.

When Danny was a baby and had that bad eczema, Dad mixed up a batch of "salve," using once again, the goose grease, and a horrible-smelling sulfur powder blended together. This salve was liberally rubbed onto the rash. It seemed to keep our baby brother from scratching at his arms and legs.

George also used plain rendered goose grease to clean the barrel of his gun and massaged it into the leather hunting boots he always wore in winter. Supposedly, this process kept the leather soft and pliable so it wouldn't crack and split in the cold weather.

Elderberry Tea: The elderberry tree grows wild in Iowa. I think of it as more of a shrub than an actual tree. White flower clusters appear in late spring and develop into a grape-like bunch of very minute purplish red—almost black berries that are much smaller than grapes. Dad would bring home at least a bushel basket of the fruit at one time, and of course would have preferred to make that into a wine, but our mom, on the other hand thought jelly would be more beneficial to our family. Needless to say, our mom always won this annual argument. She liked to have at least six or seven quarts of this precious jelly on hand every winter, and rarely were we allowed to eat it on bread as most jellies are supposed to be used. The elderberry fruit is an extremely heart-healthy food and an amazing cure for a bad cough, sore throat, flu, and even digestive problems.

To make this tea, Mother would bring a pot of water to boil on top of the stove, and then stir in a whole jar of this elderberry panacea, simmering until all the gel was completely dissolved. It was always served steaming hot, in coffee mugs just before bedtime to anyone in the family who was slightly "under the weather." It seemed to have the magic of a mulled wine and tasted every bit as delicious.

I am very lucky. I actually have elderberries currently growing in my backyard, and I try to make a few jars of jelly each fall just to have on hand. I must admit that I dearly love elderberry wine like my father did. Unfortunately, I do not know how to make it, so I must content myself with a simple cup of comforting tea.

Another cough medicine that I still make today is with vinegar and honey. Place a whole raw egg, unbroken, into an eight-ounce glass. Cover the egg with vinegar and let sit on the kitchen overnight. By morning, the shell will be soft and pliable, and the vinegar will be foamy and thickened a bit. Scoop out the whole egg and throw it away. Measure the remaining vinegar and mix it with an equal amount of honey. This works well and can be administered to patients of any age. It does not have to be refrigerated—can be kept in a lidded jar in the pantry.

Of course, we all remember Watkins' salve. No medicine cabinet was complete without that round tin can of "Watkins." It was used for anything and everything—for any ailment. You name it, and not just humans, either. It was used on cows, goats, horses, dogs, cats, rabbits, and yes, kids. Our "doctor" Dad swore by Watkins salve.

* * *

As I look back in retrospect upon those early years of my life, I realize the very important roles both of the grandmothers played in influencing me and my brothers and sisters during the "growing" years. Not only my white gram whose memory is most prominent in my mind, undoubtedly because of the fact that we lived in her home and thus had become more closely involved with her; but, my little, lame, black gram as well. I consider myself very fortunate, indeed to have known these two great ladies and to have experienced just a small part of their lives. I am grateful to have been the recipient of their unselfish love and unending kindness—to have the opportunity to observe and thus learn from their quiet strength and sedate charm.

Now it is well known that grandmothers of any era are truly special in their being. This fact is indisputable and I should never argue against it. It certainly is not my intent here to disparage against these elect ladies of the "here and now," but I cannot help but be most partial to those great-grand and glorious grandmothers of yesteryear! Perhaps it was the time, the era, or the very need itself that made these old-time grandmas so rare. We all know it was a simpler and less confusing time. I do believe the poverty that prevailed during those difficult years was most certainly reason enough for the grandmothers to be just so much more warm and loving. They were painfully cognizant of the many needs of the depression child; they attempted to make up for everything else that was lacking—however, most of those grandmothers had very little else but love to offer. This, they gave most freely and most willingly and most unselfishly!

There exists a definite demarcation line between the modern ladies of today and the grandmothers of my childhood years. Back in the 1930s, grandmas did not rush off to catch a bus or a car pool in order to report to a nine-to-five job. They stayed at home and knitted mittens and crocheted doilies, and stitched on quilts and braided rugs. They baked oatmeal cookies, gingerbread men, and apple pie. And, oh—do you remember how "good" our grandmas smelled? Like freshly laundered bedsheets dried on the clothesline in a warm summer breeze—like summer sunshine, sweet as honeysuckle and lilac blossoms—and sometimes, they even smelled like vanilla extract, lemon pudding, and hot chocolate. Whereas, today's grandmothers are surrounded by a mysterious fragrance known by some exotic name as Estee Lauder, White Shoulders, or Chantilly—a French word you've never learned to pronounce (if you are a child), let alone understand.

A grandma in the olden days most always had white or graying hair, and most often, it was piled high in a loose bun upon the crown of her head. Or perhaps it might be placed at the nape of her neck, or softly twisted into a braided circlet that coiled around and around her head creating a natural framework for a gentle and beautiful and loving face that never frowned at you, but always smiled warmly. Her hair was held neatly in its place with wiry little hairpins and tortoise shell or ivory combs. On rare occasions, a wayward curling tendril or two would naughtily escape about the forehead or around the eye area and maybe slip free from its confinement behind the ears. These sassy little curls accentuated the crinkling laughing lines that outlined a grandma's eyes and only served to add to her unique charms.

Old-time grandmas didn't know much about beauty shops and permanent waves. They were totally unfamiliar with Grecian Formula and had never ever heard of Clairol. They didn't wear Gucci shoes, Halston pants suits, or Calvin Klein jeans. The closest they ever came to donning jeans was when they went "berry-picking." Then they wore a pair of grandpa's "bib" overalls (Oshkosh b'gosh) and his old battered straw hat. Underneath the overalls they would wear one of grandpa's long-sleeved work shirts. They did, indeed, look quite ridiculous in this getup, but it served a twofold purpose. It kept the mosquitoes off as well as protected their soft skin from those prickly thorns and brambles of the berry patch. And, if you have ever gone "a'berrying," you know exactly what I mean.

Mostly grandmas wore black silk crepe dresses to church on Sunday and to weddings and funerals. In the summertime, they would add a black straw hat with a wide brim to complement their dress up costume. This hat was usually adorned with a bright red fabric rose, jauntily protruding off to one side. In the winter, their chapeaux would be exchanged for a felt black hat similar in style, only it most always boasted of a brightly colored pheasant feather or a very showy, bluish-green peacock feather. For the everyday workweek, they invariably were dressed in simple cotton housedresses, dark and depressing in color with little round peter pan collars and cuffs at the end of long sleeves. They were rarely seen without a full-length white or gray apron worn over top of these dresses.

That apron was the most versatile and useful garment, indeed. Grandmas utilized it freely—to wipe their hands off and to "shoo" flies out of the kitchen by way of the back screen door. More often than not, the apron also served to wipe a little kid's "runny" nose (in passing) or to "whack" a naughty child across the buttocks. Our own gram was extremely dexterous at grabbing the apron skirt in one hand, swinging it round and round, and with just the proper amount of speed and twist of the wrist, the child definitely felt the pain. Sometimes, it was used to dry the tearful eye of a crying baby. If, by chance, there happened to be a clean corner left on the apron, it too would be put to use polishing an apple or ripe purple plum for a hungry child to sink his or her teeth into. Whenever unexpected company showed up, Gram's apron was hurriedly whisked from her body and hung on a nail far out of sight, behind the kitchen door, as though it were an object of shame! Alas! No one wears aprons anymore. What a pity!

Of course, Grams in the 1930s rarely wore fancy jewelry—such ornamental baubles as sterling silver medallions and fourteen-karat gold zodiac symbols so popular with today's grandmothers. The only real jewelry that they possessed was their simple "band of gold" worn on the left hand that was a token of love and obedience to Grandpa and to their marriage (even though he had long since passed away).

More often than not, their faded housedress was adorned with a string of safety pins in various sizes dangling from the edge of the pristine white collar in readiness, if necessary for a quick diaper change or perhaps to replace a broken buckle or a missing button. Another item was the ever-present threaded needle that was drawn in and out in mock stitches stuck somewhere in the region of her ample bosom. This was always in readiness for a quick repair job on a ripped seam. Sometimes, the child or, perhaps I should say, victim was forced to stand perfectly still and at close attention, obscenely jutting out a certain portion of his or her anatomy, while Gram performed the most delicate operation to a rear-end seam or upon a pant's patch.

And if, by chance, the seamstress was called to another duty, such as mashing the potatoes or turning the chicken, the said child had to remain in that awkward position and wait for Gram to finish the stitching.

Yes, I did mention bosoms. And Grams of yesteryear were famous for their well-endowed upper torsos, sort of like aging Dolly Partons. Along with their wide roomy laps, they served as a source of warmth and comfort to many an ailing and hurting child. It was so comforting to crawl into a grandma's lap and close your eyes, and feel her safety and her love enveloping you in her strong arms as she held you very close. For what harm dare to touch you now while held safe within the snug security of a grandmother's protection.

In comparison, today's grandmas are into health foods, health spas, and health exercises in an attempt to retain the slim and trim appearance of their youth. These days, they are avidly dedicated to aerobic dancing and busily working out with a personal body trainer. They are rushing off to the golf course, a luncheon, a tennis match, a bridge game, or lavishing indulging themselves to an expensive shopping spree with "the girls." In contrast, olden grandmas attended quilting bees, church socials, wedding shivarees, and parish picnics. They went to church "scrubbing parties" (each lady providing her own pail, brush, and mop) and to family reunions.

Grandmas cooked, baked, and canned within the small confines of sweltering hot kitchens. They sweated and slavered over old-fashioned wood and kerosene cook stoves. The temperatures must have climbed beyond Fahrenheit's actual "boiling point," not only upon the cooking surface of the stove itself, but within the kitchen—and the entire house as well.

I always knew from the very beginning that I was Grandma Rohner's most favored child in our household. Please understand, that no one actually told me so—I was simply and rather smugly (I must admit) aware of this fact as far back as I can remember. If there existed one "spoiled child" in our midst, I am certain that that child is none other than yours truly. Grandma babied me, loved me, and pampered me. She became my fortress of strength and my stronghold of protection. She served as my personal buffer against an outside world.

She brushed and braided my long black hair and told me I was beautiful, when in actuality, I was nothing more than a skinny, freckle-faced, scrawny, knobby-kneed, leggy kid. And I had a long nose. Grandma tried to convince me that it was a "Roman" nose. But whom was she kidding? I think that was just the Latin word for "long nose." Gram lavishly sprinkled both me and my bedsheets every night (after we said our night prayers together) with Holy Water! This was an attempt to keep me pure at heart and to frighten away the devil. Somehow, I always had the feeling that "he" was hiding underneath my bed, waiting for the exact moment when my grandma would turn her back, to leap out and pounce upon me. But Grandma said she would never allow that to happen! She believed in miracles and taught me to do likewise.

One sad day, my dear gram became very sick. It was the beginning of the end. She hardly ever left her room these days and eventually was unable to get out of her bed. Her meals were carried to her room on a tray, and she slept most of the time. Many times she'd cry and at other times, she would become so angry with everyone for no apparent reason whatsoever; and then she would cuss at them. After which, she always became very remorseful and then would begin to cry some more. No matter how sick, my grandma ultimately became, she continued always to treat me as "special," and I still knew that she loved me the most. Dr. Beyer now came to our house every day to see to her health, and Father Dupont, just as often, to see to the needs of my grandmother's soul.

Grandma's illness occurred at a very inopportune time, for our mama was once again in Iowa City giving birth to Danny Lee. Mom would have preferred to forestall this birth, but it was not her choice to make. New babies are impatient and refuse to be placed on a waiting list.

Of course, we were not to worry, for we children again had our substitute mother, Mrs. Krogman. By now, our sister, Kathy was considered to be a young adult. We younger children much preferred her services rather than those of Mrs. K. One day, Kathy was dutifully hanging up the laundry in the backyard, and it seems as though she was under the impression that Mrs. K was supervising the younger children. Whereas, that lady was busy making the bed in the downstairs bedroom.

Right at that time, Father Dupont had arrived to visit Grandma and bring her Holy Communion. He knocked at the front door, and no one heard him. He decided to try the back door or hopefully meet up with one of the children. As he headed around the south side of the house, he came to face with face with little Celie, not more than three years of age. This little child had a long, sharp butcher knife clutched within her tiny hands! Now, our knives were always sharply honed, thanks to Papa's whetstone, and had this little child slipped or tripped or stumbled with this dangerous instrument on her person, the results would have been disastrous.

Father Dupont was most angry at such child neglect! Had he been a man who vented his rage with cuss words, for certain the very heavens would have been horrified. Priests never do so, however, it was very obvious that he was outraged! I'm not sure who received the worst brunt of his anger, our baby sitter, Mrs. Krogman or our sister, Kathy. I do know this—they were both the recipients of this sainted man's ire and his lecture! And both were dutifully chagrinned! Poor Kathy, she has never forgotten that day.

Mama soon came home from Iowa City with our new baby brother. Mrs. Krogman returned to her own home and to her own daughters, and our family attempted to settle back into the normalcy of our own household. But, things were different these days. We were all much more quietly subdued as we silently tiptoed about the house and spoke in soft voices. We made a special effort to refrain from slamming the doors and other loud and boisterous noises that children are compelled to do, as this would immediately disturb our ailing grandmother or our exhausted mother, who was still recuperating from her recent childbirth. Plus, she had to be up and down all night long with either the new baby or our sick gram.

On one of these days, Gram took a turn for the worse. Dr. Beyer had come to the house to see her two times already that day. He returned in the early evening right after supper. He talked at great length with Papa and Mama, and told them that Uncle Frank was on his way to our house and would be arriving any minute. They were going to have to take Grandma to the hospital in Dubuque that very same night. We were all quiet and sad as we sat or stood around in the living room. Uncle Frank soon arrived while Mama was upstairs getting Grandma ready to go. When she came back down and saw Uncle Frank, she began to cry. "She is ready, but she can't make it down those stairs. All three of you men are going to have to help her."

We listened intently and most fearfully to the footfalls coming from the stairwell as our grandmother laboriously descended the steps. Papa's and Uncle Frank's noisier and heavier footsteps echoed her own as they eased our gram down one step at a time. We could hear her wooden cane tapping on the bare stair treads and then, as though in planned accompaniment, Dr. Beyer's lighter step. Altogether, the muted sounds created an ominous rhythmic cadence that brought to mind the atonement of a funeral dirge.

We stood in silent awe as this somber and small group made its entrance into the living room—Papa and Uncle Frank on either side of Grandma, assisting her as she slowly hobbled across the room. Dr. Beyer followed directly behind carrying her old battered suitcase in one hand and his own "doctor" bag in the other. Grandma was wearing her Sunday dress and her hat with the big red rose. They worked their way past us steadily and slowly. At the front door, Gram turned and looked at us children with sick and tired eyes that were deeply set within a framework of the many weathered wrinkles that had accumulated with the passing years. These eyes now rested on each child in turn for a long time, as though she were lovingly memorizing and subconsciously immortalizing every minute detail of our features. At long last, in a weak and shaky whisper, our grandmother spoke these words, "Goodbye, my children. I know I shall never see any of you again. Be good to your ma and pa."

Did I imagine it, or for sure did my gram stand just a little straighter and square her shoulders just a bit stronger, as she turned to Uncle Frank and nodded her head. "I guess I'm ready now," she sighed. "Frances, please come outside with me." These were the last words she spoke. Sedately and majestically, this great and venerable lady turned her back to us. Slowly she walked away. We children were all speechless—we were in shock—we were awed—and, we had never been so well behaved.

Our sister Kathy, grasping the emotional impact of this scene much more readily than her younger siblings, went to our mother's side and lifted the baby brother from her arms. Mama followed Grandma out to the car. I peeked through the door and wanted to run after my grandma and hide my face in her long skirts, but Rosy placed her more wise and restraining hand upon my shoulders and cautioned me to remain where I was. I continued to watch, however, at my mama and my grandma as both ladies looked long and hard into each other's eyes. They placed their arms around one another, and I saw the shine of tears running down each face.

Our Grandmother Juliana Johll Rohner never came home to us again. She was sick for approximately one week and then died in the hospital in Dubuque. Her soul went straight to heaven (I know for sure, it did), and her earthly body was returned to us for but a little while longer. She now lay in state for the next three days in our own home, rather than a funeral parlor. This was not an uncommon practice in those days. Friends and relatives filled our house as they came to pay tribute one last time and to give their final respects to our grandmother. We all prayed for the repose of her soul, and each of us children in our own special way said our personal "goodbye" to this grand lady who had meant so much to us throughout the years.

Permit me to share one memorable goodbye with you . . . Papa and some other strong men had dismantled the bed and moved all of the furniture out of the big bedroom belonging to the parents. Over in the corner was that thing they called a casket. And Grandma was "resting" in it—Hildagarde knew for sure that her gram was just resting—and *not* dead like everyone was saying. She knew 'cause she distinctly heard Father Dupont say, “May she rest in peace,” when he prayed for her last night. And for sure, priests do not lie.

There was a kneeler in front of the casket—actually this was called a prie-dieu. Hildi was very knowledgeable about that French word, because Sister Amelia had explained to her what it meant. It had been borrowed from the church, and they were all supposed to take turns kneeling on it and say some prayers for Grandma's soul. But, Hildi was not going to pray for Grandma's soul just yet. She was going to pray that God would make Grandma wake up. All around the room were rows of folding chairs from the funeral home. Many chairs were needed to accommodate all the relatives when they sat around the room and talked about Grandma. That is what people do at “wakes you know—a lot of talking and praying.” The child thought it was cruel for the grown-ups to talk about Grandma when she was right there in the same room with them. What if she woke up and heard them? Even though they would be saying nice things it would still make her grandma feel sad. For shame, grown-ups should know better.

It was a Sunday morning, and the big people had all gone to late Mass. Hilda and Rosy had already been to the seven o'clock service. Everyone in the family was to wear their good clothes all day long—they could keep even their shoes on. Today, Mama wanted all her children to look neat and be well behaved as many relatives and friends would be dropping in throughout the day. The little girl wandered into the wake room and saw that the casket lid had been opened up. She knelt down on the kneeler but it was much too big for her short body so she just stood next to the casket and gazed upon her grandma.

She remembered that Grandma's place at the dinner table was right next to her own and recalled how Gram would always help the child “clean her plate” by eating Hildi's “yucky” vegetables like turnips and carrots. As soon as Hildi pointed to what she didn't like on her plate, the older lady would quickly whisk it off with her fork and into her own mouth. Mama never noticed this little sleight of hand because she was always so busy making sure the little ones were getting enough food to eat and/or feeding the baby at the same time. Thus, when it came time for dessert, Hildi's plate was always clean—thanks to Gram. There was an unwritten rule in our household—no clean plate, no dessert! Lots of times, Gram would share her dessert with the child as well.

Speaking of sharing, Gram always kept a white paper candy sack with lemon-drop candies right beside her bed and often rewarded the little girl with one of these tasty morsels. Lately, she'd even wake her up in the middle of the night (Rosy and Hildi slept in the other big double bed in the far corner of Grandma's room) just to give her a lemon drop. The child would only be about half-awake and wanted to lay right back down. But, the white-haired Grandmother stubbornly insisted that she remain sitting upright on the edge of the mattress until every trace of the hard candy had disappeared. When Mama heard about it, she said Grandma was just acting "senile," so naturally, Hildi thought the word senile meant "generous and giving" because isn't that exactly what Gram was doing when she shared her candy with the child? It was many years later, before the child discovered that "senile" did not mean "generous and giving."

The little girl stood by her grandmother's casket for a very long time, still wanting her to wake up. She knew she was not to disturb her, but maybe, if she spoke very quietly—"Grandma, please, wake up. Can't you open your eyes," the little voice pleaded. Grandma didn't hear her, probably 'cause she was so exhausted and worn out from being sick and all. She didn't want her gram to be dead, because Donny Rohner had told her some cemetery men were going to dig a big and very deep hole in the ground. Then they would drop the big coffin down into the hole and shovel that dirt right back in on top of her grandma. She couldn't let that happen. She knew she was not supposed to touch Gram or that casket box, but no one was around. She hesitantly brushed her fingertips across the shiny white fabric that lined the inside—it felt just the way it looked, soft and satiny. Her curiosity got the better of her, and now her fingers rested on Grandma's snow-white hair so neatly coiled around her face. It felt just like always, soft and clean—not dead! Bolder now, her fingers traveled downward, tenderly touching Grandma's eyelids that were closed in a deep and silent and strange sleep. They caressed her face—her lips—something was not the same. Gram felt, oh, so cold—so concrete! Oh, no! The child's hopes were shattered! She felt deserted and desolate!

Now, for sure, she knew! They were right! Even Donny Rohner was right! Her grandma, after all, was truly dead. No one would ever be able to wake her up. Wet tears coursed down the child's face. Quiet footsteps crept into the lonely room. A protective and gentle arm slipped comfortingly around the child's shoulders—she was no longer alone in her grief! Her dark eyes looked up, but she already knew it was Rosy, for Rosy was always there. Her older sister had come to ease the hurt the child felt, but could not fathom. Rosy led her to the prie-dieu—it was big enough for both sisters to kneel down on—side by side. Together, they folded their hands, bowed their heads, and closed their eyes. "Are you praying for Grandma's soul, Rosy?" the younger one asked.

"No, not yet," said the big sister, "but, I'm trying to. I just don't know what to say. Are you praying for Gram, Hildi?" The child shook her head. "Well then, let us try to pray together," Rose continued and once again her gentle arm encircled the slim shoulders of her little sister. "We must pray the hardest—because we loved her the most!" The sisters prayed, perhaps not for Grandma's soul (for sure such a good lady was already in heaven), but they prayed to Gram and beseeched her to help them understand their sadness.

* * *

Nothing stays the same—and nothing is as lasting as forever. Tomorrow is but yesterday's today—and death is but a journey to another world—to yet, another life. Each of us children had painfully accepted and at last came to terms (even though we didn't fully understand death) with the loss of our grandmother. We continued to live in her house for a few more years after she died. Since Rosy and I had always shared Grandma's big bedroom with her, the two of us remained therein for just a few weeks longer.

Mom and Dad kept their bedroom downstairs, and they also continued to share it with the three youngest children in the family. The youngest baby, of course, slept in the white iron crib in one corner of the room. At the opposite end of that wall was a double foldout davenport where the next two toddlers slept. Each time a new baby arrived at our door, the children played "musical beds." The older one on the davenport now graduated to the second storey, moving the occupant of the crib into his vacated spot, thus freeing the baby bed for the newest addition.

With the advent of Danny Lee, it was Larry's turn to venture upstairs. This placed four rambunctious brothers into one very small bedroom. It goes without saying that this bedroom soon became a "bedlam," and Mama declared it was much too small to accommodate so many children. Thus it was that Rose and I were moved into the smaller room just off the bathroom; Kathy and Helen remained in the same room that they had always shared, and all four boys were now in the largest bedroom which had originally been our grandmother's. Each room opened into a long hallway that led to the stairs.

The new sleeping arrangement was well suited to all the children as I recall, but I also remember, only too well that it was the beginning of the many and vicious pillow fights that were destined to go on for many years to come. This age-old art of pillow fighting had been handed down from older to younger siblings for many years. I do believe, however, that is one thing the very youngest brothers missed out on. Frances, after one "never to be forgotten" horrendous battle in which feathers were floating and flying everywhere, simply removed all of the pillows from our beds—not for just a week or a month, but, forever. From that day forth, we all learned to sleep without them.

And yes, it is this very bedroom that brings to mind those aforementioned model airplanes that my older brothers used to build with such pride. They saved their pennies and dimes from paper routes and various other odd jobs, until they had enough to pay for a "plane kit." They worked for hours bending over the small rectangular table that had once served as the pedestal stand for Grandma's prized glass-walled birdcage. Actually, it was not really a cage, more like a showcase, but Gram, herself always referred to it as a "birdcage." It was truly a work of art, and Gram was extremely proud of it. Oftentimes, she would take visitors up to her room to show it off. Our grandmother more or less inherited it from her husband. Originally it belonged to his first wife, who had received it as a special gift from her father. Our grandpa inherited it from her when she passed away and eventually left it to Gram.

Our mother was worried that this beautiful birdcage would not survive long with so many children in this household. So she contacted her half-sister, our Aunt Clara (who was actually the real daughter of the original owner), and offered it to her. Aunt Clara was delighted! For she had secretly been longing for it for many years as a memento of her own mother, but never could get up the nerve to ask Grandma for it. So it turned out that everyone was happy. Except for me. I personally loved Grandma's birdcage. As I recall it was about three or four feet long, about two feet wide, and about two feet high. The bottom floor was wooden, and all four sides along with the top were made of glass with wooden framework all around the edges. The wooden parts as I recall were a very dark wood, maybe walnut. The entire creation was sealed airtight.

The interior held a very artistically designed display of various types of birds and a squirrel with a big bushy tail sitting upon a hollow log. He even had a black walnut clutched between his two front paws. The largest bird was an owl with big round wide-open eyes. I remember a cardinal, a blue bird, a robin, a canary, and a blue jay. Grandma had told me that a taxidermist had stuffed the animals that had actually been alive at one time. It truly was a beautiful woodsy setting with a lot of stone and moss, and even clumps of tiny purple flowers on the bottom. The animals were very life-like. It was so amazing. There was also what appeared to be a real tree branch with little twigs growing out in different directions on which the birds were perched as though in a very natural setting. I used to spend hours just looking into it and wishing I could open it up and touch the little animals.

I was terribly sad the day two strange men (Aunt Clara had hired them to move the heavy cage) arrived at our house to pick it up. Mama took them upstairs and I watched as they carefully carried it all the way down the narrow stairs and out into the street where they loaded it into the back seat of a big black car. For some reason, I felt like crying as I said goodbye to this most fascinating "piece de resistance." Thus, it was that the birdcage and the last, perhaps the most poignant, memory of my dear gram had been removed from our lives. I should like one day, to see it again—I often wonder if my childish recollection is accurate.

* * *

This next incident is another funeral in our young lives. Although this one did not occur until we moved into the Alley House and the telling is a little premature, it, too belongs in this chapter.

Alas, the days were drawing to a close for our old Sport. The past winter had been unusually hard on the animal. Along with his senility, he was also suffering from an arthritic condition that crippled his old and aching bones so badly that, he could barely drag his feeble body around. He had long ago given up chasing the chickens in a teasing attempt, darting after rabbits and squirrels in hot pursuit, or nipping playfully at the feet of the children. Mostly, old Sport, nowadays, just plopped his tired body down beneath the nearest shade tree and snored away the hours. He became cantankerous and cranky in his old age and oftentimes was feisty, biting and snarling at the children when they wanted to play with him.

Poor old Sport didn't even have enough gumption to swat flies with his tail anymore. This had always been his favorite pastime, and he was exceptionally good at it. Those unfortunate flies never had a chance against the old pro. But, now he just did not care anymore. Besides that, his teeth were falling out, and he was losing his beautiful orange hair by the handful. His eyesight had deteriorated so badly that he was constantly bumping into everything and everybody. His skills as a hunting dog had long deserted him and were now, nothing more than a happy dream to our canine friend.

Papa could no longer stand to see his old hunting companion so slowly and so painfully dying in front of his very eyes. Mostly, though, George was more concerned about the safety of the little toddlers (not only his own young sons but the neighbor children as well). Thusly, he commissioned the "town cop" (Guttenberg's answer to The Humane Society) to put an end to Sport's misery.

Small-town policeman, more often than not, inherit a lot of dirty and undesirable jobs in their line of duty, and this was one of those dreaded tasks. The cop (I am not sure, but I think his name was "Boots" came to our house very early before sun-up). He and Dad coaxed Sport into the "cop car"—drove to the edge of town—George turned his face away from the very best friend a man could ever have as Boots pulled out his gun. A single shot echoed throughout the surrounding hills. Sport's misery had come to an end! With a tear in his eye, our father now tenderly wrapped the rigid body of his faithful companion within the folds of the smelly old sweater that had always been Sport's favorite blanket. Dad placed the dog on the floor of the back seat, and the two men without a single word between them returned to our home.

George slowly and sadly climbed the stairs to the boys' room and woke up Arnie and Frank. "You two get up right now. I need your help. Be quick about it and be as quiet as you can. I don't want the rest of the kids to wake up." He returned to the kitchen where he poured himself a cup of hot coffee. The two older boys came down.

"What's up? What do you want us for?" They acted as though they had done something wrong.

"The sheriff came this morning and we took the dog out south of town and put him to sleep. I asked Boots to pull the trigger. I just could not do it, myself." Dad explained. "We had to do it. He almost bit one of the little kids yesterday. My ride's gonna be here in a few minutes, so I need you two to take the body down to the Schutte garden and bury him close to the tracks. There is a big cardboard box out in the shed. I wrapped his body in that old sweater and it's out on the front step. Frank, you go get the wagon to haul him in and Arnie, go fetch the spade. Make sure you dig the hole deep enough. You'll have to have at least two feet of dirt over top of the box. Hurry up now! Get moving!"

He tossed down the rest of his coffee, grabbed his tin lunch box from the kitchen table, and hurried out the front door. Both boys came around the side of the house. Dad looked long and hard at Sport's shrouded body and gently placed it into the cardboard box. A car turned into the alley and Dad again ordered, "Hurry up, now! I don't want the little kids to view the dead body. That would only make them start to cry." He hurried to the car and the men drove off.

"Come on, Frank, let's put him in the wagon," ordered Arnie. The boys worked together as they placed the box into the wagon. It would barely fit. "I'll be right back," said Arnie again. "I just remembered something. It's in the shed." He quickly ran back to the shed that had served as Sport's "dog house" these past years. He spotted the half-empty dish of water and a rusty tin pie plate with the remainder of the dog's Last Supper from the night before. He kicked the dishes aside displaying an emotional mixture of both anger and grief at the fate of his dog. Then, he spotted it—that old braided rug that Gram Rohner had made years ago. He shoveled it onto the spade and carried it back to the front porch. "Let's cover him up with this rug. It should keep the dirt from sifting onto his body." He then tucked all four flaps of the cardboard carton neatly inside. The corpse was now respectfully and decently shrouded.

The two boys headed down the alley, with Arnie pulling the rusty old wagon that had been given to the family years ago by Aunt Martha and Uncle Pete after their own children had outgrown it. I am sure the wagon must have at one time been a bright red and shining new; but to us it had always been old and rusty. It served its purpose well. However, I'll wager it had never before been utilized as a death hearse! Its wheels had long ago worn their rubber treads off, and now as the wagon rolled down the alley with its dead weight, the metal rims scraped and scratched and scrunched and ground themselves into the gravel stones in the road. Silently and somberly this small funeral cortege wended its way at least a block and a half along the deserted alley past the house where Mrs. Ferris lived, beyond the Leliefeld home, and on past the potato patch behind Gram's old house. A lady by the name of Mrs. Scheller and her daughter Ann now lived there. The two brothers moved on past Mrs. Schutte's old, ram-shackled shed that tended to lean in a southern direction. The wind of many past years had forced it that way—against its will and weakened wood.

Frank followed his older brother at a short distance behind, dragging the spade, as it noisily clinked and clanked against the gravel rocks and the dirt of the alley. Arnie, the oldest, at least had enough foresight to put his shoes on. He did not relish the idea of digging a grave in his bare feet. Frankie, on the other hand, plodded along barefooted, paying no mind, whatsoever, to the sharp and jagged rocks beneath his feet. He was used to the rough surface and now seemingly oblivious to any pain that the nerve endings of the soles of his feet might be suffering.

"Hey! Where are you going?" he shouted to Arnie, as the older brother moved on past the garden. "Dad said to bury him back here." Arnie kept on walking. Frank had to run to catch up to his brother. "Where are you going?" he hollered again.

"Come on, Frank. I gotta better idea," shouted Arnie. "Remember how Sport used to 'run the bases' with us when we'd slug a homer? Come on, Frank. Let's bury him over there. Right under home plate!"

"All right," Frank grinned broadly. "He'd really like that! Right beneath home plate." He ran ahead of his brother. "Here it is," he shouted, as he picked up the old shingle that had served as their marker. Arnie began the digging—a rectangular hole, two feet by three feet and very deep, right on the exact same spot where many a player had touched home base on a single hit and yes, dear reader, the exact same spot where old Sport's feet had trod many times before. As Arnie laboriously lifted up the dirt and slung it over his shoulders, Frankie flopped lazily onto the weeds next to him and busied himself by poking dandelion blossoms between his bare toes and watched the cloud shapes as they changed their patterns in the sky. Arnie frowned that Frank was one shrewd kid—he hadn't exactly forgotten his shoes, as he'd like his brother to believe. He was just smart enough to know that Arnie would never force him to spade that hard ground in his bare feet!

Arnie was exasperated with his younger brother as he labored over the hard crusty earth and dug through the top layer of tangled grass and weed roots. "Git off your lazy butt and do something," he said. "Why don't cha run the bases one last time with Sport? At least you can do that much!" Frank jumped up eagerly—he was afraid Arnie might make him spade without his shoes after all, and anyway, he liked the idea of a ceremonial departure for old Sport. Pulling the wagon behind him, he took off on a run and touched first base, barely gained second, rounded third, and, at last, huffing and puffing slid into home!

By this time, Arnie had dug deep enough, and both boys lowered the coffin of cardboard gingerly into the ground. Both boys worked silently as they replaced the loose dirt over the box and tamped the soil firmly around it. They re-sod the ground with the clumps of unkempt weeds, quack grass, and dandelions and placed them neatly over the new gravesite. The old shingle was returned to the same spot and would forever serve as a permanent tombstone marking the gravesite of Old Sport.

When they had completed their task, Arnie, who knew just a little bit about priestly ceremony, due to the fact that he had recently attended the Seminary of the Divine Word at Epworth, reverently bowed his head and folded his hands. His younger brother did likewise. "Dear God," Arnie spoke. "May you forgive Sport your old and faithful servant, all his sins, if he has any—and may he rest in peace. Forever! Amen."

Frankie, accustomed as he was to prompt Altar Boy responses, quickly responded, "Amen!" Arnie picked up the spade and slung it over his shoulder. Frank grabbed the handle of the wagon. Both boys walked slowly home—wordlessly. For silence is a form of respect for the dead, you know.

During my most recent visit home, I must tell you now, that I actually stole a few moments from my busy schedule and wandered all alone and aimlessly down to this vacant lot—the old ball diamond where the bases were marked by a remnant of a fallen shingle (home plate) old broken boards for first, second, and third bases and a flat rock with a circle etched into the dirt for a pitcher's mound. It was a trip of nostalgia for me, as I stood out in left field (a familiar spot), and I had to admit that the old vacant lot looked pretty much the same. It was a bit quieter now and perhaps a little smaller than I remembered. If I listened very carefully, I could almost hear faint shouts of "Strike Three!" "You're out!" "That wasn't a strike!" "Play fair!" "Foul ball!" "We win!"

As I opened my eyes, the "voices" within my head faded into the warm still air and reality returned to me. T'was nothing more than a memory. As I glanced toward the direction of home plate, I couldn't help but notice one bright patch, approximately two feet wide by three feet long. Believe me, when I tell you that it was the brightest and most brilliant patch of dandelion blossoms

(Ahh! It greatly resembled "old Sport orange") that I have ever seen. Now I have often heard of "pushing up the daisies," but I sincerely believe that our ever dear and departed canine friend is "pushing up dandelions" in his own honor! And when summer's warm breezes blow those seeds do scatter so! Thus we learned to bury our dead.

Chapter VIII

The Spiritual Works of Mercy

As you can see, with the passage of the years, we continued to grow and develop. Not only were changes taking place within us physically, but emotionally, spiritually, and mentally as well. We children, however, were not yet free to allow our underdeveloped characters to wander at will or roll with the tide, but once again were strictly guided by another set of rules, known in our very Catholic world as "The Spiritual Works of Mercy." These Spiritual Works were a direct counterpart to the aforementioned Corporal Works of the preceding chapters. Instead of fulfilling our physical needs, The Spiritual Works apply to the needs of our hearts, our souls, and our innermost beings:

Instruct the Ignorant
Advise the Doubtful
Admonish the Sinner
Be Patient with Those in Error
Comfort Those in Need
Pray for the Living and the Dead

As we grew taller and stronger, we gradually learned to read and write and reason. We learned to laugh and cry and hope and dream. We learned to pray, to forgive, and to comfort. We learned to love. Every day of our lives, in some way or another, became just another day of education. We had, as our teachers, parents and relatives, friends and neighbors, that saintly figure Father Dupont (you are all most familiar with him, by now), the goodly nuns of the Order of St. Francis, and, yes, at times, we even learned from our enemies.

Life, as we were destined to discover in our very early years, soon became an endless journey of education. We, as little children, were oftentimes victimized by our own lack of experience and ability. Some of the adults took great delight in patronizing this ignorance and finding humor in our naïveté. We soon learned to ignore their jesting, however, and were yet able to glean valuable information from these associations.

Instruct the ignorant: Larry, at age four, had been observing our neighbor Mr. Connelly as he was busily butchering and cleaning chickens for his family's Sunday dinner. Being naturally curious, our little brother incessantly questioned the older man as to "how" and "why" and "when" and "where" and "what." Mr. Connelly, being an old, experienced, and—I might add—a patient hand at parenting, replied to every question. His answers, however, soon proved to be a bit beyond the truth—greatly exaggerated—and, if you must know, extremely embellished. The conversation went something like this:

Larry: Mr. Connelly, where do chickens come from?
Mr. C: People grow 'em.
Larry: I know that, but I mean *how* do you grow 'em?
Mr. C: In a garden. Like you grow potatoes and corn and peas and beans. You can grow anything in a garden. Even chickens.
Larry: That's dumb! I never heard of such a thing! Are you *sure*?
Mr. C: Sure, I'm sure. It's easy. You just take a chicken, like this, you see. Then you chop off his feet, like so. (He

> wielded his sharp knife and two scrawny, web-toed feet dropped to the ground.) Now, you take these here feet, you see. Then you plant 'em in a straight row in the dirt. Make sure you plant 'em in the sun and keep 'em watered. In about ten days you should have a whole garden of baby chicks peeking through the ground.

Now, Larry, you have got to remember to loosen the dirt around the ankle, like so. Otherwise they won't be able to pull their feet out of the dirt when they learn how to walk. And, pretty soon, Larry, you will have yourself a fine bunch of little chicks all over the place.

Needless to say, our gullible little brother was astounded at this revelation and never, for a single moment, doubted the word of Mr. Connelly. One last and final question from the boy—"Mr. Connelly, if you ain't gonna use these old dead chicken feet, can I have 'em? I wanna plant me a real live chicken garden!"

Mr. Connelly grinned as Larry eagerly gathered up all the "dead" chicken feet and rushed home. He carefully selected the sunniest corner in Gram's backyard garden—a spot that also happened to be conveniently located in close proximity to the pump. This was a wise move on his part, since he was not yet very big or strong, and buckets filled with water could be extremely cumbersome and difficult to carry. For the next few days, this very young but enthusiastic chicken farmer labored over his chicken patch, diligently following the instructions of his mentor, Mr. Connelly.

As you can surmise, nothing much happened. The old, dead-by-now, dried-up feet did begin to smell a little—quite a little, I might add. Eventually, they sort of shriveled up into nothing more than a row of bony sticks protruding from the earth. A few flies were momentarily attracted to the site and curiously buzzed around these unusual seedlings, but they too soon flew off to seek much greener pastures, so to speak. Old Sport, always curious as to what was going on around him, opened one eye, quizzically, as he lay in his usual bored supine position at the very edge of the garden plot. He gazed dubiously down the length of this weird row in Larry's garden, halfheartedly sniffed the foul air, and disdainfully returned to his afternoon siesta.

And the relentlessly hot summer sun continued to shine down. Alas, our industrious young poultry farmer soon lost interest in his project, and a few days later, when Mr. Connelly asked Larry if he had any luck at "growing" chickens, our little brother disappointedly replied, "Not much. Just their feet growed into sticks." As an afterthought, he added, "They don't look like very good sticks, either."

Education was also received from older brothers and sisters, and this was an experience in itself. Sometimes, it was good, and other times, it was bad. Take those pillow fights, for example. When our exasperated mother was no longer able to control those battles, she simply eliminated the source. No more pillows! Ergo, no more pillow fights. "There's more than one way to skin a cat," said our mom.

Most of the time our lessons were more of a beneficial nature, however. There was a short interim (at Gram's house) between the raising of chickens and the arrival of the goats, which left the old shed vacant, but not for long. Kathy and Rosy, armed with brooms, scrub brushes, mops, and lots and lots of hot sudsy water, and P&G soap, attacked that building with a determined vengeance. Clouds of chicken debris, loose feathers, and dust poured out of both door and windows. The girls power-scoured and scrubbed every square inch of floor and wall and ceiling space and removed every minute trace of poultry inhabitation as well as its telltale smell. At last, it was spick and span and squeaky clean. Frilly little curtains now adorned the windows and that once dirty old chicken coop had been transformed into a combination of playhouse and schoolroom.

We even had our very own blackboard, thanks to the ingenuity of our Uncle Albert Rohner. It was nothing more than the lid to an old cedar chest, which he had covered with many coats of black paint, but we children were extremely impressed. We thought it was fantastic! Kathy and Rose once again doing the honors of teaching, we younger children were now able to learn the three *R*s—reading, writing, and 'rithmetic, long before we were old enough to attend a real school.

In due time, with the arrival of the goats, we found ourselves evicted from our classroom. We simply transferred our furnishings and other paraphernalia to the hayloft above the barn at the other end of the building. This location, however, was not as easily accessible for the smaller children, as its only entrance was an opening in the floor of the loft. In order to reach the entrance, one had to climb a makeshift ladder which was nothing more than old rickety boards nailed to the wall in haphazardly spaced intervals. Climbing the boards was no problem for me, but descent was another very serious matter. My natural fear of heights proved to be a very real detriment when I looked down and saw the distance that was between my little person and the barn floor beneath. My limbs literally morphed into rubber bands. It was at this point that I would shout for my older brothers, Arnie or Joe, to come and assist me in my descent. Alas, these two older and willingly able brothers were not always at my beck and call.

Advise the doubtful: It is late at night. The little girl is very frightened. Everyone in the household is fast asleep—save for this child. She is determined to remain awake, in spite of her heavy and drooping eyelids. She is certain the moment she gives in to sleep, that awful 'Angel of Death' will sneak into the bedroom and whisk her away in the dark of night, just as he did the little baby who had been buried only this morning. Her best friend's little brother had been "taken in his sleep." It was such a sad funeral. Everyone had cried. Rosy was angry at God. She thought him very cruel to allow the Death Angel to prowl about at night and steal innocent children away from their parents.

Fear overwhelmed her as she peered out into the dark night searching the black skies for a glimpse of this ominous creature. She knew he had to be lurking out there somewhere. What was death like? Was it cold and lonely, and scary? The child shivered in the night air and rested her tired and tousled head upon the windowsill as she solemnly stared out into the vast universe.

Thus it was that Papa found her. His first impulse was to "swat her a good one" on her bottom and sternly order her back to bed, but as Rosy hesitantly expressed her fears to him, his heart went out to the troubled child. He wasn't quite sure how to handle this and decided a cigarette might help. He found his tobacco and papers in the top drawer of the buffet and couldn't help but notice his wife's Sunday missal in the corner. One of the many "holy cards" that she used for bookmarkers was protruding from its pages. He took it and returned to the bench where Rosy sat still staring out into the dark skies. Placing the card between them, he silently smoked on his cigarette, gradually edging the picture closer and closer to the child.

Her curiosity was aroused. She glanced downward at a picture of a small boy and girl holding hands as they crossed over a wooden footbridge. The bridge was old and rickety, and the wood was rotting away. The children could easily have slipped into the dangerous waters swirling beneath, but an angel with a very large wingspan protectively hovered above their heads and appeared to be guiding them safely across. Papa pointed to the printing on the other side and said, "Go ahead and read this to me, Rosy. Can you read these big words?"

Of course she could. In a childish and faltering voice, she stumbled over the following:

> Angel of God, my guardian dear,
> To whom God's love commits me here,
> Ever this day, be at my side,
> To light and guard, to rule and guide . . . Amen

Papa placed his strong yet gentle hand on top of his little daughter's thick, brown hair and softly he spoke. "Rosy, you too have a guardian angel who is watching over you. God has told him that he doesn't want you to die—at least, not yet. Your very own guardian angel is protecting you just as he protects the children in this picture. Now, it is very late. Way past your bedtime—and mine too! Take this holy card with you. It is yours to keep."

Little Rosy's bare feet pattered off to the bedroom and at the doorway, she turned. Shyly she spoke, "Thank you, Papa." No longer did she fear the Angel of Death. Nor was she ever to forget that tender and most loving lesson in prayer that her father had given her so many years ago.

That is how my older sister Rosy learned to pray. She, in turn handed down that lesson to me in much the same fashion, probably with the very same holy card. Whatever happened to those little cards with their beautifully executed artwork, oftentimes edged in gold or silver leafing on the front side and printed with a meaningful lesson in prayer on the back? Oh, I know they are still around, but not nearly as many as they used to be. They were an important part of my Catholic childhood. My friends and I collected them, swapped them, and cherished them much like kids today do baseball cards or cartoon stickers.

They weren't free, you understand. We had to earn them in various ways. Sometimes, an excellent grade on a test warranted one. Or perfect attendance at daily Mass for a month or perhaps weekly confessions with the priest would earn one. Once I even received one for staying after school and helping my teacher clean the blackboards and dust the erasers. We stashed them between the pages of our prayer books and prided ourselves on having the "fattest" books. On occasion, when Father Dupont's Sunday morning homily was exceptionally boring, we entertained ourselves by looking at and reading our holy cards. This diversion of course did not go unnoticed by the good priest, as his pulpit was directly above us. But he never admonished us. Perhaps, he too in his godlike wisdom felt that "a picture's worth a thousand words."

Admonish the sinner: Truth is, I could easily write an entire series on this subject alone, but in all due respect to my brothers and sisters, I shall refrain from doing so. However, there is one singular incident that I truly feel does warrant some documentation at this point. In the words of our dear Aunt Louise—and, I now take the liberty of quoting her verbatim—"Boy, have I got a 'good one' on Joe!"

Joe was probably around thirteen or fourteen years of age at the time. Aunt Louise and Uncle Arnie had driven up from Dubuque early on a Sunday morning. They planned to take our mom and dad and Grandma Rohner to Rockwell City to visit with Aunt Josephine, and they would not be back until suppertime. This was the very first time that we children were left at home alone. Kathleen, being the oldest child, was of course responsible for all of us. Our parents gave us all a lengthy lecture on good behavior and what we were allowed to do or not to do while they were absent. Of course the "to do" list included minding Kathy, staying in our own yard, etc. The main thing on the "not to do" list was "do not" go anywhere without having permission from our sister, and, of course, that "always in force rule" of "do not" go near the river.

Young Joe, since he was next to Kathy in age, probably felt that he was exempt from the "do not" list, and when a couple of his buddies showed up in the afternoon, they all disappeared with nary a word as to their whereabouts. Young Kathy, who took her newfound responsibility very seriously, was worried sick. She knew she could not go out and look for him because that would leave all of us without supervision. Nor could she justify sending Arnie or Rosy in search of the missing brother, for then she'd have more missing children. The closer it got to five o'clock, the more worried she became. For if Mom and Dad were to return during the absence of our oldest brother, there would, indeed, be *hell* to pay!

As fate would have it, Mom and Dad and Grandma were the first to come home. This was shortly before suppertime and still no sign of their errant son. It was totally unlike any of us to disappear like this, and our parents were justifiably concerned. In fact, Uncle Arnie had just offered to take George in the car and drive around town to look for him, when the "prodigal son" returned. Joe casually sauntered into the backyard barely in time for supper. Needless to say, Papa's parental concern quickly turned to anger! He let the screen door slam loudly as he exited from the house and accosted our oldest brother. Our father was not easily fooled, and we all knew that Joe would have to do some fast-talking to get out of this one.

Unfortunately, our brother was not very adept at cover-ups and far from experienced in outright lying. Within minutes, Papa learned all he needed to know. As always, truth will have its way out! It seems as though Joe and his friends had sort of wandered off into the direction of the forbidden Mississippi, and boys, being boys, you know, one thing led to another. In addition to their first misdemeanor, Joe and his friends had indulged in a little experimentation with tobacco that afternoon! Papa was livid! He lectured, preached, scolded, and ended up "grounding" our brother for the duration of "all the rest of his born" days. Young Joe took it like a man, I must admit. He spoke not a word in his own defense, but meekly hung his head in shame.

At last, the fracas had calmed down, and our father, as well. But as brothers and sisters are most often prone to do, we tended to be more than sympathetic to our brother Joe's cause, as we all felt his punishment to be much too severe. Perhaps it was this sibling support that prompted him to speak up just then, or perhaps, it may have been the fact that Papa had at last returned to the house and was well out of "earshot." Then, Joe boasted, "I don't care if I am grounded. It was worth it all. We smoked a real cigarette and we cussed a blue streak! We said words like 'hell' and 'damn'! We even said s.o.b. and everything else!"

Just what "everything else" was, we never found out. We were all very shocked at our older brother's open display of audacity. But, unbeknownst to any of us, the kitchen window was wide open. Aunt Louise and Uncle Arnie as well as our parents had overheard every word that Joe had spoken. This was the straw that broke the camel's back! Our father's face reappeared in the kitchen window. "Inside, young man, and on the double! We've got to have a meeting of the minds here!"

Joe winced at the angry tone of Papa's voice and knew immediately that he had way overstepped the boundary line with this one. He marched dutifully into the house. Papa met him at the back door and sternly ordered him to head up the stairs to his room. Joe did as he was told—our father was directly behind him. We could hear the bedroom door slam shut even though we were all in the backyard. And then, silence! I, at that time, was not at all sure what a "'meeting of the minds" meant, but I am most certain that my brother found out soon enough. We did not see Joe for the remainder of that day or evening—not until the following morning. When the rest of us were called into supper, he did not come downstairs. Papa carried a plate of food to him. Aunt Louie and Uncle Arnie ate supper with us, but for once we were all very quiet and well behaved. It just did not seem the same without Joe at the table.

I think that Joe received the lecture of his lifetime from our father. In conclusion, I will say that whatever punishment meted out to our brother did not go without avail. For, to this very day, I have never ever heard him indulge in such harsh and offensive language again. Not in any way, shape, or form! And as for smoking—*no way*!

The act of "cussing" was something my mother was strongly against. My father possibly could have become more lax in that area, but he refrained from doing so, because he did not want to become a victim of Mama's wrath. And even our Gram Rohner on rare occasions was known to express herself in rage, and we always knew when Grandma Spielbauer was cussing because she used German words. For example, *Ach! Mein Gott!* But, the closest thing to off-colored language that we had ever been exposed to was, no doubt, the times when Papa's cousin, Walter Brimeyer, came to visit. Walter was a most colorful character, and we kids delighted in his company. He often reminisced about the "good old days" when he and Papa were young, and when he got carried away, he'd slap his knee and loudly use that s.o.b. word. Frances did not approve of such language and told Dad that he had better tell Walter not to "cuss" in front of the children ever again or he would no longer be welcome in her home. Our mother was also very good in her delivery of ultimatums!

I don't guess that this was the first time that Walter had been admonished because of his colorful language, because he willingly agreed to stop swearing. The next time he came to visit, we children listened very carefully, because we were certain this veteran man of cuss words would surely slip up. We knew it was bound to happen! When he raised his right hand and slapped at his right knee and uttered the words "son of a," we all held our breaths. Papa frowned at him and kind of said no-o with a shake of his head. Mama's mouth was pursed in anger and disgust. Walter continued his sentence, "batch! George, but didn't we have fun?" He placed all of his emphasis on the "batch" word, accentuating this tamer and much more respectable version of an old and well-worn epithet.

Papa breathed a sigh of relief and grinned. Walter proudly grinned back. Mama's eyes went from one to the other and then to her children. Her mouth as well opened into a big smile and she began laughing out loud! From that day forth, Walter cleaned up his act, and "son of a batch" became his signature "cuss" word!

And we continue to admonish the sinner, so to speak, only this time, the "sinner" is me. Frankie and I had managed to sneak past Mama with a big bag of her prized butternuts (she considered these a rare delicacy and always saved them to be used for holiday baking only). Well, we managed to tote the butternuts, Papa's heavy claw hammer, and a flat rock (we needed the flat surface of the rock to crack the nuts on) up to the loft. Here we would be safely out of Mama's sight and hearing. Frank would climb half way up the ladder and then I would pass the objects up to him. He was tall enough that he could then place them onto the floor of the loft, then he would scamper up the rest of the way. I, in turn, would follow suit, but always counted on him to grab hold of me and literally pull me up and into the loft. I was so afraid of falling. We spent the greater part of that morning cracking and eating the butternuts to our hearts' content.

All of the older children were in school and we were not bothered by anyone, until we heard Mama's voice shouting from the back porch. "Frankie! Hildagarde! Where are you kids? Come on in the house now. It's lunch time." Well, by this time, we'd already had our fill of nuts, and neither one of us had any desire for lunch, but we knew we had better hurry up and get in here, or else! Frankie quickly hustled down the ladder, urging me to hurry up and follow him. Alas, my phobia took control and I failed to do as he commanded. "I can't make it all by myself. I'm scared! Can't you help me, please?"

My brother was becoming impatient with me. "Hurry up and just climb down," he ordered, "'fore Ma gets out here and catches us. Come on! Hand me that hammer first. And get a move on, you big sissy!" I really wanted to do as he told me. I reached for the hammer as I lay on my tummy peering down through the opening. All I could see was the floor, far below me, and my brother's face turned upward. I was *so* scared—I accidentally dropped the hammer! I was horrified as I watched it plummet downward toward Frankie's head! We both instinctively knew something terrible was going to happen, but neither one of us could do anything about it! The hammer struck him in the forehead and broke the skin wide open! Blood spurted in every direction! Frankie sagged to his knees and slid to the ground as he cried out in pain! I was so sure that I had killed him, and I truly wanted to die!

I have absolutely no idea how I managed to descend from my lofty perch, but I knew that I had to do it by myself. I remember running past Frankie, up the narrow sidewalk, shouting, "Mama! Mama! Come quick! Frankie's hurt bad! He's bleeding everywhere! I hurt him! It's all my fault! I hit him with the hammer! I didn't mean to do it!"

Mama rushed past me and managed to carry Frankie up to the house. Gram hurried next door to use the telephone, and soon the doctor came. My grandma took me into the kitchen. They laid Frankie on the dining room table, where Dr. Beyer examined and treated his injuries. I must confess the remainder of that day is a complete blank in my mind except for when my mom came into the kitchen after what seemed like hours and told us that my brother was going to live. "You can come and see him now," she said, and taking my hand, she led me into the room where Frankie now appeared to be sleeping in the big brown leather chair with the matching hassock pushed right in front of it, like a big comfy bed. His head was resting on pillows and both face and head were completely swathed in white clean bandages except for his closed eyes. There was no sign of any bleeding now, and I should have felt better, but knew I would never forgive myself for hurting my brother, and to this very day, I still feel that guilt. I was reluctant to enter the room and remained in the doorway with tears streaming down my face. I kept saying over and over, "Frankie, I didn't mean to do it! I'm sorry!"

Dr. Beyer was still there and when he had finished placing his doctor "stuff" back into his bag, he came to me and took my hand and led me to Frankie's side. "We know it was an accident, young lady. Your brother is going to be just fine. He needs to rest a while. I gave him some pain medicine." Then, he gently patted my brother on the shoulder, "Frank, your sister is here to see you. Can you say something to her so she knows you're OK?" Then, I heard my brother's muffled voice, "You're just a big old 'scaredy cat', Hilda. It doesn't even hurt, so quit bein' a cry baby!" Somehow I knew then that he was going to pull through. The doctor returned every day for a week or so to check his wounds and change the bandages.

It was just a matter of time before my brother and I managed to tuck this trauma into the deep recesses of our minds, and soon we were happily playing with each other once again. And yes, we even managed to get ourselves into additional mischief on more than one occasion. Frankie went right back to playing in the hayloft with other children, but as for yours truly, I avoided that loft like the plague, even though my other brothers and sisters teased me mercilessly and called me "sissy."

Be patient with those in error: We all had our erratic moments, yes, even yours truly. This particular day had played host to one of northeast Iowa's worst and deepest snowfalls of the season. And in its aftermath, the little town of Guttenberg was now veritably smothered in a thick blanket of snow. I probably was about seven years of age and not yet very tall, for I vividly recall that the snowdrifts along the edge of the sidewalks were higher than my head. As usual, I had stayed after school to help my favorite teacher clean the blackboards and the erasers, so by the time I headed homeward, the schoolyard was deserted. There had been so much snow that the janitor had shoveled only a single pathway from the school to the church and to the street and on down to the priest's house. This amounted to a lot of shoveling because the total distance could have easily measured up to one city block.

Unfortunately for Mr. Dorweiler, who served as custodian for St. Mary's School and Church buildings and grounds, the modern day snow blower had not been invented yet. The narrow footpath that he had shoveled was barely wide enough for one person to pass through. The only other person in sight was one of the older Leliefeld girls. It was Mary. I did not know her very well, but we were not exactly on friendly terms, you understand, because of those frequent snowball fights. And, of course, our brothers were always battling against the Leliefeld girls and teased them without mercy. So, naturally, being younger and something of a copycat, I too joined in this long-established harassment. As long as my older brothers were around me, I was fine—my only problem was not realizing when *not* to harass, that is. My brothers were nowhere in sight and this was definitely *not* the time for me to be harassing anyone.

As I followed behind Mary in the shoveled pathway, I remembered how angry she would become when my brothers called her "Skinny Minny." Suddenly, I found myself chanting,

"Skinny Minny is a ninny." What a little brat I was. I understand now that I really had no business referring to any other person as "skinny." Being somewhat angular and elongated in my own body, I certainly had no room to criticize others, and I truly deserved what came next. I continued with my cruel harassment, all the while maintaining the safe distance between us. Several times, Mary turned around and glared at me with dirty looks and demanded that I "shut up!" As long as she kept a ways ahead of me, however, I felt reasonably safe. Soon she turned at the corner of the church and I lost sight of her. I kept on trudging through the deep snow, my arms loaded down with my usual stack of books and mountains of paperwork, and allowed my mind to wander in other directions.

Naturally, being only seven years in age, my attention span was rather short-lived, and by the time that I too had turned that same corner at the church to head southward toward home, I had long forgotten about "Skinny Minny." Out of sight, out of mind. Not so, my friend. I was so deeply engrossed in my own thoughts that I never noticed her furtively lurking in the shadows of the snowdrifts.

All I know is that suddenly, out of nowhere, strong hands seized me by the back of my coat collar and forcefully shoved me, my face, my upper torso, my armload of books and papers into the nearest snow bank, head first! Books and papers flew helter-skelter, in all directions! I was totally immersed in a blinding sea of bright white, not to mention, cold, wet snow!

I managed somehow to come up sputtering and spitting through the drift and when I finally realized who my assailant was, I must admit I was literally shaking in my boots. "Don't you ever call me Skinny Minny again, you little brat!" Mary threatened. "If there is a next time, you're gonna get worse!"

I don't mind telling you I was mighty scared! In all honesty, I have never been able to look back on this incident without having very guilty feelings about my own behavior, for I must readily admit that I was in the wrong that day and have since come to see the error of my ways. I truly deserved that comeuppance (as well as that cold and wet dunking in the drift), and I eventually came to respect this older girl very much. I respected her so much, in fact, that I would actually venture blocks out of my way, or cross over to the other side of the street in order to avoid a chance encounter with her. I have often believed that there is a certain amount of fear imbedded within the meaning of that very weighty word *respect*. One more thing. Know for certain—I have never *ever* called Mary (or anyone else, for that matter) "Skinny Minny" again!

I did mention that my older brothers thoroughly enjoyed teasing those Leliefeld girls, particularly Joe. He usually got the best of them, but one Sunday afternoon (once again, one of those cold, snowy, wintry days—known only to the hinterland of northeast Iowa), three of the older Leliefeld girls (Mary, Opal, and Betty) had all ganged up on Joe. He was by himself and soon, with their combined efforts (three against one), they had him helplessly grappled to the ground. While he was in this most vulnerable position, they proceeded to wash his face and his mouth out with—what else—cold, wet, slushy snow!

When he finally did break loose of their clutches, he cowardly turned tail and ran for the safety of his own back door. He ran to shouts of "Chicken!" "Joe's a big chicken!" Alas, our oldest brother's manly pride was deeply shattered that Sunday—even more so, when he burst into the kitchen and realized that his entire family, including Aunt Louise and Uncle Arnie, had been laughingly observing his defeat from the kitchen window! Joe vowed he would get even. He allowed his revenge to seethe and smolder all winter long. Ah! Ha! One beautiful, warm spring day, the long-desired opportunity goldenly presented itself to him!

It was Joe's turn to take the "billy goat," a very mean and aggressive creature in his own right, out to the back alley garden to graze on whatever tender weeds and new spring growth that had sprouted forth from the earth. Betty L. was innocently bouncing a red rubber ball off the old barn that was adjacent to the alley. The Leliefeld yard was completely fenced in and the gate was open. Actually, the gate had been broken and swung completely free in a circle instead of stopping at the halfway point. Also, Joe was well aware of the fact that Betty had a great fear of our billy goat.

Instantaneously, a big bold grin slowly spread across his features. This was the chance he had been waiting for. Somehow (well, maybe with a little help on Joe's part) the goat broke loose and made a beeline for the girl, with head bent down in readiness to butt! Betty started screaming and ran for the gate but was not fast enough. The goat managed to "pin" her between the fence itself and the gate on the alley side. Whenever she would try to escape, the goat butted into the gate pushing Betty back up against the fence. She was literally trapped within. "Get your dumb goat outta my yard," she screamed at Joe. Our brother just kept on grinning. "My goat is not in your yard," he gloated. "This is an alley and an alley is public property. My goat has every right to be here, just as much as you. If you don't like it, why don'cha get in your own yard?" "I can't! Your dumb old goat won't let me outta here!"

Joe just grinned. "Tough," he said, enjoying every second, for he knew this moment would not last long. He was right, for at just about that precise moment, Mr. Leliefeld appeared in the doorway of their home. It was then, and only then, that our now fully avenged brother "managed" to gain control of his goat and quickly led him down the alley where he staked him out to graze. Joe wasn't just grinning anymore—now, he was smirking!

Forgive offenses: Frank, at about seven or eight years of age, was caught up in his own make-believe world of cowboys and Indians, cops and robbers, spies and espionage, etc. He became deeply involved in his role acting and would actually lose his own identity as he indulged in a fantasy of hero worship. One day, he might become the notorious "FS the Kid," or perhaps one of the very adventurous Hardy boys, or Dick Tracy, or Sherlock Holmes. The family soon learned to tolerate his playacting and to accept his various personalities. But, the acceptance of the neighborhood was another matter.

One morning, Mrs. Schutte (the little widow lady living by herself right next door) knocked on the back porch door. She was terribly distraught, very nervous, and worried. Something was deeply troubling her, and she needed a trusted friend in whom she could confide. She chose our mama. For the past week, she related to my mother, she had been the recipient of threatening, anonymous "notes" that had been secretly deposited in her flower beds, slipped underneath her front porch screen door, and brazenly "tacked" to the inside wall of her "outhouse." Clutched within her tiny hand was a whole fistful of neatly folded pieces of paper as living proof. Her name was printed on the outside of each one. So she knew they were meant for her.

One glance at the handwriting and Mama thought to herself, "Oh! Oh!" Actually, the notes were composed in the crudely formed printed lettering of a child." It was quite obvious that the dirty villain who had masterminded this caper did not possess the neatest penmanship in the world, nor could he be mistaken for a scholarly figure, for his spelling was atrocious—a fact that the distraught little widow now pointed out to my mother. "Look," she said, "Whoever did this doesn't even know how to spell my name properly!" Each note was crudely addressed to a "Mrs. Shootey," rather than Mrs. Schutte; and the messages themselves had been carelessly and sloppily printed.

One after the other, Frances read these threatening notes. Mama was very adept at "smelling a rat" when a rat was to be smelled. There was little doubt in her mind as to who the perpetrator of this crime was! Each telltale note became more incriminating!

The first one read something like this:

> "Bewear! For tonite you dy. I strike at midnite."

The second one read:

> "Kilroy was here and he stands for kill."

(Poor Mrs. Schutte had never heard of that notorious and ever-present personality!)

The very last threat was the most frightening of all:

> "Dear Mrs. Shoot, tonite is the night! Evil lurks! Remember, I strike at midnite! PS: Don't call the P! Or else, you are doomed!"
>
> (The *P* quite obviously was an abbreviated form of policemen—undoubtedly because the author did not know how to spell that word.)

There were a few more notes, but mom did not need to read further. She sighed in deep exasperation and attempted to console the frightened Mrs. Schutte as best she could. She poured her a hot cup of coffee to sooth her nerves. "Don't you worry, dear. I think I can get to the bottom of this. Drink this coffee now and I promise I'll be right back. Excuse me for just a minute." With a most determined and tight-lipped expression on her face, Mama went straight to the back door and shouted, "Frankie, you *get* in here right now!"

She marched her young son into the master bedroom and angrily yanked the curtain shut over the double doorway. This had no actual door, just a very wide curtain that provided privacy between the dining room and the bedroom. Mama's voice was almost in a whisper as she spoke to our brother—alone. We could not hear the details of this conversation and perhaps we didn't want to. Very soon, she marched a shame-faced young lad out of the bedroom and into the kitchen, where Mrs. Schutte had at last gained control of her senses. An apology was given (from our errant brother), and, most graciously granted (by Mrs. Schutte).

It was never Frank's intent, you understand, to actually frighten this old lady; he was simply a victim of his own imagination, helplessly entrapped by one of his character studies. However, from that day forth, Frank was no longer an innocent. He, guilty or not, would be blamed for every dastardly deed that took place for blocks around, at least in the eyes of Mrs. Schutte. Months later when she was again victimized by some of the more notorious Halloween pranksters in the neighborhood, she pointed her accusing finger once again at our brother, believing that he was the one responsible for tipping her outhouse over onto its sides! Even though he was proven innocent of all charges in this case, Mrs. Schutte never quite forgave that "awful" Spielbauer boy!

All morning long, strange sounds had been escaping from behind the closed doors of the old woodshed—sounds of pounding, tapping, rapping, sawing, drilling, and hammering, in addition to other muffled and mysterious noises. Whatever was going on behind that unattainable door was a secret known only to brothers Joe and Frankie. Naturally the curiosity of the rest of us was greatly aroused. All the coaxing and conniving in the world was to no avail, however. We were, in no uncertain terms, ordered to get out and stay out!

Sullenly, we stood by and observed as Frankie repeatedly opened the door just barely wide enough for him to slip through. He'd quickly close it behind him as he made countless trips to the house and cellar for various odds and ends—necessary items, we were sure, to accomplish whatever mischief was brewing within the shed. First, it was Papa's saw from the cellar; then, a handful of nails and a screwdriver. One flying trip back to the house even produced Mama's sewing scissors. Boy! Frank would be in big trouble, if Mama saw him take those. Trip after trip he made. Now, it was Papa's hammer, an old burlap bag, some rope, and even an old baby blanket and a pillow! What was going on inside that shed?

The closest thing to a clue that we ever got was an occasional "just about done" or "wait 'til you see this," as he dashed back and forth on his errands. We tried to peek through the cracks in the wall, but they did not reveal anything—just Joe's backside as he was bending over some dumb-looking contraption in the middle of the barn floor.

Frankie came out again and with a big grin spread across his face, headed for the goat house. This time he pulled and yanked and shoved a stubborn and reluctant billy goat into the woodshed and once more slammed the door shut. In a few minutes, he was right back out and headed for the house. Instead of entering the back door, he went around to the front porch, where he furtively opened the screen door and quietly snatched our baby brother Danny Lee (about one year old at the time) from where he had been happily playing on the floor. Fortunately for Frank and unfortunately for our baby, Mama did not see this sinister kidnapping. Of course, Danny thought nothing of his capture as it was an ordinary thing for him to be clumsily lugged about by one or more of his older brothers and sisters. He cooperated nicely as Frank hoisted him to his hip and ran back to the barn with him.

The next time the barn door opened wide, out walked brother Joe proudly leading the billy goat, who was more or less oblivious to the fact that he was now harnessed to a small two-wheeled cart or a reasonable facsimile of the same. This contraption had been deftly designed and created by the young mastermind, Joe Spielbauer. The cart itself was made out of an old apple crate that Joe had attached to a baby buggy axle with the two wheels still intact. He had nailed boards to each side of the crate, which acted as a set of traces and created a harness out of rope and the gunnysack. Need I tell you how tremendously impressed we all were, and of course we all wanted to "go for a ride" in our brother's cart.

The young genius patiently explained that he was not for sure just how much weight the cart would hold, so it would be tested on the little ones first, beginning with the baby. Not that he didn't have faith in his own engineering talents, but he had to admit there was a slight chance that an excessive amount of weight could present a problem. Naturally, Danny Lee, being the youngest and the lightest, was chosen to be the human guinea pig for the first trial run. The blanket and the pillow provided a padded interior for the comfort of the passenger, and little Danny just grinned happily as his big brother (whom he trusted implicitly) now lowered him gingerly into the cart.

All went according to plan as Joe slowly paraded around the house leading the goat by the leash. The animal obediently stopped and started on cue, at each command from his master, and Joe was most proud of his accomplishment. Just at the time that he was ready to give himself a congratulatory pat on the back, all *hell* suddenly broke loose!

Out of nowhere a shrill fire alarm blared loudly! A car honked! The dog barked! The goat panicked! He tore off on a run, yanking the leash from Joe's hand as he took a sharp turn around the corner of the house and headed straight for the street, still pulling the cart that held the baby behind him. Little Danny helplessly bounced along in the cart, clapping his hands and squealing with delight at this wild ride, until the precise moment that the cart hit the curb! The axle broke into two pieces. The cart came to a sudden halt and dropped into the gutter of the paved street with a loud thud! Thank goodness for the pillow that buffered the blow! One of the wheels went rolling down the street; the other circled round and round and at last fell to its side still spinning crazily! The frightened goat tore off and dashed across the street, running through Mrs. Petsche's garden with Joe in hot pursuit! It was then, and only then, that our little Danny began to cry. And it was then, and suddenly then (due to all that commotion), that Mama appeared on the scene!

When Joe returned, leading the now docile goat (still dragging the remnants of his makeshift harness behind him), Mama was waiting, with her hands angrily resting on her hips and tapping her foot in a gesture of irate impatience! I don't need to tell you just who it was that caught "holy hell"! Joe and the goat stood there silently catching the brunt of Mama's wrath. And just where, you might ask, was our brother Frank, the cohort in crime, while all this was going on? I've told you before that Frank was one shrewd kid! He had remained in the background and had by now safely obscured himself amid the branches and blossoms of Gram's bridal wreath bush that was in full bloom and lush with its delicate white clusters that cascaded down the entire length of each and every branch. Brother Frank, under this protective cover, was making a valiant, however, unsuccessful attempt at stifling his merriment with both hands (covering his mouth), and his shoulders were shaking with uncontrollable laughter!

Comfort those in need: No one knows for certain just how this relationship ever got off the ground, but from the very first, it was unique and endearing to both parties. From what my brother tells me, I can only gather that he was going through some type of sibling jealousy (probably after the birth of his new baby brother) and he did not feel that our mama loved him enough or paid enough attention to him. So-o-o, he went seeking his love and comfort elsewhere. This elsewhere turned out to be two houses to the north of us, and the object of his affection proved to be a most gorgeous young redhead! Larry was truly in love. The gorgeous redhead had recently moved into the neighborhood, and the fact that his paramour was an older woman and that she just happened to be a happily married lady presented no obstacle to our little brother.

He was most grateful that Mike (the husband) was employed on one of the Mississippi River barges and thusly was away from home for weeks at a time. This arrangement conveniently allowed our young Lochinvar to pursue his romance without restraint. Larry was an adoring little puppy as he faithfully followed Eunice wherever she went. He was always by her side as she worked in her yard—sprinkling the lawn, clipping around the hedges, and weeding in her garden and flowerbeds. I told you earlier that Larry was one of the few redheads in our family, and without a doubt he had more freckles that all the rest of us put together.

One of us older kids would usually have to go up to Eunice's and retrieve our little brother at mealtime or nap time and more often than not, we'd have to resort to physical force to bring this reluctant little boy home. Eunice often treated him to cookies and milk but cautioned him "not to tell" his brothers and sisters about that, because she did not have enough for everyone in our family.

During a recent interview with my brother, he also admitted to me that, and I quote, "indeed, Eunice was a dear person in my young life. I was in love with her, I guess. You might say, she was my 'first love.' I thought at the time that she had the most gorgeous red hair and the most beautiful smile that I had ever seen. Eunice was very special to me."

Pray for the living and the dead: Oh boy, did we pray. One of my earliest memories is that of our entire family kneeling on the floor around the supper table at the close of that meal, even before the table had been cleared of the dishes, and praying the Rosary together. In the very early years, it was Papa who led the prayers, and the family responded, but as my brothers got older, they too would take turns at leading the prayers. This was a nightly ritual during the month of May (celebrated in Catholic Liturgy as Mary's month, in honor of The Blessed Virgin Mary). We also prayed the Rosary during the month of October, which was dedicated as the Month of the Rosary and again during the Lenten season just before Easter, as well as the Advent prior to Christmas.

We literally grew up with the power of prayer and learned to rattle off a steady stream of Our Fathers, Hail Marys, and Glory Bes long before we were able to recite the alphabet or learn to spell our names. During the war years, we put forth a much greater effort at praying. For then, not only individual families and small neighborhood groups, but the entire St. Mary's community would gather in mass prayer assemblies, and, in one voice, would raise their hearts and their souls to God. Church services on Sunday evenings were held as a special plea for peace and for the safe return of our soldier boys.

Our private lives were strongly influenced by an established system of prayer, which varied little. There was always the morning and evening sessions where we knelt at the foot of our beds and offered body and soul to God—even the youngest of the toddlers soon learned to lisp his or her way through the . . .

> Now, I lay me down to sleep.
> I pray the Lord my soul to keep,
> If I should die before I wake,
> I pray the Lord, my soul to take.

This was always followed by a long list of "God blesses"—God bless Mama, God bless Papa, God bless Grandma, God bless Kathy, God bless Joe, on and on and on! The number of those "God Blesses" was usually determined by just how long the kneeling child could prolong the bedtime hour. Sooner or later, an impatient Mama, or Gram, or older sister would say, "Enough already! Into bed with you!" We prayed before and after mealtime. We began each day of school by attending Mass before classes, and without fail, at first assembly in the classroom, recited The Morning Offering. When the bell rang for noon recess, we again stood beside our desks and recited The Angelus Prayer, followed by The Memorare before we went home for lunch. As soon as afternoon class was resumed at 1:00 p.m., we recited The Apostle's Creed, and finally the Act of Contrition just before we left for the day. Believe me, by this time, even the best-behaved child among us needed to be forgiven for some sin or another—so, we all faithfully began, "Oh, my God, I am heartily sorry for having offended Thee"—ad infinitum.

This following "prayer" story has been related to me by Mrs. Ann (Scheller) Olinger and involves my brother Frank and some of his buddies. If you will recall, Mrs. Scheller (Ann's mother) is the lady who bought Grandma's house after she passed away. This incident took place in the early fifties and Frank had just been discharged from the Air Force. Mrs. Scheller had by this time been diagnosed with a bone cancer and had been confined to her bed for many years. When Ann married her first husband, Cyril (Lilly) Leliefeld, the two of them continued to live with Mrs. Scheller and take care of her. Ann and Lilly owned a gas station on the River Front Drive across the street from Dahm's Studio. Their gas station soon became a "hang out" for all the young guys in town, including my brother Frank, Billy Buechel, Squeakie Meier, Snooky Heller, Harry Nigg, and many others whose names I do not recall.

Many evenings after the station closed up for the night, the young men would go down to Lilly and Ann's house and play cards and drink a few beers. There wasn't much entertainment for the young men in town except to frequent the local taverns or gather at someone's home for cards. They knew they were always welcome at Ann and Lilly's as long as they kept the noise level down. It was just before Christmas during the Advent Season, and Frank, Snooky, and Harry had been killing time in Nigg's Tavern, which was owned by Harry's dad. They decided they would buy a couple quarts of beer and head on down to Ann and Lilly's. Lilly (he sang in the church choir) had a beautiful singing voice and loved to sing. Since it was a little late in the evening to be calling, the boys thought they needed an excuse to knock on the door. So they decided to sing Christmas carols in order to announce their arrival.

The three young men stood on the front porch and knocked on the door and began with "Silent Night! Holy Night!" Lilly answered the door and explained to them that they were just getting Mrs. Scheller ready for bedtime and were about to pray the Rosary with her. He graciously invited them in and soon added his own melodious voice to theirs as they finished their caroling. Mrs. Scheller was deeply touched with the thoughtfulness of these nice young men whom she thought had come to serenade her and insisted they now join her and her family in their evening prayer service.

I can easily picture my brother Frank and Harry Nigg as they knelt down and recited the Our Father, Hail Mary, and Glory Be prayers, for after all, they had once been pious little altar boys. However, it is very difficult for me to visualize Snooky Heller on his knees with head reverently bowed in prayer. Ann has assured me that even though Snooky did not know the words to the prayers, he did indeed kneel down, respectfully bow his head, and fold his hands as he pretended to pray along with the rest of them.

Mrs. Scheller was so pleased with these thoughtful young men and thanked them profusely for singing and praying with her. She said, "Now, you boys come back again, any time! Come back and say the Rosary with me as often as you like. You are such good boys. Your Mothers must be very proud of you!"

Well, these so-called "good old boys" then adjourned to the kitchen, where they proceeded to sit around the kitchen table with Lilly and now indulged in a game of cards and drank the beer they had brought with them from the tavern.

I well remember that as a child I did not really know what prayer was all about. It was easy enough to memorize the exact wording, but I did not actually understand the true meaning of prayer itself. The nuns told us that praying was easy. It was "like talking to God," they said. No matter how hard I tried, I never could imagine that picture of me, as a little child, conversing with this very awesome Being known as "God." However, I faithfully continued to recite my memorized prayers by rote.

Now, I am much older, not nearly as shy, and hopefully just a little bit wiser. At long last, I truly feel that I am able to really talk to God. I may no longer remember the exact wording of The Act of Contrition or The Credo of my childhood, but I can certainly communicate with God! Mostly, I admit, it is me who does the talking. I have noticed that God never says much! He just listens. In spite of the silence, He still manages to get

His point across. He always seems to let me know just what He expects of me and what He wants me to do. At times, he can be insistently demanding, and sometimes, He even upsets me and makes me angry. But most of the time, I know deep inside that He is always right! I have learned to accept His ways without question. Even though I don't always understand Him, I trust in Him, and with that trust, I shall continue to pray.

. . . Not my will, but Thine, Oh Lord!

Chapter IX

The Alley House

When Jimmy was one year old, our parents bought a home of their own. Grandma's house had been sold, and we needed another place to live. Our new home was one block to the north and in the alley—ergo, the Alley House.

The move itself was relatively uncomplicated and not really as much of an undertaking as it may sound. We all eagerly anticipated the excitement of a new venture and new surroundings. Many of the smaller pieces of furniture, the bedding and personal items, and pots and pans and dishes were transported by a steady stream of barefooted children making endless trips from Gram's house to the new one. We worked all of one day and on into the evening. Very early the following morning, Dad's good friend, Billy Vogt, showed up with his flat bed truck. The two men and my older brothers loaded the heavy furniture, including Mama's cook stove (of course, it had to be completely dismantled into many and sundry parts before they could get it onto the truck). The men removed part of the fence that separated our new yard from the alley—just enough to be able to back the truck right up to the front porch. The porch floor and the truck floor were almost even with each other, so the heavy stove and other pieces of big furniture could easily slide right into the kitchen at the new house. Mama's stove was the very last thing to be put on the truck and the very first item to be removed. She insisted that it be put back together before any other item was unloaded because she would have to use it that very day.

During all the commotion of moving boxes and furniture into the house and carrying everything to its proper room, many trips up and down the stair steps were necessary. Little Danny kept getting in everyone's way. He eagerly wanted to ascend the very narrow and steep stairway leading to the second story. But there was always so much traffic up and down those steps that some older person was always yanking him out of the way. At last, he saw the perfect time—he watched to make sure that the person coming down the stairs had gone out the front door, and when there was no sight of any grown-up coming in, he darted up the steps. This stairwell was much steeper than the one in the old house, but he almost made it to the top landing before he stumbled and fell and bounced and rolled all the way back down to the bottom. Danny always managed to have more bumps and scrapes and black and blue spots than anyone in the family. Mama could hear the little toddler bumping and banging his small body all the way down the stairs! She screamed, "George, get in here!" She ran toward Danny, fearing the worst. Before our father arrived on the scene, little Dan righted himself, laughed happily at his own clumsiness, and began the long climb once again. Mama quickly grabbed him from the third step and began scolding him. When Papa came in, he too had to laugh, and after making sure the little toddler had no broken bones, he said, "He's just curious to see what's up there. Hilda, you take him upstairs and let him look around." I did as I was ordered. Danny ran from room to room and looked out from each of the upstairs windows. Dad was right—the little toddler was simply a curious little boy.

With the setting of the sun that evening, we were, for all practical purposes, settled in and feeling right at home—all of us, that is, except baby Jimmy and our old yellow dog Sport, who was already a little senile in his dotage. Baby Jim was excited with his new surroundings and toddled all around the first floor on his short wobbly legs (he had just taken his first steps a few days ago and just as recently had learned to talk in short phrases). By now, he was becoming very sleepy and yearned for his baby bottle and his favorite "'blankie" and his little white crib. He kept running to the door and pointed down the alley toward the old house, trying to communicate with us in his limited baby language. He looked at Mama and pleadingly said, "Ba-ba" (bottle) and "bye-bye" and then wave to us, as though he were leaving. At last, he clearly pronounced "go home" and angrily stomped his foot! Mama rocked him to sleep that night.

Old Sport too kept looking longingly toward the old house and would periodically rise from his reclining position on the front porch and head on down the alley to Grandma's house. When no one joined him, he'd stop and turn around and coax and whine for someone to "go home" with him. But in a few days even these two most reluctant members of our household gradually came to accept their new surroundings.

A few days after we had moved into the house, Mom sent our little brother Larry and sister Celie up to the grocery store with a list of items she needed for lunch. They were probably around six and seven years old at that time. They each carried one sack of the groceries and headed homeward, forgetting to turn at the corner that led to our new "'alley house." They arrived at Grandma's old house, walked right in the front door, through the dining room and out into the kitchen, where they placed both sacks of groceries on the kitchen table. They did not see anyone around, so they went outside to play in the backyard, totally oblivious to the fact that they no longer lived in this house. They didn't realize it until Ann Scheller came out and asked, "Do you kids know how those groceries got on my kitchen table?"

"Yep," said Larry. "We put 'em there for our mom. We don't know where she went, but she should be home soon. You can wait for her, if you want!"

"Well, you kids don't live here anymore. Don't you remember you moved to a different house? You'd better come in and pick up your groceries. Do you know how to get to your new house in the alley? Your ma's probably wondering what happened to you two." Ann laughingly handed a sack to each of these little children and led them into the alley and pointed them in the right direction to their new home.

It was not like we had actually moved into a brand new neighborhood, where we didn't know anyone. We were already well acquainted with the Gueder boys, Doug and Jackie, as well as the Lansing kids (about seven or eight children who attended St. Mary's School and were in classes with us). The Sassen boys lived right behind us, just over the railroad tracks. The oldest Sassen daughter, Anna Mae (now married to Kenny McGuine), lived in a small house right next door to her parents. The McGuine family had at that time a little girl named Mary Ann and two young sons Dougie and Kenny, who were the same ages as my little brothers Danny and Jimmy. A few years later they also had another daughter, named Toni (after her grandfather Tony Sassen), as well as one more son, Timmy. I vaguely remember babysitting the three older McGuine children.

The Dorweilers lived directly across the alley from us, and we already knew Mr. Dorweiler very well because he was the janitor at our school and church. Mr. and Mrs. Ben Voss (they always addressed each other as "mama and papa") lived to the north of Mr. Dorweiler. Mr. Voss had a strawberry patch that ran the length of his backyard, right next to Mr. Dorweiler's garden. There was a wire fence between the two yards. As soon as the strawberries were in season and ready to be plucked, Mr. D. would often reach right through an opening in the fence and help himself to the ripe juicy fruit, as he worked in his vegetable garden. He would chuckle to himself, knowing fully well that Mr. Voss would be very upset.

At first, Mr. Voss blamed the Spielbauer boys (naturally, being the "new kids on the block," they would be prime suspect for any and all misdemeanors that took place) for stealing his strawberries, but my brothers adamantly denied any guilt on their part. As I recall, it was Mr. D. who first came up with the name of "Mama and Papa Fuss" in reference to his elderly neighbors. That pseudonym soon spread like wildfire throughout the neighborhood and henceforth Mr. and Mrs. Ben Voss became known by all as "Mama and Papa Fuss." Mama Fuss often came over to our house to have a cup of coffee with my mom, and they mostly got along very well. She was really a very nice lady and even allowed us to use her clothesline when we ran out of room in our own backyard. She also had a huge half-gallon-sized canning jar filled with thousands of buttons that she snipped off old clothing throughout the years. My Mom and Gram had done the same thing, but our "button jar" was just a quart size. Whenever we could not find the right buttons that looked nice on the blouses and dresses that our mom made for us, Mrs. Voss let us come over and go through her button jar. I recall many a pleasant afternoon when she and I sat at her kitchen table and sorted through her vast collection of buttons searching for the three or four or six that we needed for a special outfit.

On many an occasion (I must admit) she would come to our house—most often in an agitated state—complaining about something or other that my brothers "might be" involved in. She was always very nice about it, saying things like, "Frances, do you think your little boys would have been responsible for whatever had happened?" or "Something happened this morning, and I wondered if you know where your boys were." Of course, she knew that our mama would get to the bottom of it. Eventually, it got to the point that whenever the verbal warning of "Oh-oh!" was announced by our sister Helen, it meant "Mama Fuss is headed this way and it looks like she's on the warpath again!" Immediately, one and all of the little brothers disappeared! You will, I promise you, hear more about Mama and Papa Fuss a little later in this chapter.

Sammy and Babe Meyers lived adjacent (to the north) of the Voss Family on the corner. They did not have any children but later adopted a tiny baby girl and named her Margo. Sammy and Babe were the only adults that we children ever addressed by the first name. They insisted upon it. At the time of the adoption, I was already running errands for Babe and helping her with light cleaning chores around the house. She would always "pay me" for my labor in nickels, dimes, and quarters. After the adoption of the very beautiful little Margo, she often asked me to babysit. That was my favorite thing to do—especially after Sammy installed a television set in his own home. Sammy owned an electrical wiring and appliance store in town, and his pickup truck advertised his business. He would often make trips to the City Dump to get rid of yard debris and junk. Every kid on the block (at some time or another) remembers climbing into the back end of that old pickup and riding along with him.

I clearly remember when WWII ended! August 15, 1945, was declared VJ Day! Word spread rapidly throughout the small town. Sammy revved up the engine of his old pickup and honked loudly on the horn, driving down the alley, picking up every little kid along the way. We all grabbed pots and pans and lids and horns and whistles—any noisemaker we could think of. One and all, we climbed up into the back end of his truck. Sam and Babe in the front seat drove uptown, honking the horn constantly and joining an endless parade of happy citizens in their vehicles. The entire town of Guttenberg was involved in this joyful occasion and very noisily demonstrated their loyal citizenship to the United States of America! Those who were not in vehicles were on the sidewalks of the main street along the river, waving "the red, white, and blue" and triumphantly shouting, "The War is over! It is over! Our soldier boys are coming home!" We all sang this:

> When Johnnie comes marching home again!
> Hoorah! Hoorah!
> The men will cheer, the boys will shout!
> The ladies, they will all turn out!
> We'll all be gay when Johnnie comes marching home!

And the entire town did turn out! People were crying and hugging one another! I shall never forget that day—even if I live to be one hundred years old. The memory of that small town celebration in the summer of 1945 still brings tears to my eyes!

Another close neighbor was Mr. Minger, who lived right next door to the Dorweilers on the south side. Mr. Minger also owned the land directly to the north of our house. He had a big vegetable garden on that land as well as a raspberry patch that ran the entire length from the alley to the railroad tracks. Right after we moved in, he told Mama that she could pick all the berries that she could reach through the fence that separated the two properties. He was a very good neighbor and never complained when we accidentally batted our balls into his garden and one of our big brothers would lift a smaller child over the fence to retrieve it.

That happened a lot because we also had to relocate our baseball diamond to the narrow alleyway in front of the house.

Mama would not let us play down on the corner anymore as she thought that was way too far away for her to keep tabs on us. My brothers soon established home plate to be the center of the road and in a straight line with the North corner of Mr. Dorweiler's garage. First base was the front gatepost. Second base had been located directly opposite Mr. Minger's garden (both first and second bases were flat rocks that always had to be picked up and leaned against our fence whenever a car appeared in the alleyway). Of course every time a vehicle did appear, our games were forced into a time-out, and all players had to line up on one side of the alley until the car was safely out of the way. Third base was located on the southern corner of Dorweiler's garage with pitcher's mound again center alley somewhere between the first and second bases.

It was not exactly an authentic baseball diamond because of its very narrow space, but much more elongated in shape. They always say "Necessity is the mother of invention," and our ball diamond was indeed an example of that. There was a greater distance between home plate and second base than between first and third bases, but that slight problem never dampened our enthusiasm or deterred us from enjoying this sport. We usually went through two or three balls every summer and more often than not we were forced to use homemade bats made out of 2 × 4s from Dad's woodshed or old tree branches.

One summer when money was really tight, Mother Frances (at first) tried to stitch the ripped seams that encircled our tattered and well-worn ball with a heavy-duty thread (actually, she may have used fishing tackle). Of course that did not last long, so she snipped out all the seams and laid the covering out flat. This leather covering was all one piece—it reminded me of a flattened octopus in shape. She then traced this pattern onto a piece of denim and recovered the old ball, hand-stitching the intricate needlework in one continuous circular seam all around the ball. I was very impressed with the handiwork of our mother's talents, but once again am forced to admit that this effort on her part did not buy much more time for that well-worn ball. Once again, it was our Uncle Frank who came to our rescue. The following Sunday he brought his family to visit us, and since Uncle Frank had already purchased a brand new softball for his own children to play with, he told Donny to give their old one (almost like new) to their Spielbauer cousins. Thanks to Uncle Frank, our "ball diamond" in the Alley was back in business!

Let's jump ahead to the basketball season. St. Mary's basketball team was scheduled to play in a tournament in Elkader, Iowa. All the students were excited because we stood a good chance to win—of course, it was already a "gimme" that our brother Joe would be going, as he was a member of the team. The coach would see to his transportation. Many of the parents volunteered to act as driver for those students who had permission to travel to the out-of-town games. It was Rosy's first year in high school. She had never been to an out-of-town game and desperately wanted to attend, as all her classmates were going. She asked Mom for permission.

Mom said, "Ask Dad." Rosy asked Dad.

Dad said, "I don't know. Ask your ma."

Rosy said, "I already did. She said I should ask you. If it's OK with you, it is OK with her."

This was a game our parents played with us all the time. I often think their plan was to drag it out long enough and hopefully, we would eventually give up. But we soon learned that if we patiently continued with this "back and forth" volley of wordplay, they would soon tire of it before we did. Rose hung in there and finally, after much deliberation, Dad said, "Well, Rose, I guess it's OK with me, as long as they bring you all the way back home. But, now hold on here. You can go on only one condition!"

Rose was too excited to really hear what that condition was. Oh yes, she acted as if she was listening, but her mind was already figuring out what she would wear and how exciting it would be to go to a different town and see the game. Papa went on talking, "You see, Rose, your ma is gonna 'be sick,' maybe tonight yet, or sometime early in the morning. I'm probably going to have to wake you in the middle of the night and earlier than usual in the morning. If I call you during the night, I want you to get dressed and run down to Mrs. Ferris's and ask her to come up and help. If I don't call you until the morning, then just get up and start pumping water for the rinse tubs. We have to do the wash tomorrow. You'll just have to stay home from school and help me. If I can count on your help, then you have my permission to go to Elkader!"

Rosy was elated! She rode with her friend Armella Frommelt. There was a whole car full of her classmates who were able to go. Armella's dad, Ray, drove and, of course, brought Rose straight home. The house was quiet and she went straight to bed, trying to remember all the instructions her dad had previously given to her. Just before she dozed off, she wondered to herself, "how does Dad know that Mom's going to be sick?"

Sure enough, in the middle of the night Rose heard her father's voice in the hall just outside her door. "Rose, Rose, it's time to get up. Hurry up. I need your help!" She jumped out of bed, threw on her clothes, grabbed her coat and scarf off the wall hook, and dashed down the stairs with her shoes in hand. Dad was back in the bedroom getting dressed, and Rose glanced out the kitchen window and thought the sun was coming up and that it was early morning. She quickly grabbed two big water buckets and hurried out to the pump and began filling them with water. She had already dumped two buckets into the rinse tubs which had been set out the night before, and was well into the third trip when dad opened the back screen door and hollered out, "Rose, why in the heck are you pumping water in the middle of the night? You're supposed to be getting Mrs. Ferris! Now get on down there and ask her to call Dr. Beyer before she comes. Be sure to wait for her and walk back with her. Now hurry!" Rosy felt really bad for failing to comply with her father's orders. She had mistaken what was now a very obvious full moon for the rising sun. She quickly dropped her buckets of water and did as her father bid and soon both she and Mrs. Ferris returned to the house. Mrs. Ferris went straight into the bedroom and was talking to Mom. Dad said, "You might as well go back to bed now, Rose. Get some sleep. I'll be calling you early in the morning."

Rosy lay awake for a long time, wondering what was wrong with her mom. It must be serious if they needed the doctor in the middle of the night. And really serious if Dad stayed home from work and she had to stay home from school. She started to say the Rosary, when Dr. Beyer's car pulled into the alley and she could now hear muffled conversation going on downstairs. Just as she was ready to doze off, she also heard a new sound—the tiny little cry of a newborn baby! She smiled to herself. So, that's how Dad knew Mom was going to "be sick"!

It seemed she had barely fallen asleep, when once again her father was calling her name. This time my sister knew exactly what to do. Quickly she dressed and dashed down the stairs. She peeked into the bedroom where Mom appeared to be sound asleep. Both Mrs. Ferris and Dad were sitting at the kitchen table, having a cup of coffee. Her dad grinned at her and said, "Come and meet your little brother, Rose! He is the biggest baby your mother ever gave birth to! His name is Thomas!" And in the center of the large kitchen table was the bottom drawer of Mom and Dad's dresser. The drawer had been transformed into a miniature baby crib with a large white-cased pillow serving as a mattress on which lay a beautiful black-haired little boy baby who weighed almost *twelve* pounds on the baby scale! Happy Birthday, Thomas Michael Spielbauer—January 6, 1944!

Mrs. Ferris had already given little Thomas his first bath. As she donned her coat and scarf, she promised Rosy that she would be back later that afternoon to check on Mom and her new little brother. She would also then teach this fifteen-year-old (and now extremely responsible) big sister how to properly bathe a newborn babe.

It was the end of May in this same year that our oldest brother Joe graduated from high school and shortly thereafter enlisted in the Navy. Rose graduated the next spring in 1945. Our brother Arnie, who had been attending the Seminary of The Divine Word in nearby Epworth for the first two years of his high school, had now returned to Guttenberg to continue his education at St. Mary's. Normally this would have taken two more years, but his classes at the seminary had been so much more accelerated that he earned enough credits to graduate after just one more year. He worked as a gandydancer on the railroad during the summer months and was now finishing up his final year of high school.

This next incident happened about a year after Joe had left for basic training in Waukegan, Illinois. The boys' room to the right of the upstairs hall now served as bedroom for all the big brothers—Arnie, Frank, and Larry, and now little John moved into the spot vacated by Joe. This left Danny and Jim on the davenport downstairs and little Tommy in the crib. The girls' room was to the left of the stairs and occupied by all the sisters. Rosy and Hildi shared one double bed and Helen and Celie the other . . .

The house was very quiet. We were all supposed to be sleeping, but the girls could hear the older boys plotting some sort of mischief from across the hall and they too were soon very much involved. "Arnie, you go! You're the biggest one and the only one who can handle it," said Rosy. "No, no! Let Frankie do it. He knows exactly where the creaky steps are. He'll be more quiet," Hildi advised.

"Frankie's too little. He'll drop the cookies," Helen spoke critically. "I will *not*!" Frank insisted. "I'll go! I'll go!" chimed in freckle-faced little Larry, as usual more than eager to be a part of whatever mischief was brewing.

"You guys, listen—just let Frank do it. He's more experienced. He does it all the time," said Hildi knowingly. "Yeah! I can do it better than any of you guys! I've been sneaking down for a week at least, and Mom and Dad don't have a clue!" Frank proudly boasted of his previous success. And then another voice was heard; this time little Celie cautioned all of us, "I don't think we should be stealing cookies. That is very naughty!" Our little sister never indulged in naughty behavior.

"Well, Frank," pursued Helen relentlessly and testily, "Are you sure you can carry eight cookies at one time? You'd better not drop them. For sure, Ma will hear!"

"I want a cookie," whined little John as he rubbed the sleep out of his eyes. All this arguing had awakened the youngest child, who was not yet used to all the clandestine activity of the upper level. The older kids smiled tolerantly at his babyhood as Rose put her arm around his shoulders and cautioned him with "Shush, Johnny! In just a minute."

"I'm going," whispered Frank. "I'll show you guys!" He was already two steps down the stairway that separated the two rooms when he said, "You guys just be quiet now and turn out the lights!" He was not to be detained with petty arguing any longer. We all scurried back to our rooms, doused the lights, and kept our silence.

Frankie proceeded down the staircase. He was confident in his knowledge that he knew exactly where and when and how to avoid those creaky areas. He hugged the wall on the far side of our parents' bedroom. He thought he heard something and stopped instantly. He did not dare to breathe! He was very nervous as he approached his destination—the pantry at the foot of the stairs to the left, directly opposite Mom and Dad's sleeping quarters. This pantry was where Mom had hidden (at least this particular year—for she was forced to select a new hiding spot every Christmas) her special date-filled cookies, which by now had become a family tradition. Frank knew he was one step away from the third step at the bottom. This was the noisiest one. There was only one small spot where he could place his foot that wouldn't give him away. He had to feel for it, but then quickly decided to avoid it totally. Luckily he made it—one—and then, one more and he was inside the pantry! Whew! He breathed a deep sigh of relief!

Now for the tricky part: he dare not turn the light on—that would be a dead giveaway. But he knew exactly where the cookie crock was on the highest shelf, which he was unable to reach. Not a problem, as he knew that he was standing just in front of a big cardboard box stacked to the brim with the old magazines that Aunt Louise always saved for our family to read. This now served as a handy footstool for Frank to complete his mission. He easily found it with his foot and was standing on top of the magazines that provided secure footage as he burglarized Mama's cookie stash!

Our brother worked well in the dark. He secretly prided himself on his own ingenuity as he began counting cookies and placing them into the little pouch that he had formed out of the tails of his pajama shirt. He grinned as he recalled that Helen had claimed that "he couldn't do it." I'll show her, he thought.

Suddenly he sensed a something—or a "someone"! It was an ominous presence! Right here—in the pantry—with him! He did not move a muscle—he could not! He didn't even breathe—he could not! He froze! It was darker than a grave in here. Something brushed across his hair. That hair was now standing straight upright in fear! A hand touched his face and traveled downward attempting to identify the object of its contact. Suddenly, that hand reached up and yanked on his hair! Curses! There was no escape! The light flashed on!

"It" was Dad! He viewed the entire scene in one swift glance—the cookies stashed in Frankie's shirt pouch and the guilty look written all over his son's face, shining so frightfully in the young boy's eyes! Frank had blown it! He had been caught red-handed! "What do you think you're doing?" whispered our father.

The boy stuttered and stammered. "J-j-just st-stealing a couple of cookies," he shamefully whispered back. "Well, you must not be able to count very well," Dad shook his head in disgust. "Looks like more than a 'couple' to me."

"Well, just one of 'em is for me. The rest are for the kids upstairs. We're all still awake." After all, our brother was not exactly a superhero—if he was going down in shame, rather than glory, he definitely was not going to go alone! "Well, son," drawled our father, silently suppressing a chuckle, "Don't you know it's a sin to steal?"

"Yeah, I do," admitted Frank with a great deal of embarrassment. He knew he was gonna get it, for sure. "Next time," Dad continued, "Don't 'steal' the cookies. If you want a cookie, why not just *take* it—that way it won't be stealing, and you won't be committing a sin. Now, here," Dad's hand reached into the cookie jar, "How many more do you need?" Frank held up two fingers. Dad grabbed a whole handful of cookies, dropped two of them into Frank's shirt tail, and once again cautioned his young son, "Now get back up those stairs before your ma wakes up, or we're both gonna be in big trouble!" With that last bit of admonishment, Dad turned and left the room, but not before Frank noticed that his Father had "taken" more than one cookie for his own consumption!

Our brother breathed a sigh of relief as he quietly slipped back up the stair, once again sidestepping that telltale step third from the bottom. He hastily delivered one cookie to the bedside of each of his siblings. There were a few whispered messages of "Thank you" as he softly crept back to his own bed. Then began the silent sound of crunching and munching as all the children happily and hungrily indulged in their midnight snack—that "taken" as opposed to "stolen" booty. When we learned a lesson, we learned it well, and surely there is a lesson in this story—I should like to think!

Kathy was living in Dubuque with Rita Leppert (Aunt Martha and Uncle Pete's oldest daughter. Rita's husband was in the service during this time, so Kathy and Rita shared a small apartment together. Our oldest sister would often come home on weekends and spend time with the family. On one of these Sundays the Hutters drove up from Dubuque and took Mom, Dad, and Kathy to Garnavillo to visit with Aunt Irene and Uncle Frank for the day. They were sitting on the front porch of the farmhouse, sipping on a glass of lemonade when someone noticed an automobile coming up the lane. It pulled into the Rohner yard and out stepped a tall, handsome young Soldier boy in uniform. At first glance, no one recognized him, but then, Aunt Irene said, "Why, Frank, I know who that is. That's that Lowell Eilers. Don't you remember him? He used to work for Johnny Auer and they came over and helped us with the threshing. He was such a nice young man!" She jumped up and waved invitingly to the young soldier. Then she turned to our oldest sister and said, "You ought to know him, Kathy! Don't you remember him? Why, you even went out with him a few times, as I recall. Now, didn't you?"

Kathy suddenly turned very shy and felt her face flush as her heart began a crazy fluttering deep inside. She gave the young man a great big beautiful smile, and his eyes lit up as he took her hand and would not let go. He spoke, "Hello, Kathleen! I didn't expect you to be here. It's been a long time! It's good to see you again. How have you been?" He let go of her hand just long enough to shake hands with all the grown-ups, most of whom he had met before, and then sat down beside Kathy on the front steps where they began to get reacquainted. She was a little disappointed when Uncle Arnie looked at his watch and announced that they had better be "heading on back down the road." They all made their good-byes and Lowell walked with her out to the car. He then asked Kathy if he could come and see her in Dubuque the following weekend. She agreed. Thus began their courtship. It is true that she and Lowell had been on friendly terms prior to his enlistment. But, as is often the case, the young couple had sort of drifted apart during the time that he was in the Army. Lowell was discharged the following October, and once again went to visit Kathy in Dubuque. Rita's husband Ray Leppert had also recently arrived home and the two couples went to East Dubuque to celebrate his homecoming.

Lowell proposed to Kathy during the floor show! Just as Lowell popped the big question, she heard the MC saying, "I have no idea what those young people at the table with the two soldiers are talking about, but they are most certainly not paying any attention to me!" Everyone in the audience began to laugh and look toward the two couples. In all the commotion, Kathy found herself turning to her boyfriend and answering, "Oh my god! Yes! Yes!" Then, Lowell kissed her in front of the whole room.

Ray stood up and announced to the entire audience that both he and Lowell had just been mustered out of the Army and this was the first time he and his wife Rita had been out together in two years. "My buddy just asked his girlfriend to marry him and she said, 'yes'!" Everyone clapped. The MC came to their table and shook hands, and the whole room full of people followed suit, extending their congratulations to the young couple! Even the bartender brought them a round of "drinks on the house"!

Lowell picked up Kathy early the following morning. He took her to a jewelry store in Dubuque and bought her an engagement ring. Then they went home to Guttenberg to tell her family of their "soon-to-be" wedding plans. Kathy was the center of attention that day as her family and friends admired her beautiful ring and wished her joy and happiness. That Saturday night, she and Lowell went out with their close friends, Bob and Jean Parker. When she came home rather late, Dad got up and stuck his head into the kitchen, "Kathleen, wait up a bit, I'm gonna throw some clothes on and I'll be right out. I want to talk to you!"

Surely, Kathy thought to herself, he's not going to "scold" me for coming home so late, certainly not when I am already engaged. But she waited. He came out and put his arm around her (something he had not done in many years) and spoke gently to her, "I just need to ask you one thing, Kathy. Are you sure that this is what you really want? Marriage is a very serious commitment. Are you sure this is the man you want to spend the rest of your life with?"

Our sister responded with a very affirmative "Yes, Dad, Lowell is the man I want to marry." Dad smiled at her and said, "Then, it is fine with me. That is all I need to hear!" The very next day, they began to make the wedding arrangements. They both wanted to keep the wedding small—just family and close friends. The date was set for January 7, 1946, in St. Mary's Catholic Church, with Father Dupont officiating. Of course, Kathy had already told Rosy she wanted her to be the bridesmaid. Lowell decided to ask Butch (Eugene) Kann to serve as his best man. Mom and Dad offered to have their reception at our house, which is what Kathy really wanted. Kathy continued with her job in Dubuque and planned to quit a week before the wedding. Lowell was again working as a hired hand for Johnny Auer, who lived on a neighboring farm next to Uncle Frank's in Garnavillo. Once they got married, the couple was going to move back to Guttenberg and live in a very small apartment in a house owned by Lowell's mother located directly across the street from St. Mary's Grade School, right next to the railroad tracks. The next few months went by very quickly—actually too quickly.

One day in mid December, Dad was waiting for Kathy as she came out from her job at the Box Factory. She knew right away that something was wrong but could not imagine what it was. He informed her that Mom was pregnant again and she had been having a lot of problems with this pregnancy. The doctor had told them she would have to be completely off her feet and remain bedridden for the next few weeks. "Since you are going to be quitting this job in another couple of weeks anyway, I was wondering if you couldn't quit now and come home and take care of the family while your ma is laid up." He really hated to ask this of her, Kathy knew. Of course, she could not refuse him, and assured her father that he could count on her. She promised she'd give notice tomorrow and would plan to return home this coming weekend. Dad gave her a parting hug and thanked her immensely: "It's a big load off my mind, Kathleen. You're a good girl—I knew I could count on you, and your ma'll be pleased. I'd better get back to the car—the men are anxious to get home."

True to her word, Kathy did come home to Guttenberg the following weekend. She already had bought her wedding dress. She and Rose had gone on a shopping trip to Dubuque several weeks ago. Rose also had purchased a blue bridesmaid dress. My sister's bridal dress was of white tulle with a satin underlay on the bodice. Of course, Kathy's artistic eye prompted her to add her own personal touch to the already beautiful gown. She decided to add a satin skirt lining between the tulle layer and the slip. The shiny satin was visible through the tulle. It was beautiful. She also made her own veil out of tulle. Lowell bought a new suit for the occasion as well as one for his best man. Butch Kann too had recently been discharged and was as yet unemployed, so Lowell graciously paid for his suit. Lowell's mother had volunteered to bring the wedding cake all the way from Chicago, where she lived with her second husband. Everything seemed to be falling into place.

About three days had passed since Kathy's return, and Mom ended up having a miscarriage. The doctor insisted she remain in bed for at least another week, so this left Kathy not only doing the daily cooking, washing, and ironing but a lot of deep and thorough housecleaning as well. Lowell would come down from Garnavillo every evening to see her, and always saw his soon-to-be bride slaving over the ironing board. He was appalled at the sight of the endless stack of ironing that she had to do. It's a good thing that he was working during the day, and of course, never saw that she also washed all of that clothing, as well. Kathy put her younger sisters to work as best she could. Rosy was working at The Button Factory and living in her own apartment, but she returned to the house in the evenings and on weekends to help with the cleaning. The last week before the big day, Mom received permission from Dr. Beyer to "get out of bed, now" and cautioned her to do "light work" only. So, the planning and preparation of the food had begun. Close friends and neighbor ladies volunteered their services and specialty dishes to the reception. Ma Jaeger, who was the absolute "*queen* of fried chicken" (and she raised her own), informed my sister that she planned on not only providing five chickens for the reception—but butchering, dressing, and frying them in her home the morning of the wedding as well. She would also deliver them to the house for the reception. "This will be my wedding present to you and Lowell," she told Kathy. "Why, you're just like one of my own kids!"

The wedding itself went wonderfully well and was a very happy occasion for everyone! The beautiful bride and the handsome groom exchanged their marriage vows, and Father Dupont introduced Kathy and Lowell to the audience as Mr. and Mrs. Lowell Eilers! As the couple walked down the aisle, the voices of our brother Arnie and his classmate Cyril Elsinger reverently sang "Jesu Bambino," which is actually a Christmas song; however, this particular selection was one of Sister Petrina's (the organist) favorite holiday hymns. As the boys were singing, my friend Evelyn Jaeger and I grabbed hands and ran out of the side door all the way to the big front doors. At the same time, the altar boys (including my brothers Frank and Larry) had run out the opposite side door and were already standing in the church vestibule. Frank and Larry each had a firm grip on a white braided rope that stretched across the center aisle in the last row. It was a tradition for the groom to hand over some ready cash (preferably in bills, rather than small change (thank you very much!) to the young Mass servers in order to "buy" an escape for the newly married couple. Once the boys pocketed this donation, they dropped the rope, and the bride and groom now embraced and kissed one another! True story—I was the witness!

The bridal party walked over to Father Dupont's house to sign the marriage certificate. Father gave them a fraktur as proof of their now legal marriage contract. A fraktur is a very ornate document with calligraphy-style printing certifying to the legality of baptisms, marriages, etc. As I recall, frakturs are historically of a German heritage and are sentimentally valued in German family trees. Marriage frakturs usually depicted Mary and Joseph in a kneeling position before God, as he blesses their union. These documents commonly have gilt edging around the borders. The word *fraktur* actually means "fracture" or a break and describes the lettering on the document. The letters are often broken or in separated segments.

When the wedding group left Father Dupont's house, they drove up to the Main Street in town, to Dahms Studio, where they had an appointment with Mr. Dahms to have their pictures taken. Butch and Rosy climbed into the back seat. The first thing that Butch did was reach under the seat and pull out a flask of whiskey. He smiled at Rosy and took a long sip straight from the bottle. He explained that it was "to steady his nerves" and politely offered it to Rose, who shook her head negatively. This time he stuffed the whiskey bottle into the inside breast pocket of his coat just in case he might find himself in further need of moral support as the day moved on. On the way into the building, the little flask fell out of his pocket. Thankfully, it landed in a mound of slushy snow that was already partially melted and did not break. Now that the official duties of this very nervous best man were over, he fully intended to relax and join in the festivities!

By the time the bride and groom returned to our home, the reception party was in full swing! The house was literally wall to wall with people. Lucille Jaeger had completely taken charge of Mama's kitchen. She ordered her own daughters to act as servers and waitresses, making sure the bowls and platters of food were constantly replenished. She put Helen along with Marcella and Marie Rohner in charge of cleanup duties, seeing that there was a steady supply of clean plates, glasses, coffee cups, and silverware, as the guests came through the food line. Celie and myself, along with Evvie and Marita Jaeger and Betty Ann Rohner, helped the little children carry plates upstairs where most of the kids ate. We had little children sitting on the floor on bed sheets in the girls' room, pretending we were having a January picnic in the park. All the younger brothers and male cousins were in the boys' room across the hall, lying on the beds or the floor on their bellies, spying on the grown-ups through the floor register that allowed the heat from the pot-bellied stove to warm the upstairs.

Both cigarette smoke and music, along with muted conversation and laughter, wafted their way upward as well. As the late afternoon waned into the evening hours, the guests began to diminish in number and the party noises were greatly reduced in volume. The music had been turned down and the voices of the last minute stragglers now subdued into whispers. Babies and toddlers were bedded down for the night and one by one the older children disappeared to their beds.

Sleeping arrangements had been altered for this night only. The newlyweds would be spending their first night in the girls' room. Rosy had already moved into her own apartment. Helen went home with the Rohner family to spend the night, so that just left Celie and myself to share one bed. Each of us was more than determined to stay awake until our sister and her new husband came upstairs. We were both romantic little girls and wanted to watch Lowell put his arms around our sister and kiss her "good night" as all those Hollywood stars did in the movies. Alas, this was not meant to be. By the time the bride and groom climbed the narrow stairs, both of us were "dead to the world."

Kathy and Lowell settled into their little apartment by the school the following day and continued to live in Guttenberg for about another year and a half. We saw a lot of them as they would often come down in the evenings just to visit, and Kathy would bring their laundry to our house and use Mama's washing machine and her iron. They usually joined us for Sunday dinner and Kathy would always bring yummy desserts and salads. She loved to bake and had many new recipes she wanted to try; however, she did not have a stove in her apartment for at least the first four months of their marriage. She had to do all her cooking on a very small hot plate, so whenever she wanted to bake something, she would come to our house and use Mom's oven. On one of these visits, she and Lowell drove down in their car. Kathy asked if she could use the stove and Mom, of course, said yes. Kathy mixed up the cake batter and popped it into the oven. This was in the summertime, and whenever something was baking in the oven, the kitchen became very warm, so everyone moved out onto the front porch. As soon as that chocolate cake was done and properly cooled, Kathy asked me to come back into the kitchen and help her decorate it. She made a white coconut frosting and spread it between the layers and then frosted the top and sides generously. She allowed me to sprinkle more coconut over the top and sides. It was beautiful! And smelled delicious! I said, "Is this for a birthday party?" She responded, "No, we're going to eat it here, right now. Do you want a piece?"

Boy, did I ever! Then, Kathy said, "Well, now that you mention it, I guess you could think of it as a 'birth-day cake!'" Then, she went to the door and called through the screen, "Honey, you can go now. We're about ready in here." Mom came in and said, "Kathy, you guys don't have to leave already, do you?"

"Oh no, not me," replied my sister. "Lowell just has to run an errand. He'll be right back. Come on, Mom. Let's go back out on the porch. It's cooler out there. As soon as Lowell gets back, we'll all have a piece of chocolate coconut cake. We are going to have a party, aren't we, Hildi? Hey, maybe Hildi can make us a pitcher of Kool-Aid if you have any."

Mom nodded toward me with that "go-ahead" look, as they once again exited to the front porch. By the time I finished making the Kool-Aid, Lowell had returned with a half gallon of ice cream from Nigg's grocery store, which was the one closest to our house. Wow! This was going to be a real party with ice cream. Since we only had an icebox to keep our food cold, we were surely going to have to consume that entire carton of ice cream before it melted!

Kathy cut her beautiful chocolate coconut cake. Mom scooped out generous portions of ice cream, and I poured the Kool-Aid. "This is so nice," said my mom. "Do you feel that cool breeze? Isn't it wonderful? We should be celebrating something."

"We are celebrating something," Kathy quickly responded. "This is kind of like a birthday party for someone who is not yet born, but," my sister had tears in her eyes, "he's on his way. Lowell and I are going to have a baby!" *Wow*! You coulda heard a pin drop!

Papa said, "Well, I'll be! I'll be danged!" Mama looked at Kathy and she said, "When?" She too had tears in her eyes. Kathy replied, "In October. And the doctor says everything is just fine. Oh, Mom, we are so excited. Lowell wants a little boy, of course, and so do I."

What we did *not* find out that warm summer evening so many years ago was that my mother was also expecting another child. Her baby wasn't due until December, and she did not want to say anything about it to anyone because she was afraid that she might have another miscarriage. Also, she wanted her firstborn child (daughter) to be able to bask in her own glory, and not have to share the awesome wonder of that most precious first pregnancy with an experienced lady (in this case, her own mother), who would soon be delivering her fourteenth child. I also suspect that my mother was eagerly looking forward to holding her very first grandchild in her arms. Indeed, she was.

On October 12, 1946, early on a Saturday morning, my brother-in-law knocked on the front door. I let him in and he was grinning from ear to ear and proudly announced to everyone that he was a "daddy"! Kathy had given birth to a beautiful, black-haired little boy, Gene Lowell Eilers. How exciting this was for all of us—our very first nephew! We were all aunts and uncles, and George and Frances now had their very first grandchild!

And, just when we thought things could not get any better than this, on one very cold day in December, I bounced down the stair steps earlier than my siblings, as at that time in my life, it was always my job to stoke the fire and start the coffee. Lo and behold! The very first thing I noticed was, once again, the bottom drawer of Mom and Dad's dresser sitting smack dab in the middle of the kitchen table! I immediately knew what that meant. Yes, we too had a new baby in our family. "Uncle" David Spielbauer was born on December 20, 1946. His nephew, Genie (as we now referred to Kathy's little boy), had beaten our brother into this world by a mere two months and eight days.

This time, Mrs. Ferris was unable to come to my mother's assistance—I think her husband was very sick, and she needed to stay home with him. So, Mom had prearranged for Mrs. Adams, who lived on our same block just across the street from the Dorweilers' to come and help. As soon as I came downstairs, she rushed home to fix breakfast for her husband. She assured me that she would be back in about thirty to forty minutes, and if the little kids came down before she returned, either Helen or I would have to fix their breakfast. She already had Tommy in the high chair. "You better feed this little guy first. He's been up for quite a while. I know he must be hungry."

It was a regular school day, and I already heard Helen coming down the stairs. She started setting out bowls and bread for the school kids. Of course, as each of our younger siblings entered the room, they oohed and aahed over their little brother and nobody had any desire to eat breakfast. At last, Mrs. Adams walked in the front door and said, "OK, kids! You have to get to school, so hurry up and eat your breakfast. I am going to give your little brother his first bath. You can all watch, but you better make sure that you are eating at the same time, or you'll all be late for school. Helen, you get that bath water ready." Mrs. Adams rolled up the sleeves of her sweater and went to work. Now, in all honesty I must tell you that I did not see what happened next. I must have been too busy feeding little Tommy. My sister Celie is the one who told me this story:

We were all sitting there watching Mrs. Adams and the little baby, who was not really little. David was a big baby, almost as big as Tommy, but not quite. First, she removed the swaddling blankets from the baby and very carefully held him in one arm, cradling his head in her hand over the basin of soapy water and with a wash rag soaped up his hair, then she gently washed his face. She then held him over another basin of warm water and rinsed his hair. She placed him on the towel, tummy side down and soaped and rinsed his back and legs. Please remember that our little David was bare ass naked! When she turned him over and laid him on his backside (he must have had to "go" really, really bad because), suddenly a stream of fluid arced upward. Mrs. Adams screamed and grabbed for a corner of the towel and hastily covered up his "privates"! "Helen, fetch me a clean cloth and wipe off my glasses," she shouted! All the children began to laugh! Mrs. Adams shook her finger at our little brother and scolded, "Why, you little rascal! Shame on you!" She laughed, too.

Our baby brother was in direct contrast to our little nephew in coloring. Both little boys had what our father described as a "ton of hair"! David had blonde curly tendrils that in about a year or so would darken into a reddish brown hue, whereas Gene had lots of thick black hair, and his eyes had already turned to brown. He was the "spittin' image" (another "dad" description) of his mother. I recall that Celie and I were especially excited with both of these little boys and coddled to their every whim. The two babies often took their naps as they lay side by side in the same crib. They were almost identical in size, and we pretended they were twins.

When Gene was about five months old, Kathy and Lowell made the decision to move to the Chicago area. Lowell's stepfather had been employed by The Chicago-Northwestern Railroad. He told Lowell that one of the Chicago positions would soon be available. Lowell applied for it and was hired. We all felt very sad at their departure and did not want our sister and her family to move so far away, but we soon learned to live with it.

In late August 1949, my parents celebrated their twenty-fifth Silver Wedding Anniversary with a great big bang! All the relatives from both sides of the family, as well as many neighbors and good friends, had been invited. The weather was cooperative—thank goodness—allowing the many guests to spill out onto the front and back porches and the yard itself. Kathy and her family arrived a few days ahead of time and she baked a beautiful tiered anniversary cake for the big day. It, of course, took center stage in the very center of the big kitchen table that was laden with bowls of potato salad, veggie dishes, platters of ham and fried chicken, all kinds of salads, and other desserts. Both of Mom's huge rinse tubs were filled with floating chunks of ice in very cold water that held bottled beer in one and Johnny Pop's soda in the other.

I am really not sure which of my little brothers were involved in this next escapade, but I am thinking that Larry, maybe Frank, and maybe Johnny were in on it or at the very least well aware of what was going on behind the grown-ups' backs. I am also thinking my cousin Gary Hanson was in on this prank, as well.

The adult men of course were all gathered around the tub of ice-cold beer, laughing and joking and catching up on the latest happenings. As each man finished off a bottle of beer, he would place the empty container back into a heavy cardboard case that held twenty-four bottles and then freely helped themselves to the contents of the beer tub.

Unbeknownst to the adult male guests, those "crazy brothers of mine" had taken some of the empty bottles, immersed them into the tub, and refilled them with ice water. They then securely recapped the bottles, slipped them back down into the water, sat back, and patiently waited for their first victim. This first victim turned out to be our Uncle Ed Blaser. He was not a very good sport about it. Uncle Ed took one sip and immediately spat it on the ground. He was *not* a bit happy. He did not think it was the least bit funny! "What the hell, George," he shouted! "What kind of 'rotgut booze' is this?" He handed the bottle to my dad. "Go on, you taste it! Something is wrong with it." By this time everyone was laughing. My brothers and Gary were all hiding behind the trees in hysterics.

Dad tasted the beer. "Those damn kids must be up to no good, again!" He dumped the water out, searched through the tub, grabbed another bottle, and opened it for Uncle Ed. "Here, try this one, Ed. See if that's any better." Our angry uncle hesitantly took a small sip and nodded his head in satisfaction. He started to say more to my dad, but Dad had already left the circle of men and had rounded up all of my little brothers along with Gary. He had them over by the rabbit hutches, obviously giving them (yet another) one of his "how-to-behave" parental lectures! The next victim of the "water beer" was our brother-in-law, Lowell. As soon as he popped the lid, Lowell didn't think it sounded right. He sniffed at the contents, then looked over at the boys. Of course all eyes were on him, except dad's, who now had his back turned as he talked with Uncle Pete. Lowell cautiously took a sip from the bottle, grinned at the boys, then went behind the tree and dumped the contents onto the ground. He helped himself to another fresh bottle and placed his finger to his lip to indicate silence on his part. Lowell was a good sport!

I remember that all of Dad's sisters (Martha, Louise, Edwina, and Tootsie) went together and gave my parents a brand new beautiful bedspread for an anniversary present. They didn't bother to wrap it. They waited until our mother had gone out into the backyard, where everyone was taking pictures. They took pictures of Mom and Dad and all of the children; four-generation pictures of Grandma Spielbauer, Dad, Kathy, and little Genie; and also one of Grandma, Dad, Rosy, and her little Dean. During this time, Aunt Tootsie motioned for me to come with her into the house. She asked me to help her take the old patchwork quilt off of Mom and Dad's bed. We folded it up and laid it on the cedar chest. Then the two of us carefully remade Mama's bed with the new coverlet, gently smoothing out the top. It was a beautiful dusty rose color with deeper rose flowers at the top part where the spread lay over the pillows, and again all around the border on the skirt part that hung clear to the floor. Never before did my mother ever have a bedspread on the bed. She always just made due with homemade quilts. This was truly beautiful!

Aunt Tootsie told me to go outside and call my mother to the house. She stood on the back porch and motioned for the rest of her sisters to come in. All four of them were standing around the bed. "Happy Anniversary," they shouted to my mom as she walked into the room. I know she loved it, because she had tears in her eyes. But Mother was happiest over the fact that her favorite nephew, Eddie Blaser, and his wife, Leota, had traveled all the way from California to attend their anniversary party! That was the highlight of her party as far as she was concerned.

At the time of this party, our grandmother Mary Spielbauer was eighty years old and now living with Aunt Martha and Uncle Pete in Dubuque. She had four daughters—Martha (Peter Duehr), Edwina (Ed Blaser), Louise (Arnie Hutter), and Bernice (Larry Hanson). We of course always called Bernice Aunt Tootsie. Grandma also had two sons—our father, George, and John, whom we knew as Uncle Jack. Uncle Jack had been married to Marie Schmidt. Shortly after the birth of their only child, Marie passed away. At this point in time, Uncle Jack moved back into his mother's home with his little tiny daughter, Velma. From that time on, Grandma Mary served as both mother and grandmother to this child. When Velma was fifteen years old, her father was involved in a terrible train accident that took his life.

The accident occurred on a Saturday night, and I don't know exactly how my father was informed of his brother's death, but I do remember coming home from Sunday Mass and seeing my father standing in the kitchen with tears running down his face. I also remember my whole family kneeling around the bed in our parents' bedroom that evening as we prayed the Rosary together for "the repose of our uncle's soul." Papa led the prayers.

My parents were the only ones in our family who were able to attend his funeral because of transportation. Mom said it was very sad for everyone. He was given a Military service because he had served in the Army during the war. When the officer presented the American flag to his now orphaned, fifteen-year-old daughter, everyone in the church was crying. Years later, my cousin Velma told me more details of the funeral that I never knew before. As all the cars were lining up for the funeral procession headed for the church, the Funeral Director took both Grandma and Velma into the room where Uncle Jack's casket was. He closed the door behind him and led them to the casket for a final good-bye. When the accident had happened, one of Uncle Jack's hands and part of one lower limb had been severed from his body. They brought them back to the funeral home and had carefully wrapped them in something like freezer paper and kept them in the freezer. He wanted both the mother and the child to know that the severed parts of their loved one were placed alongside his body and would be buried along with him. This was comforting to both of them.

Shortly after Uncle Jack's death, Gram and Velma moved in with Aunt Martha and her family. Martha's youngest daughter, Ginny, was the only one still living at home. She was very close to Velma in age. These two cousins were already good friends and soon became as close as sisters. It is interesting to note here that one day they actually would know each other as sisters-in-law. Velma married Jim Hoppman and Ginny married Jim's brother, Lloyd.

Our dear little "black" grandmother passed away in October 1949. Her funeral Mass was held at the Immaculate Conception Church in Buenie, and she was laid to rest beside her husband's grave in the cemetery located at the top of the hill behind the church. I do recall being at the church services. But my brother Frank and I had to remain at the church instead of going to the cemetery. There were several older lady friends of our grandma who wanted to ride out to the cemetery. I don't know who they were but they came to us later and thanked Frankie and me for being such "good kids." My younger brother Larry did manage to get into one of the first cars behind the hearse and recalls that part way up the hill, the hearse got stuck in the still wet and muddy gravel road (due to a recent rainstorm). About six or seven men in suits and ties, white shirts and shiny shoes had to get out and actually push the hearse to the top of the hill. This cemetery is located high on the hill overlooking a beautiful view of the Mississippi River Valley far below.

Many years later, both my Aunt Louise and my cousin, now Velma Hoppman, had gone to this same cemetery to visit the gravesites of our family. The tombstones of our grandparents (Joseph and Mary Spielbauer) and those of Velma's parents (John (Jack) and Marie Spielbauer) had begun to show signs of deterioration. Aunt Louise immediately ordered new stones for our grandparents' graves, and Velma replaced the tombstones on her mother and father's gravesites.

The next few years saw many changes in our own family. Rosy was now married to Earl Schultz (a Guttenberg native) and had already given birth to her first son, Dean. They lived in a small apartment on the north side of town over on the hill. As soon as Arnie was old enough, he enlisted in the Navy at just about the same time that our brother Joe was discharged. Joe got a job in Dubuque, working at the same factory as our father. He continued to live at home and commuted back and forth with Dad and his buddies until he had saved enough money to purchase his own car. Shortly thereafter, he met his future wife, Delores Wilker, who lived up around Volga, Iowa. They were married in The Rectory of the Sacred Heart Catholic Church in Volga, Iowa, on May 8, 1950. This was a private ceremony witnessed by our sister Helen and Delores's brother, William Wilker. Her mother and father hosted a small reception for the newlyweds at their farmhouse near Volga. It was an evening reception—just the family members of the bride and groom and also our Uncle Frank and Aunt Irene. Uncle Frank came to Guttenberg and picked up Mom and Dad, Helen, Frankie, and myself because we did not have a car.

Just as the sun began to set and twilight dusk settled into early evening, the until now quiet reception was interrupted by loud honking horns and other noises. A steady stream of vehicles—automobiles, pickup trucks, and even a tractor rolled down the lane and pulled into the Wilker farmyard. What had begun as a very small private gathering soon developed into a full-blown country jamboree. These "party crashers" turned out to be friends and neighbors of the Wilker family who lived in the surrounding community. They had come to congratulate the bride and groom. Men, women, and children convened in the frontyard, armed with pots and pans and lids, dinner bells, cow bells, and even wash boards and horns—anything that made a lot of noise. They had come to shivaree my brother and his new bride! They shouted, "Joe and Delores! Joe and Delores!"

The bride and the groom shyly came outside to greet their uninvited guests, who presented the newlyweds with an envelope of money as a token of their friendship and gave their best wishes! The shivaree, even back in 1950, was a form of celebration that had already seen its better days, and today, it is practically extinct. I was fifteen years old at that time, and it was the very first time in my life that I had the experience of participating in one—as well as my last! I am so glad I did not miss that experience.

Our brother Arnie met and married his bride, Laurie (Delores) Seib while still in the service. They continued to live in Illinois (Waukegan area) after his discharge. Our sister Helen worked at The Button Factory in Guttenberg after her graduation and she remained at home until she married Don Bolsinger from Colesburg. Don and Helen resided in Guttenberg for a few more years and eventually moved back to Colesburg to work on his dad's farmstead. Our older brothers and sisters were leaving us, and sadly, our once very large family was becoming smaller and smaller, unless one can count the ever growing number of little grandbabies that were now steadily increasing our fold.

My brother Frank was a junior in high school when I became a freshman. He was an outstanding basketball player and truly loved the game. He was always trying to convince our dad that we "needed" a place to play basketball in our own yard. He suggested that we make Dad's garden a little smaller on the alley side and put the poles up right in the center. My brother's dream finally became a reality. He at last gained permission from our father. The boys bought two very long poles from Livingston's Lumber Company and began to dig very deep holes about four feet apart. Dad actually helped them with this project and made a homemade backboard on which the hoop would be attached. Most of the time, as I recall, this hoop did not even have a net.

Now even the sisters joined in the family basketball games. Frank became our "coach" and taught us all how to play the game. Our yard soon turned into a playground for all the neighborhood kids for blocks around. Mom was happy about it because it kept her own kids at home, where she could easily keep an eye on them. And she never minded the extra kids hanging about. These neighbor boys continued to play basketball even during our mealtimes. Our brothers would rush to the table, gobble their food down dash back outside, and get right back in the game. They even played basketball in the winter months with snow on the ground. They didn't mind in the least shoveling the snow off their so-called basketball court.

As soon as Frank graduated, he enlisted in the Air Force. In September of that year, Larry became a freshman. During my senior year at St. Mary's, both Larry and I had part-time jobs. I worked for Charles Millham at The Guttenberg Press, and Larry was employed at Fukey's Gas Station. In 1952, there were three Spielbauer kids in our high school at the same time—Celie as a freshman, Larry now a sophomore, and me a senior. That's enough to frighten any teacher! Following my graduation in early June, I went to work for the Button Factory. This was, at that time and still is, the job I disliked most. Fortunately, I did not have to tolerate it for very long, because Sammy Meyers came to my rescue. He offered me a "girl Friday" job at Meyers Electric.

Of course, I jumped at the opportunity. Sammy and Babe had always been my friends. And I loved working for him.

I had only been working there about one month and decided that I would like to buy my mother a brand new refrigerator. Up to this point, we were still using nothing but the old icebox which was extremely archaic, even back in 1952! Sammy gave me a good discount off the original purchase price of a Frigidaire floor model that he'd had for some time. Frank Fukey, Larry's boss, also owned an appliance shop that offered only gas appliances for sale. Larry and I often had friendly arguments going on between us as to which of these services was most efficient—gas or electric. He also decided that he would buy our mom a brand new gas stove from his boss. Larry selected a Roper Dri-gas model for his gift to Mom. Mr. and Mrs. Fukey lived right across the street from Sammy and Babe. Even though the two appliance dealers were competitors in the business world, they were very good friends as well. We worked out an agreement with both of our bosses to deliver the stove and the refrigerator on the very same day, almost at the same time. Our mother was in seventh heaven! Welcome to the modern world, Mom! My Dad liked the convenience of the new refrigerator almost as much as did Mom, especially when Sammy told him, "Now, George, the bottom shelf in the refrigerator always belongs to the 'man of the house'! It is 'off-limits' to everyone else in the family. That shelf is strictly for the man's beer supply!"

Sammy and Babe were very good to me, but after about four years, I decided to move to Cedar Rapids with Alice Tujetsch—both of us worked for the same company, in the same department at The Cryovac Corporation. We had the same friends and the same bosses. And we had a lot of fun! I must admit I was a little "homesick" at first and missed my little brothers and baby sister. We came home almost every weekend, and I continued to do Sammy's bookwork and what little typing there was on Saturday mornings. Eventually, Sammy closed his appliance business and went into a semiretirement. He still did electrical wiring and repair work out of his home on a limited basis.

On a Sunday evening, just one week before Larry's HS graduation (Class of '54), he was involved in a very bad auto accident. His best friend, Eddie Lowell, had, after much coaxing, received permission to use his dad's car for the evening. Their initial plan was to attend the movie in town, but either they had already seen it or it did not appeal to them, so they decided to drive up to Elkader. They had already seen that one, as well. They drove around for a while, cruisin' the downtown area and ran into our brother Frank and a couple of his buddies who were up to the very same thing—just "messin' around." Eddie and Larry headed south toward Guttenberg, and just a little way north of The Ceres Church the accident happened! There was a spot in the road where the highway makes a very sharp turn to the left and almost another immediate sharp curve to the right.

They came face to face with another vehicle that had lost control as it came around the curve and crossed over the centerline. Eddie's car collided head on! Larry on the passenger side was thrown right through the windshield and received a multitude of cuts and gashes on his face and head. Eddie's hands were both gripped in a deadlock on both sides of the steering wheel. Another vehicle was close behind Eddie's car. They did not actually see the accident happen, but helped the boys into their vehicle and took them straight into town to the hospital. There were two men in the oncoming car, but no one seems to know who they were or where they came from. Larry seems to think they were also taken to the hospital but were then transferred to a hospital in Dubuque. His also thinks one of them might have died a few days later but never did find out anymore information. Eddie was kept overnight and released the next day. Dr. Goddard had contacted a surgeon from Dubuque, and he came up that same night. He worked over him a long time and Larry ended up with over two hundred stitches on his face and head alone.

It just happened that Frank and his buddies were about ten minutes behind Eddie and Larry. When they came upon the scene of the accident, they recognized the car immediately and drove straight to the hospital. About this time, I was walking home from the theater with Germaine and Arlene Hoeger, and we noticed a large crowd in front of the hospital. Someone broke out of the group and said, "Hilda, your brother's in there. He's been in a bad accident!"

"Which one?" I waited just long enough to hear her say, "Larry" and ran into the hospital, breaking my way through the crowd. A nurse stopped me just as soon as I got inside and told me to leave. "But, I came to see my brother. Is he OK? I *have* to see him!" I never would have gotten by her, if it hadn't been for Betty Nieland, who was also a nurse.

Betty recognized me and said, "It's OK. Let her come in. She is his sister." She turned to me and continued, "Larry is sitting up and he is OK. You can talk to him a bit, but don't wear him out. We have a doctor coming from Dubuque. Larry is going to need some stitches—quite a few of them." She opened another door and took me inside. My brother was sitting upright in an examining chair. His eyes were tightly shut and his face was bleeding badly. I began to cry.

"Now, don't start up with that cry-baby stuff," he scolded! Just then, the door opened again and Dad walked in. He took one look at Larry, turned to me, and said, "You need to get out of here. Your ma's on her way. Stop her at the front door and don't let her in here. She can't see him like this. She'll be hysterical! You have got to keep her out, understand!"

I returned to the waiting room, and my mother was already shoving her way through the crowd. When push comes to shove, my mother can be quite aggressive. I knew there was no way I could have stopped her from entering that room by myself. But the same nurse who had denied my entrance was still on duty and she was a bigger lady than my mother. A few minutes later, Frank walked in the front door and Dad came out of the examining room, almost at the same time. The surgeon from Dubuque had arrived, and they were now taking Larry to surgery. Dad tried to talk Mom into going home, but of course she refused. So he then gave me strict orders to go straight home and help Celie with the younger kids. It's a good thing I did. Everyone was so worried about our brother. We actually knelt down and prayed the Rosary.

My brother remained in the hospital for that whole week. I know my parents and all of us worried over his vision. Of course his face was always swathed in bandages that covered his eyes, so he couldn't even open them. He later confided in me that he had really been afraid to open his eyes at that time, because he did not want to face the possibility of not being able to see.

Needless to say, there were a lot of prayers that following week. About the fifth day out of surgery, the bandages were removed, and my brother was given a thorough visual examination. He could see! Our mother cried with relief! He was temporarily released from the hospital on Sunday late afternoon and marched down the aisle of St. Mary's Church that evening at the graduation service, donned in his cap and gown and received his high school diploma with the rest of his classmates. After the services and a short graduation celebration at our house, he had to return to the hospital for about another week.

Larry also chose to enlist in the Air Force right after his graduation. This left only Celie and the little brothers now at home. One of the last things my little sister did before she graduated from St. Mary's was to give all five of the younger boys a "how-to-do" lesson—how to do the dirty dishes. Up until now there had been enough sisters to handle this task—well, now you know who inherited that most dreadful household chore! Of course, they grumbled and griped about it, as any teenager would do, but eventually the boys proved that they too were very capable of performing this otherwise feminine task. They loved to play "snap the dish towel" at each other and, of course, invented lots of water splash and spray games behind our mother's back. As you can well imagine, these little brothers were every bit as full of mischief as their older siblings had been—and then, some!

Actually, I sort of hold my brother Frank somewhat responsible for this next misdemeanor that was committed by the now famous Spielbauer "gang of little hoodlums," as my mother often called them. As soon as we had moved into the Alley house, Frank discovered that he could readily gain access to the roof of the woodshed at the back of the yard. This roof slanted downward to the tracks and was not at all visible from our house or yard. Conveniently, there just happened to be a fence post located right next to the back corner of the shed—part of Mr. Minger's garden fence. This post served as a stepping-stone to the rooftop. Even I ("fraidy cat" that I was, and still very fearful of heights) managed to get on top of that roof now and then. Frank would sneak up to the roof with his BB gun, entice the rats and the sparrows by putting some kind of bait out, and as soon as whatever animal approached the bait, Frank fired away.

Of course, you all remember that our brother had the reputation of being an expert sharpshooter and never missed his target. The sparrows (he called them "spatzies") dropped to the ground like flies, whereas those tough-skinned rats barely flinched upon impact and the tiny BB shot just bounced right off their backsides.

It goes without saying that Frank passed his knowledge and pursuit of this particular sport on down the line to each of his little brothers in turn. My brothers and the McGuine boys were good friends and partners in crime on many occasions. Of course, they were all very adept at reaching that rooftop, and since it was practically invisible, it was the perfect spot to experiment with smoking! Mama would never know! Mrs. McGuine would never know! Grandma Sassen would never know! Mama could not see the slanted backside of the roof. Mrs. McGuine and Grandma Sassen could not see because the trees around their yard cut off the view. It was foolproof. Finding the cigarettes would be no problem. By now, George was buying them in packages and cartons and if, by happenstance, an occasional cigarette came up missing, he probably would not ever notice. And maybe Digger and Kenny could find a few more. I really don't know where the cigarettes came from, but this little gang of hoodlums for a long time thought they had it made!

One evening after supper, Dad made Danny help him dig potatoes in the garden and brought up the subject of cigarettes. "Danny, I've been missing cigarettes from my packs lately and I was wondering if you've seen anybody taking them?" Of course, Danny knew nothing about this. He had never seen anybody take any, and for sure, he would never do such a thing. "Well, keep your eyes open and let me know if you ever see or hear anything," our father warned. The illegal smoking ceased for a few days. And nothing more was said. But these boys weren't smart enough to quit while they were ahead of the game. And within a week or so, the whole gang was once again indulging in their illicit activity!

This time, Dad talked to all of them. "I know that you boys have been climbing up on the roof of the woodshed where your ma can't see you—you and the McGuine boys. You have been sittin' up there like a bunch of dumb pigeons passing the cigarette butts back and forth. You think you're pulling a fast one, but I got news for you. Now, you all better listen to me," pointing his finger at Johnny, Danny, Jimmy, and even Tommy. David was too young to be a suspect. Dad continued admonishing them. "First of all, you are much too young to be smoking. Secondly, you could accidentally burn down my shed, and worse yet, one or all of you kids could be burnt badly! And don't be trying to lie out of it! I know you are involved! And I want it stopped right now. You have been seen and I have been missing cigarettes. I know that you are all guilty! There will be *hell* to pay if you try it again! That's it for now!"

The brothers never could figure out who "ratted" on them. It wasn't until years later that they found out. The owner of that "long arm of the law" who had turned them into the authority (namely, our dad) was none other than kind, old Grandpa Sassen. Mr. Sassen always worked in his cornfield in the early morning before it got steamy hot and often spotted his own grandsons and those Spielbauer boys perched on the roof "like dumb pigeons" (his description) puffing away to their hearts' content. He did not want to turn his own flesh and blood in, but knew it had to be called to a halt. He also knew our father would put an immediate stop to the problem. I have no way of knowing if my little brothers ever indulged in their "smoking habit" again. I strongly suspect they have. If so, they must have found a different location, and for sure, they made certain that Grandpa Sassen and Papa George never knew about it.

The McGuine family somehow inherited a parrot that was named Sammy. Not only was Sammy a very colorful bird, but a most colorful character, as well. It was the very first time in my life that I had ever seen a real live parrot and I was truly fascinated by him, especially when he looked right at me and clearly spoke, "Polly wants a cracker!" Mrs. Sassen handed me a soda cracker and urged me to hold it by the corner and slide it into the cage. The parrot immediately grabbed it with his beak and gobbled it up. Sammy was always "running off at the mouth" and had quite an extensive repertoire of phrases to his credit. He especially loved to perform right around bedtime. As soon as the sun went down and the moon came up, it was "show time" for Sammy! We always kept our bedroom windows wide open during the hot summer months and were often entertained by Sammy's raucous and rather colorful vocabulary. Grandma Sassen often threatened to "wash his mouth out with soap," if he didn't clean up his act. Sammy would act very contrite and plead with her, "No-o, Grra-maw! No-o, Grra-maw!" Sammy also loved to shout out a series of "Good-nights!" to everyone in the neighborhood.

My brother John tells me of a situation wherein Mr. McGuine became very angry at the loud-mouthed Sammy and literally kicked him out of the house just so he could get some sleep. I believe Mr. McGuine at this time was working the night shift at The Lock and Dam and, therefore, had to catch his shut eye during the daytime hours. After many attempts to silence the bird, Mr. McGuine got out of bed, stormed into the kitchen, and grabbed Sammy, birdcage, and all. He then stomped outdoors in his bare feet—clad only in his underwear—tromped clear out into Grandpa Sassen's cornfield that was almost half a block from his house, and plopped the cage on the ground behind the shed. "Now, you stupid blankety-blank-blank bird, go ahead and talk—talk a blue-streak, if you want! You can talk to the 'coons' for all I care! But you're *not* keeping me awake any longer!" Sammy yelled for "Grra-maw!" to come and save him. Alas, nobody heard him. Sammy's voice was very hoarse most of the next day, and he was unusually silent. Grandma Sassen wondered if the "poor parrot might be sick." Her son-in-law responded, "Well, if he ain't sick yet, he sure is gonna be! I know I am damn sick of him!" I think, eventually, Mr. McGuine totally banished

Sammy from the household, and poor Sammy was forced to seek shelter with Grandma Sassen right next door.

Sammy even got the best of our own Mother one day. And trust me, getting the best of Mother Frances was quite an accomplishment, indeed! Our youngest brother, David, was probably around six months old and Mom had put him in the crib for an afternoon nap. Tommy had already fallen asleep on the davenport. She needed to go over to the garden on Mr. Sassen's land and pick peas for supper. So, she instructed John to stay in the house and keep an eye on the little ones. "When Tommy wakes up, just keep him inside and play with him. But, when the baby wakes up, be sure to call me right away. Just yell out the back door really loud, and I'll come right home."

Mom sets off over the railroad tracks with her basket in hand and begins to pick the peas. No sooner does she get started than she hears someone (of course, she thinks it's John) calling, "Moth-err! Moth-err!" She's thinking to herself, "He can't be awake already." Then, she again hears, "Moth-err! Moth-err!" Quickly she grabs her basket and hurries back over the tracks. When she gets in the house, she finds John with his nose in a book, Tommy still in dreamland on the davenport, and little Davie blissfully sleeping in his crib. "Did you call me, John? I thought I heard you calling for me!"

John replied, "No! You must be hearing things, Ma. It wasn't me! I didn't hear nothin'." "Well, I'll be," she said! I swear I distinctly heard someone calling Mother! "Well, if you don't need me, then I'm going back." Back over the tracks she goes and once again starts picking the peas. And once again, she's down on her hands and knees and hears, "Moth-err! Moth-err!" By this time, Mom is really puzzled. She listens very carefully and is thinking, "It doesn't really sound like John's voice," but decided she better check it out, anyway. Sure enough, when she got back in the house, all was quiet and the babies were still sleeping. By this time, she is thinking that maybe John might be playing a trick on her, but it wasn't like John to do stuff like that. He was such a good boy. She hears the back screen door slamming shut and in walks Danny Lee. "Where have you been?" she questions.

"Over at McGuine's—playing with Digger and Kenny. Why, what's up?" he innocently asked. Mom gave him a very suspicious look, "Danny, were you calling for me? Did you see me working in the garden? Are you the one who kept yelling 'Moth-er' at me?"

Danny started laughing. He shook his head, "I didn't even know you were over there. It wasn't me, Ma—I swear! I heard it too. Did it sound like, (and he mimicked a squawking, guttural sound) 'Moth-err'?" Mom nodded. Danny said, "That was Sammy, McGuine's parrot. He always yells at Mrs. McGuine when she's out working in her garden. He probably thought you were Mrs. McGuine." Needless to say, by this time, Danny Lee and Johnnie were both laughing—loudly! And both little babies woke up crying! And Ma was embarrassed, but she was laughing as well.

I am not certain when or from whom we acquired little David's dog, Jinxie. The dog was David's pet from the very beginning, and they both seemed to sense that. By this time, our sister Kathy and Lowell were living in Freeport, Illinois. They came home often for the weekends, especially in the summertime. Little Gene also had a small black-haired dog, named Pepper. It was such fun to see these two little boys, our mother's very first grandchild and our baby brother, running around the yard with both little puppies chasing after them in hot pursuit. There was only two months' difference in the ages of the little boys and I would guess just about the same with the puppies' ages. David—the uncle, and Genie—the nephew, never realized their unusual kinship. They were more like brothers or best friends in those toddler years and, of course, both of them were in kindergarten at the same time. David was a student at St. Mary's and Genie attended school in Freeport, Illinois. They were too little to compare notes on this important time in their young lives, but trust me—the two mothers did. Every time they got together, the proud mommies would tell their stories.

On the very first day of school, Kathy and Gene walked into the kindergarten classroom. It was already crowded with shy five-year-old children and proud mothers. One of the little boys pointed his finger at Kathy and said to his mom, "Whose big, fat mommy is that?" Kathy's mouth dropped open! She was terribly embarrassed! Everyone in the room was staring at her. The boy's mother was equally embarrassed and tried to shush her son. Then, Gene went right up to the curious little boy. Kathy held her breath—she was worried that her son might fist up his hand and lash out at the other child, but Gene smiled at him and proudly replied, "That's my mommy and she's big and fat 'cause she is gonna have a brand new baby!" These two little boys became best friends and so did their mommies.

David's kindergarten teacher ran into our mother at the Post Office one Saturday morning and Mom asked her how Davie was doing in school. Sister replied, "Oh, Mrs. Spielbauer, that little boy is just so precious. Why, just the other day, David and another little boy were down on the floor underneath the kindergarten table, crawling around on their bellies trying to pick up some crayons. One of them had dropped his whole box and they were rolling everywhere. I scolded the boys because I didn't want them to get their clothes dirty. 'You two sit back down in your chairs. I'll have one of the big boys pick the crayons up. Why just look how dirty your clothes are. Your mothers are going to be very upset because now they are going to have to wash them again! Shame on you!'"

David innocently looked up at his teacher and said, "Oh, that's OK, Sister. My ma won't care if my clothes get dirty. She likes to do the 'wash.' She likes to do the 'wash' so much, she does it at least three times a week." This is very true. David's Ma did do the laundry three times a week, but as to actually "liking" it—little brother, I think *not*!

During the early childhood of the older children, we rarely had good cuts of meat on the dinner table, other than at butchering time. Most of our supper meals consisted of hot dogs, bologna, and some of the side pork that was always preserved in crocks of lard. Roast beef, pork roast, ham, and pork chops were rarely served as an entrée; these were a much more expensive cut of meat to purchase. My brother Joe tells me that about the only time we were able to enjoy a roast beef dinner with all the trimmings was when Aunt Louise and Uncle Arnie came up on Sundays. Aunt Louise often supplied the meat portion of the meal. We also ate a lot of chicken and wild game, thanks to Dad's hunting endeavors.

By the time Tommy and David had entered into our family, our parents could afford to purchase a quarter of beef or half a porker and preserve it in a rented locker. Many people had already purchased freezers for their own personal use, but they were quite expensive. Renting a locker box was much more affordable. Now the family was able to sit down to meals that consisted of roast beef, pork chops, and, once in a great while, even steak.

Sunday arrives. It is dinnertime. Little Davie—probably five years old at the time—sits down at the table. "What's for dinner?" he asks.

Proudly Mama replies, "Roast beef, mashed potatoes, and gravy and green beans!"

"Yuck!" David gripes. "Not again! Why can't we ever have any good meat anymore, like wieners and bologna?" Is this kid spoiled or what?

Back to "Mama and Papa Fuss." Aunt Louise and Uncle Arnie had driven up from Dubuque on a Sunday morning, picked up Mom and Dad, and they all went up to the Island where the Hansons were spending the weekend. The Island was a popular tourist haven for many out-of-town people who had little cabins and weekend homes. Aunt Tootsie and Uncle Larry were very close friends with a couple who owned one of the cottages, and they had given them the key to it with permission to use it whenever they wished. Mom and Dad left Helen in charge of the youngest boys, Tommy and David. They had already planned to take Danny and Jimmy with them so they could go fishing up at the cottage. With our sister in command, there would surely be no problems, because she kept a tight rein on her little brothers.

It was about three thirty in the afternoon when they returned. Aunt Louise and Uncle Arnie had been asked to stay for supper. We always had a huge Sunday dinner at noon, so our evening meal was usually quite simple—something we older girls could easily prepare. Our mom surely deserved to have a break from that tedious task of meal preparation. Helen and I busied ourselves in the kitchen, while all the grown-ups sat in the living room and visited. Both Tommy and David were sitting on the floor, reading the "funny" papers and politely tolerating Aunt Louise's constant teasing. She happened to glance out the window and noticed our neighbor Mrs. Ben Voss coming across the alley. "Oh! Oh!" she warned. "Here comes that old Mama Fuss, headed this way. She looks like she's upset. Did you boys do something to make her mad?" David looked at Tom and Tom looked at David. They both said, "No, we didn't do anything. We weren't even in her yard." Both the boys quickly ran out the back entrance just as Mama Fuss knocked on the front door. Mama got up to see what she wanted.

"Mrs. Spielbauer, I know you have company, and normally I wouldn't bother you, but I just have to get to the bottom of this. And Papa's really upset! I had my glass jars sitting out on the pump stoop, making a batch of 'sun tea'. You know, Papa loves that sun tea. I can never keep enough of it on hand. He drinks it like water. Anyway, I just went to get some for his supper, and all my jars are broken into smithereens and all my tea leaked out into little puddles on the stoop. I just want to know if maybe your boys are involved."

Our mother, of course, was embarrassed and truly did not know what might have happened, since she had not been home all afternoon, but assured Mrs. Voss that she would talk to the boys and see what she could find out. "Well, I don't think my two little ones would do that," she said. "And they were the only ones here. The older boys were with us on the island." Mrs. Voss thanked our mother and left. Mom looked at Helen and said, "Do you think Tom and David broke her jars? Were they over there at all?"

Helen, always in charge, responded, "I can't say for sure, Mom, but I intend to find out! Right now!" She went to the back door and called out, "Tommy, Dave, you guys can come back in now. The coast is clear. Mrs. Fuss went home." Both little boys came into the house, somewhat reluctantly, for they knew Aunt Louise and Uncle Arnie would surely tease them, even *if* they were not guilty. Of course, they continued to maintain their innocence throughout the grueling questioning from not just their aunt and uncle, but their mom and dad as well. I actually felt sorry for my baby brothers. I did not believe they were guilty, but my sister Helen, on the other hand, was most suspicious. She never said a word all the while we finished getting the meal on the table.

The family gathered around the kitchen table and as the bowls of food were passed around, Helen went around and poured Kool-Aid for everyone. She took her place at the table right next to David and helped him cut his ham into bite-size pieces. What a nice big sister! "So, Dave," she slyly asked, "Just how many of those jars of sun tea did Mama Fuss have on her stoop? I know she usually makes a lot of it." This "innocent" little five-year-old let out a deep sigh, looked up at his sister, and said, "They wasn't jars, Helen. They were jugs—those big glass jugs with the handle!"

Everyone stopped eating and placed their forks beside their plates and looked at the little boy. Helen fixed her bold stare directly on the eyes of her baby brother, "So, you guys must have done it, or you wouldn't know what kind they were!" Tommy said, "Aw! David! She tricked you! Now, we're gonna get it!" David burst into tears. And "get it," they did. But, not before one more incriminating question was answered. "And just how did you guys break those jugs?" asked Helen. The little boy just hung his head. "David, do I have to ask you again?"

Every eye was on him! "We just whacked 'em with a bat and a big stick," he reluctantly replied.

Mama marched both boys over to Mrs. Fuss's—one armed with a broom and the other with a dustpan. After a very shame-faced and tearful apology, they went quickly—if rather reluctantly—to work, cleaning up the shattered glass. Our mother also kept some of the glass "jugs with the handle" stashed in our basement. As I recall, the grocery stores sold vinegar in these containers. We saved them for Papa's wine. The boys finally answered Helen's question and admitted that there had been three jugs on the stoop. Mom made the culprits replace the broken ones with three of her own.

I am sure, you can see what a difficult task it was for our mother to know exactly where her boys were and just what they were doing at all times. It simply wasn't possible, but she honestly did try. I am certain that my dear, sainted mother never had any knowledge of this next incident. This involves Danny Lee and Jimmy. They were probably in their very early teens and were supposed to be hoeing in Dad's cornfield on Mr. Sassen's land across the tracks. They each had a hoe in hand and headed over the tracks.

On the way to the cornfield they met up with Artie Hoeger and Jerry Handke. "Hey, you guys wanna come with us? We're gonna take Clarence Cassutt's fishing boat and head on downstream to that slough behind the Creamery."

"Nah, we gotta get that corn hoed this morning," Jimmy replied. "Ma'll be fit to be tied if we don't get it done today." Well, my brothers did have good intentions. But like most boys their age, it was very easy for them to become sidetracked. So they hid their hoes in between the rows of corn, and the four buddies headed for the river. Clarence Cassutt was a commercial fisherman who made his living from the Mississippi River. Artie knew him quite well, and Clarence had given him permission to use his "duck boat" whenever he wanted. The duck boat was tied up on the shoreline, and they all got in and headed downstream. They did not have any definite plans except to "mess around"—maybe do a little swimmin', some fishin', look for snakes or some frogs, whatever it is that boys do when they mess around.

There were willow trees on both sides of the slough—huge ones with branches hanging almost into the water. Jimmy did not know how to swim, and was now walking along the edge of the sand bar, barefooted with his pant legs rolled up, sometimes wading in the water. Artie and Jerry did not know he couldn't swim, and they were coaxing him to grab hold of the pliable willow branches and swing over to the other side. Jim thought it did look like fun, but he refrained from doing so. Danny of course knew his little brother did not know how to swim. The three older boys continued to play at being Tarzan, swinging their bodies and yelling out jungle screams to their hearts' content. At last exhausted, they plopped down on the shore and rested. Suddenly, Jim let out a large yelp and disappeared into the water on the other side of the sand bar, where he began floundering and bobbing up and down.

Artie and Jerry thought he was playacting and just faking a drowning scene. They sat on the sandy shore and laughed at him. Thank God, Danny knew very well that his brother was not pretending, and quickly jumped into the nearby boat. He rowed out to the edge of the sand bar. It all happened so fast. He could see that Jim was struggling against the current and flailing wildly. He quickly pulled his sopping wet and very sick brother into the boat and back to shore. Artie and Jerry still thought Jim was joking until they saw him bend over and spew out what appeared to be gallons of water! At last he was able to explain that his feet were on sand one minute and in the very next second, he must have stepped into a hole and totally lost control as he fought against the current. Dan and Jim decided that they had messed around long enough. They had better get back to their hoeing.

They hurried back to the cornfield, retrieved their hoes, and went straight to work. Jim's clothing was dripping wet. He took off his shirt and draped it over the top of the tall corn stalks and spread his dungarees on some low brush. He was clad only in his underwear as he labored with his hoe completely concealed between the rows of corn and unseen by human eye. Both boys made a silent pact to keep this near-drowning incident to themselves. They continued to hoe until the sun had dried Jim's clothes. He put them back on, and the boys hung their tools in the shed and went up to the house where mom fixed them both a sandwich. This was the only time they ever succeeded in "pulling the wool over my mother's eyes."

It is very true that our little brothers got away with a lot of shenanigans and into a great deal of trouble at times. But, just once in a while, they found themselves to be the victims of someone else's pranks. The year was 1953. The coronation of England's new Queen Elizabeth was soon to take place. This was definitely a most historical event and was highly publicized all over the world. Our younger brother Tom was about eight years old at that time, probably in third grade. His teacher had brought up the topic in the classroom, and Tom was fascinated by it. Even more historical was the fact that for the first time in History, this event was going to be globally televised! Alas, the Spielbauer family did not own a TV set. Tom was devastated. Our Aunt Louise and Uncle Arnie came to visit one Sunday afternoon. Aunt Louise was quite impressed with Tommy's knowledge of the upcoming ceremony as well as his interest in its occurrence. "I just wish we could buy one of those television sets, then at least, we could watch it," he said wistfully.

Aunt Louise immediately jumped on this bandwagon and replied, "Well, Tommy, I heard that some Americans are going to be invited to go to London and see the actual coronation for themselves. Maybe the new Queen will send you an invitation!"

"No way! She doesn't even know we exist." A week or two went by. One Saturday morning, Mom sent Danny Lee and Tommy to pick up the mail from the Post Office. There seemed to be more than usual—a bunch of seed catalogs and The Farm Bureau paper, some bills, and what in the world is *this*? A square-shaped white envelope addressed to Mr. and Mrs. George Spielbauer and Family. The return address indicated it had been mailed from Buckingham Palace in London! Tommy remembered that London was located in the country of England! It looked like an invitation. Both little boys ran all the way home. They insisted that Mama open that envelope first!

Coronation of Her Majesty
Queen Elizabeth II

By Command of the Queen

Sir George Spielbauer and Frances Spielbauer and children are
directed to be present at the Abbey Church of
Westminster on the second day of June 1953

Norfolk

Wow! My little brothers could not believe it! "Do you and Dad *know* the new Queen? Why would she invite us? I bet we can't go. We'd have to cross the ocean and that would cost way too much money." Tommy simply could not stop thinking about it or, for that matter, talking about it. Of course, he went to school and told his teacher, all of his classmates, and all of his friends—anyone who would listen to him.

He asked Mom if he could take the "invitation" to school and show his teacher and the kids in his class that it really existed. Mom said that was not a good idea. By this time, everyone in the family, even Danny Lee, realized the invitation for what it truly was—just another one of Aunt Louise's practical jokes. She had seen a picture of the Royal invitation in a magazine article and had somebody (I think Uncle Arnie's secretary at the factory) type it for her. She then performed a "cut and paste" technique onto a blank card, addressed the envelope, slapped a three-cent stamp on it, and dropped it in the mail. Knowing our dear sweet Aunt Louise Hutter, she was no doubt chuckling all the while!

I guess, in retrospect, none of us wanted to tell Tommy it was a joke because we all felt that he would be very embarrassed at his own naïveté and would feel like some sort of a "chump."

Mom even went so far as to destroy the "evidence," namely, the invitation itself, by burning it in the cook stove, because she was worried that Tom might find it and take it to school without her permission. She was trying to save her little boy from embarrassment.

Eventually, the coronation incident was pretty much forgotten. The only allusion ever made to it was when Aunt Louise came to visit. She often, in a teasing manner, introduced the topic into the conversation and would question Tom about it. After one such visit from the Hutters, while Celie was helping the little brothers with dishes, Tom said, "I always wondered what happened to that invitation. I really wanted to take it to school and show everybody. I can't imagine that Mom would throw it away. She should have framed it or something."

Celie looked at John. John looked at Celie and nodded his head. Danny started laughing. David did not even know what they were talking about—he was too young to remember. Celie and John finally told their younger brother that he had been just another victim of one of our dear Aunt Louise's practical jokes. Welcome to the club, Tom. This club has a big membership!

Upon her graduation from high school, Celie went to work as a receptionist for Dr. Don Meder in his dental office. She was there for several years, and when her boyfriend, Vern Steger from Dyersville, went into the service, she also came to Cedar Rapids, and we shared an apartment together with Sandi Whitlock. Celie was employed at Quaker Oats Company during that time.

It was around this time that I met and married my husband, Dick Brooks. We continued to live in Cedar Rapids. Celie and Vern got married when he came home from the service, and they made their home in Dyersville. Frank was still living in Guttenberg with our parents, but was employed at John Deere in Dubuque, Iowa. He met his future wife, Jackie Wessels, and eventually married her in St. Mary's Church in Guttenberg. They continued to make their home in Guttenberg. By this time, Larry was also living in Cedar Rapids and was employed by The Cedar Rapids Fire Department. He married Ellie Hemesath a few years later, and they too made Cedar Rapids their home.

John stayed pretty much around the Guttenberg area and continued to live with our parents. He worked for a factory in Dyersville for many years and still resides in the family home in Guttenberg. All four of the youngest brothers enlisted in the Air Force right out of high school. Danny married Georgia Hines from up around the Clayton area. They have a country home close to Osterdock. Jim met his wife, Dorcas Post, when he was a student at The University of Iowa. They did live near Guttenberg for a short time, but made their home in Riverside, which is a small town near Iowa City. The two youngest boys are the furthest away from home. Tom and his wife Ginger live in Amarillo, Texas, where he is currently employed by the local Fire Department. Our youngest brother, David, works in a factory and lives in Amarillo as well.

These days we try to get together as often as we can. Of course, we always reminisce about the good old days, when we were nothing more than a passel of little children living and loving and learning, as we trod barefoot through the streets of Guttenberg and along the sandy shores of The Mighty Mississippi. That "ole man river" keeps calling us home.

Chapter X

Aftermath

As a little child, I remember my family and relatives gathering around Mom's kitchen table and reminiscing about the good old days. Mother was an exceptionally good storyteller; so were my dad's two sisters Aunt Tootsie and Aunt Louise. Even Dad often joined in with a few good tales about himself. As each of the fourteen children grew and developed into adults, we too began to participate in this ancient form of entertainment. Please let me remind you that this was a time before TV land, and in our case, before the ownership of a radio for many years. There was never enough extra money for movies, so storytelling and the reading of books from the local library were the only sources of entertainment that existed.

"There are many more stories," my mother would often say. "So many of them—we should write them all down some day." It wasn't until 1981, after the death of my firstborn child, Todd Steven, when my mother's words came back to haunt me. It was the morning of my son's funeral. We were all ready—just waiting for the limo from the funeral home to come and take us to the services. In all honesty we were physically ready—certainly not mentally or emotionally. My husband and I and Tanya and Trent were sitting in the living room waiting silently—like zombies—each one of us trying to come to terms with the loss of our son and brother. We were devastated. I truly did not think we would be able to get through this day. It was, indeed, our darkest hour, and I prayed for strength and guidance from above.

The doorbell rang, and I, of course, assumed it was the funeral director coming to pick us up. Instead, it turned out to be my younger brother Jimmy and his wife Dorcas. At the sight of one of my own siblings, I immediately burst into tears. Jim explained that they had arrived in town much sooner than they had anticipated, and rather than wait for another hour at the funeral home, they came straight to our house. The presence of family was such a comfort to me. I already knew that some of my brothers and sisters were planning to attend the funeral, but had not been expecting Jim. I invited them in and served them coffee and doughnuts. My next door neighbor had brought the pastries over earlier that morning. Of course, they extended their condolences to each of us, and we talked about Todd's untimely death. It was a good thing for my family, because now we were actually communicating with one another instead of sitting, each caught up in our silent and personal pain. Just knowing that someone was there to share that pain was very consoling to all of us.

Soon the limousine did arrive, and my brother and his wife followed us to the funeral home. I knew there were a lot of people around us, but we were quickly escorted into a small, curtained family room for the services. We were ushered past other folks already seated clear down to the front row. As I turned to follow my children into the pew, I became aware that Dick's sisters, Shirley and Bev, were seated directly behind us with their husbands. They reached their hands out to each of us in turn and again the tears began to flow. Once again, I felt the comforting feeling that only the presence of family can provide in times of sorrow.

Oh yes, I remember every minute detail of my young son's funeral, but I cannot share it. It is too difficult to speak of. I am a person who readily shares my joy with the world, but when it comes to sorrow, it is mine alone to deal with. The service is now over and once again our young escort is motioning for my family to be ushered out first. We now face the people sitting behind and again I touch the outstretched hands of Shirley and Don and Bev and Bob and their children. I look beyond them searching for Jim and Dorcas. I was just so amazed at what I saw. Directly behind Dick's family, there they were—row upon row—my own brothers and sisters! Jim and Dorcas, Johnny, Joe and Delores, Rosy, Danny and Georgia, Larry and Ellie! I was overcome with emotion!

I have never forgotten that sight of so many of my siblings on this saddest day of my life and what their presence meant to me and to my family. Of course, it was impossible for all of them to attend the funeral, but I did hear from every one. They called and sent flowers and cards and contributions. Everyone was there for us. At that particular point in time, I felt compelled to write something special to each family member. I wanted them to know how I felt about each one and let them know how special they are to me. And I wanted to thank them for coming to me in my hour of need. My thoughts returned to those age-old memories of storytelling around my mother's kitchen table, and once again, my mother's words came back to haunt me. At that moment, I made a solemn vow to myself and to my mom, who was then a patient in The Care Center on top of the Guttenberg Hill. I promised to make my mother's wish come true! Somehow, I felt it was my duty to write the family stories down.

Thus, the story of *Living Arrows* began to blossom. *Mom, this is for you!* I began writing the initial draft shortly after Todd's death. It served as a kind of catharsis that helped me in my journey through the grieving process. All of part I and the first eight chapters of part II were initially written in longhand and then typed on an ancient manual typewriter (Royal). I contacted my sister Kathy, and she readily agreed to supply all the artwork that I needed. My whole family soon became involved in this project, filling in the gaps where my own memory failed me, always encouraging me to complete it. My initial intent was to simply make little booklet copies of the manuscript and present one to each member in my family.

Admittedly, these booklets could only (at their best) be described as "rough copy." But alas, this was the closest thing to "the family story" that my mother would ever see. At this point in time, she had already been diagnosed with late-onset diabetes, a disease that greatly affected her entire body, including her vision. She suffered from iritis in one eye and macular degeneration in the other. Sadly (this is not meant to be funny or silly or sarcastic), my mother was literally blind in one eye and could not see out of the other. My sister Helen offered to read "the story" to Mom (just a few pages at a time) when she visited her at The Care Center. Helen assured me that Mom loved it! Sometimes, her eyes would well up into tears and other times she would laugh out loud. After each session, she would always say, "But, there is so much more!" As usual, my mom was right. There is so much more—far too much to fit into one book.

My life at this point was very busy, with working at a full-time job and taking care of my home and family, and for many years, this manuscript lay stashed away in the bottom drawer of my dresser. I always did have the plan "to finish it someday." But it wasn't until I retired and learned to use a computer that I actually began to work on it once again. This time, I knew I had to complete it!

I do feel that now is the time to bring this story to its close. As of this date, July 12, 2009, there are a total of thirteen surviving children born of George and Frances Spielbauer. We currently range in ages from sixty-three to eighty-three. Oh yes, there are those among us who can complain of the usual aches and pains relative to our ages, and others who freely discuss recent bypass surgeries, pacemakers, cataracts, and knee replacements. But, for the time being, we are all still hanging in there.

I can only take *Living Arrows* as far as its final chapter. I am not capable of ending it. This ending can only occur when the last of the living children is called to his or her heavenly home. You see, only God can end this story. We do not know when, where, or how this will happen; but we do know that our days are numbered. We have had quite a journey, we have had a good life, and we have no regrets. We shall leave this world, one by one, just as we entered it so many long years ago.

Thank you for reading our story,
Hildi

In Memoriam

I should like to have a private moment of prayer here for those who have gone before us. I want to say "thank you" to each one of these people for having been a part of our lives and for having touched our hearts. We now pray for the repose of their souls.

Relationship	Name	Spouse	Date of Death
Aunt	Marie (Schmidt) Spielbauer	Jack	11/20/1930
Grandma	Juliana (Johll) Rohner	Matt	06/02/1941
Uncle	Jack Spielbauer	Marie	06/08/1946
Grandma	Mary (Brimeyer) Spielbauer	Joseph	10/10/1949
Aunt	Edwina (Spielbauer) Blaser	Ed	01/04/1957
Uncle	Peter Duehr	Martha	01/22/1965
Uncle	Edward Blaser	Edwina	03/04/1967
Father	George Spielbauer	Frances	11/14/1972
Uncle	Frank Rohner	Irene	01/20/1975
Aunt	Martha (Spielbauer) Duehr	Peter	08/19/1976
Son	Todd Steven Brooks		06/07/1981
Uncle	Larry Hanson	Tootsie	04/13/1986
Mother	Frances (Rohner) Spielbauer	George	12/06/1986
Aunt	Irene (Miller) Rohner	Frank	01/04/1989
Uncle	Arnold Hutter	Louise	01/20/1994

Sister	Kathy (Spielbauer) Eilers	Lowell	08/24/1994
Aunt	Louise (Spielbauer) Hutter	Arnie	01/04/1999
Brother-in-law	Lowell Eilers	Kathy	02/18/1999
Aunt	Tootsie (Spielbauer) Hanson	Larry	09/22/2002
Brother-in-law	Earl Schultz	Rose	03/24/2007
Brother-in-law	Donald Bolsinger	Helen	06/23/2008

May they rest in peace,
Amen.

Living Arrows has been a labor of love for my family, my friends, my relatives, and all those dear hearts and gentle people who live and love in my hometown—
Guttenberg, Iowa.

Acknowledgments

Thank you,

To my immediate family—Dick, Tanya, and Trent, Tim (son-in-law), Hunter and Staci, Travis and Danny, Riley and Macey (grandchildren)—for sharing my hope and dream with me. And thank you for your love.

To my brothers and sisters and all of my very large extended family—you all know who you are and what you have done. I love each and every one of you.

To my brother Loras John and to my husband, Dick Brooks, for the financial support. I couldn't have done it without you.

To Melissa Richards, my dear young friend (like my second daughter), for the beautiful cover design. My sister Kathy also thanks you.

Last, but not least, a special thank you to my "lunch lady" friends, Dorothy Johnsen and Vickie McVey, for their expert computer knowledge and the willingness to bail me out of all my little "technical glitches." May God bless you both!

LaVergne, TN USA
12 December 2009
166782LV00003B/1/P